forbidden bread

forbidden bread

a memoir

ERICA JOHNSON DEBELJAK

North Atlantic Books
Berkeley, California

Published by   Cover photograph © PeskyMonkey,
North Atlantic Books   iStock.com
P.O. Box 12327   Cover and book design © Ayelet Maida
Berkeley, California 94712   Printed in the United States of America

Photograph copyrights noted on page vi. All other photographs copyright © 2009 by Erica Johnson Debeljak.

The City and the Child translation copyright © 2009 by Chris Merrill. Five Little Negroes and All the Wreathes Are White translation copyright © 2009 by Erica Johnson Debeljak.

The characters, events, and places depicted in the memoir Forbidden Bread are treated as creative nonfiction, with certain facts restructured where necessary for the benefit of the overall narrative.

Forbidden Bread is sponsored by the Society for the Study of Native Arts and Sciences, a nonprofit educational corporation whose goals are to develop an educational and cross-cultural perspective linking various scientific, social, and artistic fields; to nurture a holistic view of arts, sciences, humanities, and healing; and to publish and distribute literature on the relationship of mind, body, and nature.

North Atlantic Books' publications are available through most bookstores. For further information, call 800-733-3000 or visit our Web site at www.northatlanticbooks.com.

Library of Congress Cataloging-in-Publication Data
Johnson Debeljak, Erica.
    Forbidden bread : a memoir / by Erica Johnson Debeljak.
      p. cm.
    ISBN 978-1-55643-740-3
    1. Johnson-Debeljak, Erica. 2. Immigrants—Slovenia—Biography.
3. Americans—Slovenia—Biography. 4. Man-woman relationships—
Slovenia. 5. Investment advisors—New York (State)—New York—
Biography. 6. Slovenia—Biography. 7. New York (N.Y.)—Biography.
I. Title.
    CT1448.J64A3 2009
    949.73'02092—dc22
    [B]
                                                                2008039617

1 2 3 4 5 6 7 8 9 UNITED 14 13 12 11 10 09

for Tanja

ACKNOWLEDGMENTS

I would like to thank my friend and agent, Judy Heiblum, whose help and support was invaluable on this project; Hanno Hardt, whose photographs and excellent advice give the book its visual flair; and, of course, Aleš and our children, who served not only as inspiration for this book but for everyday life as well.

I would also like to thank the photographers and translators featured in this work.

Photographs copyright © 2009 by Hanno Hardt, p. 33, 57, 99, 109, 134, 170, 224; Žiga Koritnik, p. 144; Borut Krajnc, p. 85; Toni Lombar/ Delo, p. 3, 157; Mary Beth Schaye, p. 259; Damijan Zibert/Delo, p. 146.

A NOTE ON PRONUNCIATION

Most letters in the Slovenian alphabet are pronounced roughly the same as in English. The main exceptions are as follows:

c as the ts in *curtsey*
č as the ch in *church*
š as the sh in *she*
ž as the s in *pleasure*
j as the y in *year*

CONTENTS

PART THREE: Plural

PART ONE

Singular

Ljubljana
MARCH 1993

Ljubljana Castle

"Let's go to the top."

I am standing at the bottom of a cobblestone lane and looking up a steep curving incline toward an unseen castle. My black-
haired poet-lover stands beside me, scowling up the hill. I
traveled halfway across the world to see him. The season is a late
gray snowless winter.

"I want to get the lay of the land."

And so we head up. After a short while, the narrow lane turns
into narrow stairs. The artists' quarter disappears behind Saint
Florjan Church to the right, and the old city falls away to our left,
a cascade of crumbling red rooftops. When we started our ascent
we were holding hands, but as we approach the summit and the
outer fortifications of the castle come into view, we let go of each
other and start taking two, even three, breathless steps at a time.
Standing on the ramparts a few minutes later, Aleš takes me by

3

the shoulders and turns me roughly round. Lover no longer, he is captain of the ship indicating the four points of the navigational compass: crucial information for any traveler.

"There," he says, pointing his finger, "that's Dunajska." Dunaj means Vienna in Slovenian. It is the road to Vienna. We drove in on it three days before.

"And to the southwest," he turns me round 180 degrees, "Tržaška." The road to Trieste and the sea.

"And there," he makes a quarter turn of the compass, "Celovška." Klagenfurt, the border town in Austria where Slovenians go to shop for Western goods that are not yet widely available here: Levi's and Ray-Bans and two-ply toilet paper.

"And on the other side of castle hill, Karlovška." He jabs a finger eastward. Karlovac is in Croatia, on the other side of Slovenia's new border. There is a hot war going on there right now. The explosions of mortars and the steady report of machine gun fire can be heard for miles around.

These are the four roads, the four fraying threads that connect Ljubljana to its vanished and vanishing empires. But my captain is not done with me yet. We are alone on the hill, sharing it only with the leafless chestnut trees that tower above us, the abandoned hulls of their fruit giving way beneath our feet, and Ljubljana Castle, of course—a dull squat affair with a single tower that has never housed royalty but over the centuries has served as a refuge from marauding Turks, a mint, a prison, and, most recently, coldwater flats.

"That's the *toplarna*." He points to the garish red-and-white chimney stack of the coal-burning works that dominates the view from the studio apartment where I have shared his bed the last three nights.

"And the old Yugoslav army barracks."

I know what he is doing. He is giving me what I said I wanted and what he thinks I need: the lay of the land, a higher vantage

4

point, a new perspective on the sights that I have seen at eye level during the last few days.

"*Nebotičnik.*" The word means skyscraper. The building is thirteen stories high, once the tallest in the Balkans, now an obsolete source of municipal pride.

"The Ministry of Finance." The building where I had an interview with a ragtag central banker earlier this morning. One Mr. Klemenčič, curious to catch sight of the young female investment analyst who had blown into town from New York City, the financial capital of the world, ostensibly, fantastically, in search of a job. When I entered his office, he reached a slender hand toward the bow that emerged from my navy blue suit jacket.

"A touch of white," he giggled. I suspect he doesn't have the authority to hire me, still less the energy to incorporate a bird as strange as me into the shadowy affairs of the new ministry. If he does, my mind can only reel at the prospect of an everyday professional life with Mr. Klemenčič at the helm.

Aleš turns me round to face him, hands now gripping my upper arms, his tone making a quick and heartbreaking swerve from ferocity to melancholy.

"You don't really think you could live here, do you?"

I return his gaze. I prefer not to *really* think about it at all. It's too much of a strain to think about what it would *really* be like to pick up and leave everything—family, friends, country, job, language, income, independence. What it would *really* be like to settle in this tiny new country that is just beginning the hard-luck scramble out of the known indignities of communism and into the lesser known indignities of capitalism and mass consumerism. Or for that matter what it would *really* be like to occupy the front-row balcony seat at the edge of that hot little war going on in Karlovac and points beyond. And perhaps most alarming of all, what would happen if the threads connecting me to the vanished and vanishing empires of my own childhood and youth were to fray. As for the "here" in his question, as for Ljubljana, who can say? I have always lived in brash self-confident American coastal cities—New York and San Francisco—cities that, with their restaurants and theater guides, museums and nightclubs, generously take up the slack when one's confidence in the meaning of life begins to falter.

Here, I sense, I'd be left to my own resources.

I prefer not to think about that either. I shake my lover's hands from my shoulders and lean in to kiss him on those warm lips of his that are just now asking too much of me. I have always preferred to focus on the positive aspects of any decision.

"No," he pushes me away. "You need to think about it, to *really* think about it."

Stymied, I turn my back to him and lean my elbows against the damp stone ramparts, scanning the city's avenues, trying to remember their names. A green river spools quietly round the hill. The *toplarna*, vaguely ridiculous, winks at me from a distance. A drop of condensation breaks loose from the bare branch of a chestnut tree and lands on my cheek. A solitary truck rumbles out of town in the direction of Vienna.

Or at least I think it's Vienna. I've never had a very good sense of direction.

New York City

Aleš and me

I met my black-haired poet-lover at a loft party in Brooklyn, New York, in September 1991, a party I should not have attended. It was Thursday, a work night. My girlfriend Tina had canceled at the last minute, citing cramps, and I was the kind of New York woman who made it a point not to go to parties alone, especially if they lay beyond the protective moats of Manhattan. But for some strange reason—and to this day I cannot recall exactly why—I went, alone and on the subway, no less, and there I met him. This was the first in a series of coincidences, mishaps, and thunder-bolts that landed me here, on these ramparts, in my current situation.

He told me many things about himself that night in Brooklyn. It was a subject he clearly enjoyed talking about. The first thing he told me was his name: Aleš spelled not with a *sh* as it is pro-nounced, but with a diacritical mark, a little hat or inverted roof, over the *s*. Then he told me, in his colloquial and nearly unac-cented English, that he had been living in the United States for

7

five years already, was finishing up his PhD in social thought at Syracuse University, writing his dissertation at his roommate Igor's apartment in the East Village. He told me that his heart wasn't really in academia, that he was more of a poet than an academic, the leading poet of his generation as a matter of fact, a winner of his country's national poetry award. He told me that the country in question was called Slovenia and that it had officially existed as a nation-state for less than three months, since June 25, 1991, to be exact, after having fought and won the Ten Day War with the Yugoslav National Army, a David-versus-Goliath conflict that he had witnessed firsthand working as a translator for CNN.

Finally (and this last point seemed most germane to me as I was already getting sucked in by his immense gravitational pull), he told me that he was leaving New York and the United States in a few months' time. He had already booked a ticket on a Romanian charter plane to Vienna. He was returning permanently, taking up a university post in the newly minted nation of Slovenia—the land, if not the country, of his birth.

Aleš waited nearly three weeks after the loft party in Brooklyn to call me. I had nearly forgotten his slate-blue eyes, his appealing brand of egotism, his vaguely foreign turn of phrase, when one day I found a message slip in my inbox. Back then I worked as an analyst for a French government bank, and my new secretary was having trouble with some of the unfamiliar names. *Alich* was the word she had written down on the pink slip of paper followed by a question mark in parentheses.

"Alich (?) called when you were out. Call back." Then a phone number.

Alich? It could have been Alice in legal, but she was on her honeymoon that week. She'd be unlikely to call me from the Bahamas—nothing was that urgent. Besides, the number had a

Manhattan area code. Then it dawned on me: Alich = Alesh = Aleš with a diacritical mark, a little inverted roof, over the s.

I picked up the phone and dialed.

One ring and right away *"halo"* in that faintly accented English.

"Hi, it's me," I said.

"You?"

"Yes, me. Erica."

"Oh, you. Erica. Do you want to meet?" He wasn't one for beating around the bush. I loved the way he said my name.

"Yes."

"When?"

"Tonight."

"Where?"

"Marion's at eight o'clock. Dinner. I'll make a reservation."

Marion's Continental Restaurant and Lounge was a low-budget low-lit dinner place in the East Village. Aleš had mentioned he was living in that neighborhood with a Slovenian roommate named Igor. I figured as a student and an Eastern European, he'd appreciate the low-budget element, and I would appreciate the low lights. After I got off the phone with Aleš, I called Marion's and made an eight-o'clock reservation. For a lark, I used the name Debeljak, the *j* pronounced "y," as Aleš had informed me. I spelled the name out twice, letter by letter, for the blasé voice on the other end of the line.

Several hours later, sitting across the table at Marion's, I recalled in a rush exactly what it was that I liked about him the first time around. He had short-cropped black hair, eyes that were playful and sad at the same time, a nose that would have been aquiline except for the slight Slavic twist at the end of it, and a short scar above his right eye that erased about a third of his eyebrow and gave his face an appealing asymmetry. He was not a large man, but what he lacked in size he made up for in sheer energy and self-confidence. He was completely and utterly full of himself, and yet the same quality that was unbearable, I knew from experience, in an investment banker, seemed almost endearing in a poet.

The first thing Aleš did that night—and in retrospect I recognize it as the first of many things he would do to discourage me, to divert our shared fate—was go all cocky and macho and politically incorrect on me. He told me that the reason it had taken him three weeks to call was that he had collected other numbers at the party and that he had called them first, thinking that they would be less complicated than me, less of a challenge. One was considerably younger and the other considerably older. This was an allusion, I figured, to the one small piece of information about myself that I had managed to impart at the party: that I had just passed my thirtieth birthday. At the same time, it confirmed what I'd already guessed about him: that he had methods of breaking the monotony of drafting a dissertation on social thought. That he got around. He bedded women.

At that moment, I didn't care.

Over dinner he told me the names of his poetry collections—*Anxious Moments, Chronicle of Melancholy, Dictionary of Silence*—and said that he was not a romantic poet but a melancholy one. He didn't write about love but about existential anxiety, that indeed melancholy and existential anxiety were pervasive and persistent conditions not only in his soul but in the soul of his country.

"Everyone in Slovenia falls victim to melancholy," he said, "especially during the long winter months. Slovenia competes," he continued with a perverse sort of national pride, "with Hungary for the highest per capita suicide rate in the world."

"Well, it can't be too hard," I parried, "with such a small population."

By then I knew the population figures, and they were dire. Tina had provided me with the numbers when I gave her a report on the party she had missed and the interesting man I had met there. She was of Croatian descent and had recently been getting up a head of steam about the evolving situation in Yugoslavia. Plus she was a master of sports trivia and so knew, for example, that Slovenia had a sharpshooting medalist in the most recent Olympic Games. The figure she had mentioned during that conversation was a number just slightly under two million. Less than a quarter of the population of New York City. Smaller, come to think of it, than the entire population of Brooklyn. The capital, Ljubljana, had a population just slightly under three hundred thousand inhabitants.

And yet the Slovenian sitting across the table from me did not seem particularly melancholy at the moment. To the contrary, he looked sly and self-satisfied, like a cat perched on a tree branch, contemplating a small snack-sized bird on a lower branch. I assured him that I, along with everybody else in New York, had read *The Unbearable Lightness of Being*, seen the movie, adored Milan Kundera and Daniel Day Lewis, and knew all I needed to know about melancholy and existential anxiety and womanizing being pervasive and persistent conditions in communist and now post-communist countries.

"Not much else to do there, I suppose. Here we actually have to work for a living."

"There's an old saying in my country," he said, suddenly changing both the subject and his tone of voice. "It goes like this: *zarečenega kruh se največ poje*."

I can no longer recall how that phrase sounded to me then when I first heard it, how it appeared floating before my mind's eye, how I imagined the sentence might be broken into words, the words broken into letters. I could master my dinner companion's first name and, with a little difficulty, his last, but this saying sounded like nothing more than a tumult of undifferentiated syllables. And yet I do recall thrilling to the sound of such

11

an unfamiliar language, wanting to hear it again and again. Unlike most European languages, it evoked a place that was actually unknown to me: a real terra incognita. The sound of the words, the hard consonants, the way he ran them together in a staccato blur, all seemed to confirm that this man was like no one else I'd ever met before.

"What does it mean?" I asked.

"It's hard to translate, like a lot of things are hard to translate."

"Try me," I persisted.

"Well," he paused, "it means something like: you always eat the bread that you've forbidden yourself."

"Oh," I said, and sent a wicked smile across the table. We were still playing games, I thought. "Here we call it forbidden fruit. But then we didn't have food shortages."

"I'm serious," he said. And he looked serious, even a bit melancholy after all, not playful or predatory anymore.

"It means that you always end up doing what you say you won't do. But I'm not going to end up doing that. I'm going home in three months' time. To Slovenia. It's a new beginning over there, and I'm going to be part of it. So don't get any ideas about me. We're just having dinner."

Eventually we finished the dinner that we were just having, and we paid for it. We went Dutch that first night. I paid for the cab up to my place. We could have walked, but we were suddenly in a hurry. When we arrived at my corner—East Twenty-Fourth and Third—we stepped out of the cab and into the busy neon street. We crossed the street and entered my building. We crossed the lobby, my high-heeled shoes clicking on the smooth marble floor, his Converse tennis shoes making a soft padding sound. We marched up the five flights of stairs to my apartment. I unlocked the door, and we slipped into the waiting darkness, and from there the few steps to the bedroom, and from there to the bed. After all that sparring at dinner, we had nothing left to say. It was as if the game had gone out of us. We had agreed to something back at Marion's—or probably before that, at the party in Brooklyn—and now it was time to put our unspoken agreement into action. All I remember was the darkness, the folding into one another, easily, effortlessly. And I remember not caring anymore that he had waited three weeks to call me, not caring about the younger woman he called first or the older one he called next, not caring that he was scheduled to leave in three months' time, not even caring that for him I was forbidden bread.

Lying in bed afterwards, I rolled up onto my side and regarded his profile, the long, slightly twisted nose of this poet, this man I had just made love to. I watched the rising and falling of his chest.

"Are you this passionate with other women?" I have no idea from what primal pit of female possession that question came.

He rolled up onto his side and looked at me. He smiled into the darkness. "What other women?"

Twenty-Fourth Street

Marion's

After the first night at Marion's, Aleš and I dispensed with the inessential: with dinner, the taxi cab, the neon street. In short, with any trace of the outside world.

We retained only the essential: the bed, the darkness, and the two of us. The division of the world into essential and inessential comes naturally enough in a love affair, and in this case it had the added benefit of shielding us from the more irksome elements of our situation: elements like nationality, cultural background, permanent place of residence, and that eternally ticking clock, the countdown, three months to go. I kept the kitchen stocked with fuel to keep us going—cheese, bread, olives, wine— and Aleš took care of our more ephemeral needs. He arrived each evening armed with books and Xerox copies of things that he wanted to show me—an article, for example, called "Voices From Yugoslavia," an anthology titled *Child of Europe: A New Anthology of East European Poetry* in which his poetry appeared in English translation, a slender tour guidebook with a picture of Ljubljana's

Three Bridges on the cover—and a dollar rose purchased from the twenty-four-hour Korean grocery on the corner below my apartment.

We slept little those nights. When we weren't doing the essential thing, we talked and talked and talked some more. He told me about the city of his birth, Ljubljana. It was, he said, the only city he knew of whose name derived from the word love: *ljubiti*. He told me about the country of his childhood: not Slovenia, but Yugoslavia, a country he had belonged to without ever much thinking about it, just as most children do. American children start their day with the Pledge of Allegiance, while Aleš and his Yugoslav schoolmates started theirs with one of their number standing up in front of the class, raising a clenched fist and shouting *"za domovino!"*—For the homeland!—and the rest of the children shouted in response *"s Titom naprej!"*—Onward with Tito!

That, of course, was only the most obviously jingoistic element of his childhood, though also recalled with affection and nostalgia, but there were countless other galvanizing moments: his trips crisscrossing the country—Belgrade, Zagreb, Sarajevo, Novi Sad—with the Yugoslav judo team; the communist youth projects that had been launched in the postwar years to rebuild roads and bridges and villages destroyed during the war, but by the sixties and seventies had transformed into a sort of socialist Burning Man festival imbuing the young not only with the rousing collective power of the international working class and brotherly love toward their fellow Slavs, but with ample opportunity to get drunk and have lots of sex. During those years, Yugo rock was huge. In the West we had the Who, the Rolling Stones, Roxy Music, Fleetwood Mac, all of it. But Yugoslav kids were actually better off. They not only had the world but their own private little kingdom that no one else understood. They had the Who, the Rolling Stones, Roxy Music, Fleetwood Mac, *and* the Sarajevan band Bijelo Dugme, the Serbian Bajaga, Azra with its charismatic

15

lead-singer Johnny Štulić. We graffitied the words ENO IS GOD on the sides of San Francisco's stucco buildings; in Ljubljana it was ŠTULIĆ IS GOD. Yugoslavia was the air Aleš breathed growing up, the milk he drank, a more pungent and intoxicating sort of milk than what was on offer either in the capitals of the West or in provincial and pastoral Slovenia. He never thought of himself as anything but Yugoslav, ethnically Slovenian too, of course, but Yugoslav more than anything else.

Aleš read me translations of his poetry, and I read him love letters that James Joyce had written to his wife, Nora, when he traveled home to Dublin and she remained behind in Trieste, their shared city of exile. I was reading her biography that fall and was enthralled by it. Aleš told me that, in fact, Trieste was only an hour's drive from Ljubljana and that, yeah, it was known for James Joyce, but in the universe of his childhood it was where, when they didn't drive over the Alps to chilly Klagenfurt, they went to buy blue jeans and Illy coffee and washing detergent, and to catch a glimpse of the glistening Miramare Castle and its formal gardens at the far end of Barcola Beach. Trieste was a beautiful sore in their side. It should have been theirs after World War II. Trieste was their lost maritime capital, their shopping mall, the backyard fence through which they caught a glimpse not only of the sea but of Western beauty and abundance.

He told me an apocryphal story about James Joyce and Ljubljana and Trieste, a story that says a lot more about Ljubljana than it does about the now legendary Irish writer. On Joyce's first trip to Trieste, he rode the Southern Railroad line through what was then still Austro-Hungary. The Southern Railroad ran from the empire's most important city, the capital, Vienna, to the empire's most important Adriatic seaport, Trieste. Tired from the long journey and unfamiliar with his surroundings, Joyce disembarked from the train too early. He stumbled down the steps and into the dim light of Ljubljana's train station. When he realized his mistake, he wandered out of the station and found a park bench across the street. He had no money, so he curled up on the bench and slept until morning when he boarded the next southbound train to Trieste. Today Joyce plaques are sprinkled throughout the city of Trieste—the Berlitz school where he taught English, the countless pubs where he drank, the countless apartments where he lived until being evicted for failing to pay the rent.

And all that Ljubljana has is a park bench.

But that, Aleš told me with a sad smile, is no trifling matter to Slovenians. That park bench is the subject of periodic anthologies and anguished poetic musings.

"I have an old friend," Aleš said, "a great poet named Tomaž who grew up on the Slovenian seacoast. His grandmother used to ride with him and his brother and sister on the old Vienna-Trieste railway line. After they got on the train in Vienna and crossed the Austrian border into what was then Yugoslavia, she would stroke their silky heads and croon to them. 'Go to sleep, children. Go to sleep from Vienna to Trieste. There's nothing in between.'" Aleš sighed.

"That's where I'm from," he said, "from that nothing-in-between."

By that time, of course, I was already besotted with my black-haired poet-lover. I could hardly imagine how my workaday life in Manhattan had had any meaning before I'd met him. I pushed aside the duvet cover and moved across to Aleš. I slid up on to his lap and wrapped my bare legs around his waist.

"It's all right," I said, kissing the scar above his eye, the shadow that lay across his cheek. "I think I'm starting to love that nothing-in-between."

I meant, of course, that I was starting to love him, though I didn't dare say so. Which in retrospect was a good thing because he broke up with me the very next day.

17

My Yugo

New Year's Eve 1992

"How is your Yugo?"

It was the night before Thanksgiving, and I was having dinner with my friend, Milena. Back in the fall of 1991, during the initial ups and downs of the affair, I tended to gravitate toward people who got the whole Eastern European thing, got the whole Yugoslav thing. In those days I knew only two of them. One was Tina, who kept me posted, in between cocktail parties and gallery openings, on events unfolding in that part of the world: the bombardment of Dubrovnik, the fall of Vukovar, and not least what Goran Ivanišević, the hot young Croatian tennis player from Split, had to say about them. She was my crash course on Yugoslavia. Then there was Milena, who had defected from Czechoslovakia in the seventies, worked at Citibank for a decade, and was now employed at a venture capital firm, going back and forth between New York and Prague, trawling for deals in the emerging market that had sprung up only yesterday on the territory of what had once been the evil empire. She was my crash course in communism.

For the most part, Milena disdained those who remained behind in the Eastern Bloc. She thought they were lazy or incompetent or worse, but she did retain a soft spot for Yugoslavia. She remembered it in much the same way Aleš remembered Trieste: as a playground of sorts, a balcony onto the West, a place to breathe away from the communist authorities at home. Sure, Yugoslavia had been communist too, but it had been a softer communism. Its leaders had been relatively lax, its jail sentences relatively short, its borders relatively porous. It had access to Western goods and culture, and most importantly for the gray landlocked hinterland of communist Central Europe, it had a seaside. Czechs and Poles and Hungarians, prohibited from going to the French or Italian Riviera, could occasionally get a visa to travel to the Dalmatian coast in communist Yugoslavia.

"My Yugo?"

"Yeah, your Slovenian. Aleš."

She had a low smoky voice and pronounced the name— "Aaah-leš"—a long diphthong extending the first syllable. He, in contrast, rushed through the first syllable of his name, coming down decisively on the ultimate one. Likewise he said his family name, Debeljak, with all the clattering emphasis of a machine gun, the stress landing heavily on the final *jak*.

What could I say?

My Yugo had dumped me in the most humiliating fashion, said he had to get back to his dissertation on social thought, that there weren't enough sparks between us. That was the first inkling I got that maybe his knowledge of English wasn't as perfect as it seemed, that he relied too heavily on clichés. But what difference did it make? He was gone, clichés and all.

He hadn't called since that night. He had deposited a single unstamped postcard in my mailbox. It featured a black-and-white photograph of a jazz legend on the front and Aleš's almost illegible scrawl on the back. His strict "onward-with-Tito!" elementary school teachers had forced him, even though he was left-handed, to write with his right. I decoded the words as well as I could: he was sorry, he had liked being with me, he didn't know how to explain, something along those lines. I don't remember exactly because I threw the card in the trash can outside my building and couldn't find it when I went back the next day to look.

"It didn't last," I shrugged.

Now I too had caught the melancholy bug. To be honest, though, I'm not really cut out for it. When it comes right down to it, shuddering misery suits me more than the resignation of melancholy.

"He just wanted to have sex with me." That's how I explained the inexplicable to Milena.

"So-o-o?" she drawled. She was very tall and blond with slanted gold eyes. She looked, I had always thought, just the way beautiful world-weary Slavic women are supposed to look. "Was he good in bed?"

I already knew from previous conversations with her that Eastern Europeans, or at least Czechs, or at least Milena, had a pragmatic and unsentimental approach to sex and sexual partners, more like the approach one might have to fitness and fitness instructors. When I had told Milena, before her most recent trip to Prague, about my encounter with Aleš at the party in Brooklyn, she had smiled nostalgically. She even looked a little homesick, something that was highly unusual for her, fanatically committed as she was to the American way of life. She told me that throughout the former communist countries Yugoslav men had enjoyed a reputation for their sexual prowess. The farther south, the better they got. Rebecca West, the British author who put Yugoslavia on the map with her travelogue *Black Lamb and Gray Falcon*, was positively weak-kneed by the time she arrived in Serbia. West considered Slovenians, who merit hardly a mention in the nearly thousand-page tome, to be ersatz Austrians. But in Milena's eyes there were still Yugos, even after the Ten Day War of independence.

"Yeah," I said mournfully, remembering one particular kiss on my ankle, the fragrant darkness lingering in the bedroom, the red wine bottle that stood guard on the hardwood floor until morning. Not enough sparks indeed.

"So?" she drawled. "What's the problem?"

And for some reason, at that particular moment, I found her approach liberating, brilliant even. My misery suddenly evaporated, and I got an idea. Again I can't remember how exactly I justified it to myself. It was another one of those elisions, one more of the many obstacles—his status as a penniless poet, his impending return to Slovenia, his unrepentant womanizing—swept aside or momentarily ignored. It struck me then—and maybe I had already had one glass of wine too many—that Milena was absolutely right. What *was* the problem? She'd never thought of Aleš as anything other than a passing lover for me, a vehicle for pleasure, a Yugo in a word. She'd never dreamed of that nothing-in-between, never thought I'd be crazy enough to fall in love with a man from nowhere, that I'd be crazy enough to even think of leaving New York and following him over there to the rim of that crazy war. She wouldn't dream of it. Aleš wouldn't dream of it. So why should I? The clock was ticking, it was almost Thanksgiving, he was leaving this country forever after New Year's. Why not seize the day? There were so few of them left.

I still had my pink message slip.

"While you were out. Alich." Followed by a question mark.

I still had the number.

"Halo," came the familiar faintly-accented voice.

"It's me," I said.

This time he didn't need to ask who "me" was.

That was just one more in the series of chance incidents that managed to keep Aleš and me together, despite all the personal and geographical elements that augured against the connection. The "How is your Yugo?" incident was followed by the "I think I'm falling in love with you at the Veselka Diner" incident and the "kissing Igor on Fourteenth Street" incident and, most improbably of all, the case of the "crossed letter to the Ministry of Finance." This unlikely combination of accident, alchemy, and fate would bring me directly to the top of Ljubljana's castle hill on that gloomy day in March 1993, to the X that marks the spot of Europe's dead and dying empires, to the moment when I, at last, without the help of accident or destiny, would have to decide which way to jump.

The "I think I'm falling in love with you at the Veselka Diner" incident took place in January 1992, a little over a month later after my dinner with Milena and on the eve of Aleš's departure to Vienna on a Romanian charter flight. During that cold, passionate winter, the only place Aleš and I regularly ventured outside the apartment on Twenty-Fourth Street was the row of Polish eateries on Second Avenue. The food was cheap and warm and filling. The kielbasa and dumplings presumably reminded Aleš of his mother's cooking, and I had the chance to prove again and again that I was not such a complicated bourgeois female after all, that I could easily live without haute cuisine. Polish home cooking suited me fine.

Our favorite diner was Veselka's at the corner of East Ninth. Aleš had told me that in the Slovenian language *vesel* meant happy, and we generally did feel happy there, although on this particular January morning Aleš looked anything but. He didn't seem to have much of an appetite, pushing a cold sliver of un-eaten yolk from one side of his plate to the other.

"What's the matter?" I asked. He glared across the table at me. "Did I do something wrong?"

He delivered the bit of yolk to his mouth and chewed morosely.

"Are you mad at me?"

I'd seen him like this a few times before, grim and angry at the whole world. Usually it was when he was reading of the latest outrage in his former homeland. At last he spoke. His voice was flat and expressionless.

"I think I've fallen in love with you." He wasn't looking at me anymore but down at the cold remains on his plate.

"Pardon me?" I wanted to hear him say it again.

"I said," he articulated the words fiercely now, looking directly at me, his eyes icy blue shards, "I think I've fallen in love with you."

Of course, what I really longed to do was rush around the table to him, hold his head in my arms, cradle it against my breast, assure him that I loved him too, that I loved him more than I'd ever loved anyone. I wanted to tell him that I'd happily spend the rest of my life with him, in a hovel if necessary, in a hovel located in the remotest corner of the world, even. I wanted to spend the rest of my life making love to him, giving birth to little Slavic babies with long twisted noses, cooking kielbasa and dumplings. I longed to tell him all of that, but I didn't, not a word. Some canny feminine instinct instructed me not to. Instead I reached a cool and comforting hand across the table and gently squeezed his, more the gesture of a social worker than a lover.

"Look," I said calmly, "let's not get too worked up about this right now. Let's just see how things go. I'll call you every Wednesday from my office, we'll meet in Rome in the spring, you'll come back to New York in a year to defend your dissertation, and maybe one day I'll visit you in Ljubljana."

The Wednesday phone call was my idea; Rome in the spring was his. It had appeared out of the blue on another one of his postcards. It turned out that postcards were Aleš's preferred method of written communication, the poet's condensed version of the novelist's epistolary urge. He bought postcards by the booklet and carried them around with him, always ready to scribble out a passing burst of emotion. He deposited them in the mailbox, on the duvet cover, on the burner where he knew I would find them in the morning before I went to work. The messages were usually short and sentimental.

"I miss you already, and I'm not yet gone." This postcard featured the photograph of a topless Brigitte Nielsen.

"Here's another picture of my sadness and longing." This one the face of a melancholy young man by the artist Franciabigio.

He'd left the one about Rome on New Year's Eve, his departure looming ever closer. "The best is yet to come!" he'd scrawled euphorically. "To love and to Rome and to love in Rome in 1992!" This on an ordinary Hallmark greeting card.

Rome, as it happened, was a turning point. Before Rome the reverse culture shock Aleš suffered in Ljubljana and his consequent despondency had been palpable in our Wednesday telephone conversations. It was still winter, the new country was in disarray, the politicians attempting to run it foolish, vain, and incompetent. Worse, Aleš fretted, with characteristic egotism, nobody remembered him after his five-year absence. But more than anything else, he viscerally realized in those first months that Ljubljana was not New York, not by a long shot, and could never hope to be. It lacked me, among countless other things.

Rome, in contrast, lacked nothing. The city was beautiful, the weather balmy and bright, our passion intact. We were even reading the same book when we met on a sunny April morning in the Piazza Navona: Milan Kundera's *Immortality*, Aleš in Slovenian translation, me in English. It seemed as if we were literally in the grip of a shared destiny. We stayed in a small hotel near the piazza. Each midday we set out to see a sight—the Spanish

Steps, the Sistine Chapel, Trevi Fountain—and each afternoon we returned to the hotel for a long sleepless siesta. Each morning I went down to fetch Aleš's breakfast—he preferred to sleep in—and the patroness handed me the tray and said *per tuo marito*, for your husband.

I never bothered to correct her.

But Aleš's return to Ljubljana was marred. The train connections had changed because of the war in Yugoslavia, and as a result he had to walk from Trieste to Sežana, across the Italian-Slovenian border. The Italian police, nonsensically figuring him for a refugee (he was walking in the wrong direction for that), gave him trouble. I got all the way across the ocean to New York nearly a day before he got to nearby Ljubljana, and nothing was ever the same again. Rome, or perhaps the tortuous route back from it, had cured him of his disease, and the disease was me. The week had worked like a powerful inoculation on his system. The walk home had reminded him of who was who in the world, where he belonged and where I did, who was likely to be harassed by border police and who likely to be left alone. As spring finally arrived in Slovenia, Aleš was often not home when I called on Wednesday, and when he was I could feel him slipping away. I knew there were other women then. I could feel them too, hovering in the background each time I called. It was probably this knowledge that led to the "kissing Igor on Fourteenth Street" incident.

He called me in July.

"*Halo.*" It was the exact same accent. The exact same accent saying the exact same word. I could have sworn it was Aleš, but the caller ID showed a Manhattan number. Still, my heart jumped. Maybe it was him. Maybe he had flown to New York without telling me.

"It's Igor. Don't you remember me? Aleš's roommate?"

My heart plummeted. I did remember him. Of course I did. I remembered everything about Aleš. We had already been apart longer than we'd been together, and I had had plenty of time to catalog each evening, each telephone conversation, each nuance that could be read into each memorable and not-so-memorable event. Naturally Igor occupied his own small space in that catalogue. He asked me out to dinner, and I accepted without hesitation. I was delighted to go, and it turned out to be fun. The food was excellent, Igor having transcended the Polish diner phase of his New York existence, the conversation flowed smoothly, and Igor's accent was pitch-perfect throughout. The slightly off intonation, the accidental reversal of word order here and there, the *h* rasped out from the bottom of his throat. If I closed my eyes, I could almost imagine I was having dinner with Aleš.

After dinner he walked me home. At the corner of Fourteenth Street, Igor put his hands on my shoulders and leaned his face down into mine. He was a good bit taller than Aleš. His intention was unambiguous. He clearly meant to kiss me, and from the tilt of his head, I could tell it was not just a peck on the cheek he wanted, but the real thing.

And I let him. I didn't resist.

I even parted my lips and enthusiastically participated. There were two million Slovenians on this earth, and I think by that time, by the heat of mid-summer, I missed Aleš so much that I would have kissed any one of them just as eagerly, figuring that somehow, by some strange process of osmosis, it would bring me closer to him.

Human nature being what it is, I can't help but think that that kiss played its own part in leading us to our present pass. Though not from me, Aleš heard about the kiss and afterwards I detected a little more proprietary interest during our phone calls. For a while there he had been willing to let me go, but he wasn't, as it turned out, willing to let someone else have me. During that autumn he even started to drop weighty hints that he might have viewed as harmless flirtation but I took to have life-changing significance.

Once after a government official mentioned the opening of a Slovenian consulate in New York and noted that he would be well-suited to the post of cultural attaché, Aleš boasted happily on the phone. "Imagine! You'll be married to an ambassador."

Another time he reported that he had had lunch with his mother and had informed her that she would have an American daughter-in-law. Poor Aleš; he might not have been aware of the English expression "Give her an inch and she'll take a mile," but he surely must have known the Slovenian equivalent, "Give her a finger and she'll take your whole arm."

He also didn't count on the *New York Times* playing a hand in his fate. The next day in its finance section the paper ran a three-page special supplement on Slovenia, the plucky new country that had defeated the Serbian war machine, and was now sitting gamely at the edge of the Balkan volcano, ready to do business. I told my secretary to hold my calls and read the section word for word, scouring it for possible clues to my future. One particular box advertisement caught my eyes. The largest Slovenian bank, called Ljubljanska Banka, had a representative office in Midtown Manhattan on Fifty-Sixth Street, not three blocks away from where I was sitting. I picked up the phone and placed a call. A man's voice answered, an American voice, and I explained that I was a high-level financial analyst, working at a reputable European firm, and happened to be moving to Slovenia. Was his boss available to speak to me? Would he or anyone else in the Ljubljanska Banka New York representative office have any idea what Slovenian financial institutions might be interested in giving a job to someone with my skills and experience?

There was, predictably enough, I suppose, no one else in the office to speak to.

The Ljubljanska Banka New York representative office was strictly a one-man operation, and when I sauntered into the bank's small suite of offices room at five fifteen that same day, a tall pockmarked middle-aged man practically rocketed out of his swivel chair to greet me. The office was unadorned and nearly unfurnished. It held two chairs, a file cabinet, and a desk with a few pieces of paper on its otherwise uncluttered surface. A silent telephone and the *New York Times* Slovenia supplement occupied pride of place. I might have been his first visitor all week. He suggested we go for a drink, which we did on that evening and on several others in the coming weeks. On these occasions he bought the drinks and I pumped him for information about the financial landscape in Slovenia. It was a somewhat barren landscape, it turned out, with only three domestic banks operating in Ljubljana—Ljubljanska Banka, Abanka, and SKB—along with one or two foreign banks (and, he added with a sigh, one or two movie theaters, two or three bars, a single decent hotel). The banks and indeed the whole financial system were struggling to survive because when Slovenia beat Yugoslavia in that ten-day war, the central bank in Belgrade peevishly locked the vault on all foreign reserves while sticking Yugoslavia's substantial foreign debt to the disloyal republics. The resulting balance of payments was dire, and Slovenia, having been the most developed and richest of the erstwhile republics, had the highest standard of living to lose.

But developed or not, he told me, the business environment was brutal for women. They were rare birds in the financial sector, and the men were not suave and dull like their New York counterparts but were real cowboys. They drank prodigious amounts (as did he, I discovered), didn't wear ties, and worked short hours, going home at three for a big midday meal cooked by their stay-at-home wives. Ljubljana itself was a provincial city, lovely and green with lots of outdoor cafés in the summertime but depressing and sunless in the winter, and winter lasted half the year.

"Sounds great," I beamed.

On our third rendezvous, I asked what the chances were that any of those three banks, his in particular, would hire me. He told me that the banks had had it up to their eyeballs with the foreign consultants and world bankers and venture capitalists that had flooded the country after 1989, scattered during the Ten Day War, and now had come back to stay, seeing Slovenia as perfectly poised on the newly expanding European continent. All the Western financial interests were sitting out the war, waiting for the big market that was once Yugoslavia to emerge, hopefully not too depleted by ethnic cleansing, and desperate for the oblivion offered by a plentiful supply of consumer goods. From that standpoint, a foreign institution or even the Ministry of Finance might be my best bet.

"Would you help me?" I asked him.

He snaked a hand across the table, gave mine a fraternal squeeze—he knew I was in love with some Slovenian poet—and promised he would. He was going on a business trip to Ljubljana in December and would personally deliver my résumé to potential employers. Under the table he pressed his knees against mine. It seemed a small price to pay. Aleš was coming to New York in late December with plans to defend his dissertation in January, and I wanted to surprise him with all the useful contacts I was making in his country.

On December 30, 1992, Aleš landed at JFK International Airport. It was a little less than a year since the "I love you in Veselka" incident and nearly eight months since Rome, when I'd said good-bye to him at the hotel near the Piazza Navona.

On December 31, 1992, New Year's Eve, Aleš broke up with me for the third, or perhaps the fourth, time; I'd lost count by then. It was a little less than twenty-four hours after his arrival. He wasn't cruel, wasn't indifferent to my tears. He just couldn't get around the fact that any real future between us was impossible.

He had no desire to settle in the United States, and it was inconceivable to him that I would settle in Slovenia. He was immovable, and this time at last I knew it was well and truly over.

It was time for me to stop: to stop all the phone calls, stop all the plotting, stop the fantasizing about ways we could somehow make it work. Time to give up. Time to say good-bye to my black-haired poet-lover.

At eleven o'clock that night, we wandered, sad and hungry, out of the apartment and into the dissonant merrymaking of New York's streets and avenues. We walked down to the West Village and stumbled into a little Cuban restaurant squeezed in between other eateries on a narrow alleyway, that however narrow, I couldn't help but notice, had considerably more than three restaurants and three bars beckoning from both sidewalks. The Cuban place was a charming hole-in-the-wall with six or seven small tables, colored paper lanterns hanging from the ceiling, the tiny place presided over by a serious black-bereted waiter who looked to us like a handsome version of Jean-Paul Sartre, if such a creature is even possible.

Miraculously, for it was just before midnight, one table was free and we sat down and ordered paella and a bottle of champagne from our philosopher-waiter. At midnight the press of people in the alley outside and the streets beyond exploded, and the dozen or so patrons in the Cuban restaurant stood up, and though they were strangers, moved around the small place hugging and kissing each other, wishing each other well in the New Year. They hugged and kissed Aleš and me too. We stood looking at each other under the bright paper shades, our champagne flutes clasped in our hands, one stranger after another coming to our table and bestowing on us their hopes for our happy future.

"I loved you so much," Aleš said to me.

"You love me." I insisted on the present tense.

"I do," he said, "but it's over. Rome's over. This is over," he gestured around him at the colorful room, the laughing strangers. "It's all over."

Jean-Paul sidled over to our table. First he topped up our champagne flutes. Then he put down the bottle and solemnly embraced us, pressing his black-bereted head between ours. "It's just begun," he whispered into our ears.

After finishing our paella and another bottle of champagne, Aleš and I floated out of the little restaurant and into the confetti-strewn streets. For some crazy reason we felt absolutely elated. It seemed to us like the most beautiful New Year's Eve ever, the most beautiful breakup ever. Sensations of euphoria and nobility puffed us up and sent us on our way. We had loved profoundly; that alone is an accomplishment in this world, and now amazingly we were able to let go of that love, to let it slip away into the neon Manhattan night from which it had first come. To have tried to hold on to it at any cost, to have let reality taint the perfection of what we had had, what we had tonight, what we had this minute, would have been an abomination. Even at that moment, though, as wonderful and noble as I felt, I knew, walking home with Aleš to the Twenty-Fourth Street apartment, that the euphoria would last only as long as he was there beside me, his breath on my cheek, his playful-melancholy eyes taking me in.

And true enough, on January 1, 1993, alone in bed, nursing a hangover, Aleš having departed for Igor's and then on to Syracuse to prepare his dissertation defense, I felt not the faintest trace of euphoria. The new year gaped before me. No love, no man, not even a dream of a man. I didn't bother getting out of bed.

On January 2, 1993, a phone call woke me at five in the morning.

"*Halo?*"

This time I knew it couldn't be Aleš. He was never awake at five in the morning. Plus he wouldn't call me Miss Johnson as the person on the line was doing and, if he did, he wouldn't have mispronounced it.

"*Halo*? Miss Yonson? Miss Yonson?"

I sat up in bed and rubbed my eyes.

"Yes?" I could barely manage the single word, though upon hearing it, the voice on the other end of the line lurched into high bureaucratic gear.

"Mr. Klemenčič here. Pleased to talk to you. Mr. Klemenčič calling on behalf of Ministry of Finance of independent Democratic Republic of Slovenia, formerly constituent republic of People's Federal Yugoslavia, but now independent and so entitled to raise money on international debt markets." He dropped all his articles. He pronounced the *b* in debt.

"Mr. Klemenčič calling to request your presence at employment interview at Ministry of Finance of democratic Republic of Slovenia located at number twelve Župančičeva Street in city of Ljubljana."

I held the phone away from my ear and stared at it. Then I placed it back against my ear.

"I'm sorry."

"Do not be sorry, Miss Yonson. Minister will be available to see you in March."

And then I remembered: the résumés, the personally delivered résumés. They must have crossed paths with Aleš somewhere over the Atlantic Ocean. Looking back now, the most absurd thing about the whole early morning telephone call was that I actually took Mr. Klemenčič at his word.

But then again, why would I have done otherwise? That was before I'd set foot in that nothing-in-between. That was when I still believed that a skyscraper was a skyscraper and that a job interview had some remote chance of leading to a job.

Vienna

MARCH 1993

Coffee cup and Saturday newspaper

"I was thinking, you know, talking to an old girlfriend of mine last night, about this whole forbidden bread thing, that I swore never to spend my life with a woman who didn't know who Johnny Štulić was. Maybe that was silly. Maybe now is the right time for me. I've played the field long enough. Maybe it would be a good time for me to get married. Anyhow: that's what me and my ex-girlfriend were talking about last night."

It was March 13, 1993. Aleš and I were sitting next to each other on the edge of a narrow bed in a narrow room in the Korotan youth hostel on Albertgasse in Vienna, Austria. The receptionist had described the room as a double with two single beds, but had failed to mention that the room was shaped like a corridor, that the beds were arranged not side by side as one would expect, but lined up rather unromantically from head to foot.

I had arrived at the Vienna Airport several hours before, in the early morning, having spent a sleepless night on an airplane flipping through a number of badly translated books about

Slovenian life and culture. A handful of common themes and sites and figures recurred in the books. The stunning Lake Bled, the visionary architect Jože Plečnik, the whole notion of being at the crossroads which, had I bothered to open the in-flight magazine, I would have realized was shared by virtually every city of significance in Central Europe and points east: Vienna, Prague, Budapest, Timişoara.

In this part of the world, brochure writers seemed to share a conviction that it was infinitely better to be located at the cusp of empires than right in the heart of them. In one section with the existential title *Where Are We?* the authors described Slovenia as being at nearly ten different significant meeting points: at the intersection of Warsaw Pact countries and NATO countries, of Balkan trade routes, of capitalism and socialism, of the Catholic, Muslim, and Orthodox faiths, of mountain and sea (Alps and Adriatic), mountain and plains (Alps and Pannonia), mountain and mountain (Alps and Dinaric ranges).

Language was another recurrent obsession. The streets of the capital, Ljubljana, were named after lexicographers and grammarians, its squares adorned with the statues not of mounted military leaders waving swords but of poets turning the pages of books. France Prešeren, the first poet to abandon the German vernacular of the imperial Habsburgs and write in the Slovenian language, was a national icon: two major streets named after him, the national arts award—the one Aleš won for his poetry—named after him, even the national chocolate bearing his name. His melancholy and slightly corpulent face gazed out from the most commonly used banknote, the thousand-tolar bill, the tolar being the Slovenian currency that replaced the Yugoslav dinar. Prešeren had written poems to his beloved Julia, herself a member of the German-speaking elite, in his own language, the language of farmhands and milkmaids. Perhaps he thought she would like it, would thrill to it as I had when Aleš first spoke it to me. But Julia ended up spurning Prešeren's advances, Prešeren became an incurable drunk, and the Slovenian people remain eternally in his thrall.

And now, if I was not mistaken, another Slovenian poet, an heir to Prešeren, was proposing to his own foreign beloved, though this time resorting to a language other than Slovenian and to words that fell far short of the lyrical.

"You were talking to an ex-girlfriend?" I echoed his last words.

He nodded nervously.

"About getting married?"

"Hm-hmm."

"Did you have anyone particular in mind?"

He turned to me with a tired smile. He too had spent a sleepless night driving the five hours from Ljubljana to Vienna to pick me up at the airport. We had decided to meet in Vienna rather than Ljubljana itself, ostensibly because the airplane ticket was cheaper—and because we could also pay a quick visit to the Kunsthistorische Museum—but really because it would be a more gradual way of easing ourselves into his world. Up until then, we had only known mine—the four walls of the apartment on Twenty-Fourth and Third Avenue, the continent of the bed. He answered my question by covering my lips with his fingers, pressing his body against my beating heart, and pushing me back onto the narrow continent of the Korotan's bed, more of an archipelago really.

That first day was easy.

The thrill of his fumbling proposal, which, fumbling or not, was a marriage proposal nonetheless; the stroll from the hostel on Albertgasse to Saint Stephen's Cathedral; the anonymity of Vienna; the German language that neither of us understood well floating around our ears, wrapping us in our own cocoon. The next day, toting my suitcase, I slid into the passenger seat of Aleš's gray Renault Clio, and we set out on the same path that James Joyce had traveled nearly a century before when he had accidentally disembarked in Ljubljana. Only this time it would not be accidental. We would not reboard the train the next day. This time we were going there intentionally, following the Austrian autobahn that ran parallel to the old imperial railroad, following the tracks leading from Vienna to the Slovenian border and onward to Ljubljana and Trieste, a passage that would bring me from the tame periphery right into the wild heart of the land of ex-girlfriends.

Back in New York, I had been warned by those who knew that winter was not the best time to visit Central Europe. But I hadn't wanted to wait for better weather. I hadn't wanted to wait to see Aleš and Ljubljana. The time had come, and besides, Mr. Klemenčič had said March. But once we put the austere grandeur of imperial Vienna behind us, impressive in any weather, I began to have doubts about the plan. An anemic sun hung low over the land. It wasn't that the sky was so gray or overcast, though it could hardly be said to be blue either. It was more that the sun seemed to lack any oomph here, the air to lack oxygen. The autobahn traversed a flat featureless countryside, the Austrian Alps being farther to the west. We passed beneath one highway sign after another, one settlement after another: Baden, Neustadt, Kapfenberg, Gloggnitz. As we got farther south, closer to our destination, I felt a growing sense of unease. Perhaps it was simply the proximity of the place I'd been thinking about for so long, reading about, daydreaming about, or perhaps it was because there were no signs for *it*, no permanent signs at any rate.

We were almost at the border when I spotted the first one: a green highway sign with the word YUGOSLAVIA deleted with a single strip of black weatherproof tape. Next to the crossed-out

word, three letters—SLO—appeared, formed with more of the
same tape. On the next sign, the highway workers had forgotten
to add the SLO. The signs painted directly on the asphalt were
hardly more encouraging. From a bird's-eye perspective one
would have seen the gray Clio sliding over the gray asphalt and
consuming the two faded letters YU. Again the two letters had
been effaced, this time with a sloppy painted x, and nothing else
lettered in to replace it.

It was as if nobody really knew what lay beyond Austria's
southern border anymore. All of this gave our destination a distinctly provisional feel, as if it might not exist at all; or if it did
exist, it might be gone by the time we got there. Yugoslavia had
disappeared into the ether and nothing had come along to take
its place. We were about to drive off the map.

"Where are we indeed?" I wondered aloud.

I glanced over at Aleš. He had always spoken of Slovenia as if
it were a real country—as if it had a real government, however incompetent; a postal service, a constitution, all the trappings of a
nation state. In three months time, it would be the second an-
niversary of the Ten Day War that severed Slovenia from Yugoslavia. Germany had recognized the country. The rest of the
European Union and America and the United Nations had reluctantly followed suit. Two years and its neighbors hadn't seen
fit to put up permanent markers. Maybe they knew something
Aleš didn't know. Maybe they thought of Slovenia as a temporary
phenomenon. Perhaps they were waiting for Yugoslavia to make
a comeback. Politicians and diplomats dislike change. It's inconvenient. You have to rewrite the treaties, the history books, the
signs along the roads. You have to reprint all the maps, come up
with new colors for the new countries. No wonder they were waiting to see how things would turn out in the end.

Aleš slowed at the border crossing.

The Austrians nonchalantly waved us through. What did they care? We were the ones leaving, crossing over to the other side, heading into that nothing-in-between.

The Slovenian officials, on the other hand, clearly relished their new jobs. Their uniforms were crisp and well-ironed. Below the shoulder epaulet the Slovenian coat of arms shone from their sleeves: three bright stars in a dark blue field above the three-headed Mount Triglav, once the tallest mountain in Yugoslavia and now by definition the tallest in Slovenia, and below three wavy lines indicating the Adriatic Sea. Later I would learn that Slovenia, a land of peasants, had never really had its own nobility or its own coat of arms. This one had been generated like a corporate logo with the help of designers and publicists. The coat of arms was featured in the corner of the Slovenia tricolor flag, another national emblem that had had to be rushed from the drafting board to the tops of the flag poles.

Unlike his Austrian counterpart, the Slovenian customs officer made a busy show of performing his duties, like a child playing make-believe border crossing. No detail was deemed too irrelevant. No page of the passport too empty for at least a brief perusal. The official flipped through Aleš's Slovenian passport and handed it back. Then he dedicated several long minutes to my American passport, turning it this way and that, rubbing a curious finger over the perforated identification number along the top, gazing into the smiling face of the girl in the photograph. He lowered his head and peered at me through the glass window of the little house.

"*Američanka?*" he called out over the driver's seat.

"Yes," I patted my chest to confirm and repeated the word, "*Američanka*."

It seemed like a good start. We were communicating, almost speaking the same language. After a brief exchange with Aleš— in a very different language, a language of which I could not make out a single comprehensible word—and the payment of a small fee, he issued me a one-month tourist visa, stamped my passport, handed it back, and Aleš and I were on our way.

The highway had ended at the border, but it wasn't far to go to Ljubljana, not more than two more hours even on a two-lane regional road. Aleš informed me that it took about five hours to drive from the east to the west of the country at its widest point, three to drive from north to south. Slovenia, as one inhabitant once put it, was about the size of a family burial vault. By that measure we only needed to skip over a few marble tombstones and we'd be there.

But for some reason Aleš was pulling over to the side of the road again.

"What are you doing?" I asked.

He nodded toward two gangly male hitchhikers standing on the shoulder, one carrying a sign that said LJ.

"Oh, no," I pleaded.

It struck me with the most terrible urgency. He mustn't pick them up. It had always been just us, always. First in my apartment on Twenty-Fourth Street, then in the hotel at the Piazza Navona amidst the singsong tones of Italian speakers, then the Korotan youth hostel on Albertgasse, and now the shelter of his little gray Clio, this little bubble of ours gliding silently through the gray Central European landscape. It was our last refuge.

"I always pick up hitchhikers," he said. "I hitchhiked all over Europe. You know that."

I did know that. He had regaled me with tales of his crossings: sleeping at truck stops, creepy Bulgarian long-haul drivers hitting on ex-girlfriends, the single tin of sardines that kept him alive all the way up the Italian boot from Sardinia to Slovenia. His stories always made me feel slightly chastened. I couldn't help but think of my own stays in Parisian hotels, my Eurail train travels, Eurail in fact being the reason I'd never made it to Yugoslavia back when it was Yugoslavia, a time when young Western tourists viewed it as a badge of honor to go there, to venture behind the Iron Curtain, though not very far. And the people who went always said the same things about it: spectacular landscape, gorgeous seaside, grim architecture, terrible food, unsmiling people. So I didn't go, ostensibly because Eurail didn't cover the communist countries, but really because I doubted that spectacular landscape and the thrill of being behind the Iron Curtain could make up for everything else.

"I know, but just this once . . ."

He shot me a disapproving look. We didn't know each other very well, not really. We hadn't socialized with other people. We had barely been out in public together. But nevertheless two particular roles had begun to gel in our still-fluid relationship: he the poor and noble son of socialism, and me the pampered daughter of capitalism, the selfish child who doesn't even want a couple of hitchhikers to sit in the empty backseat, all because of some bourgeois notion of privacy.

But in this particular case he misunderstood me. It wasn't hitchhikers I didn't want. It was these hitchhikers. It was Slovenian hitchhikers. It was people who spoke his language. Aleš would chat with them all the way to Ljubljana, asking where they'd been, what they'd seen, what school they went to. And I would have to give him up, to share him two hours earlier than scheduled. I would be plunged into the isolation that I already knew awaited me in Ljubljana. If we picked them up, Aleš would be with them and not with me anymore. They would share a language, a history, a culture, all of which were obscure to me. I would become what I already knew I was: stranger, foreigner, outsider. The spell would be broken, the illusion that all lovers cherish while they can, that there are only two in the world, only two that matter.

The boys clambered into the back seat with their packs, bobbing their heads gratefully. Aleš pulled away from the shoulder.

After a while he asked them in Slovenian what I presumed meant: Where to? Where do you need to be dropped off exactly? One of the boys bobbed his head up and down some more, smiled goofily, and handed the LJ sign forward.

I turned my head back sharply and looked at them. They didn't speak Slovenian. They were foreigners too.

"Where are you from?" I asked in English.

They shrugged and shook their heads.

"D'*ou venez-vous*?" I summoned my banker's French.

"D*a dove sei*?" Aleš chimed in from the driver's seat.

Nothing.

Then one of the boys held up his hands and communicated something to the other in sign language, and I realized that, yes, they may have been Slovenian, but they were also deaf and mute, a different kind of outsider than me, but outsiders all the same. I sent them a collegial smile and a clumsy little wave, not quite international sign language but a stab at communication.

I turned back around and faced the road, grinning sheepishly. All that fuss for nothing. Aleš and I could hear the boys in the back seat laughing among themselves in their awkward, infectious, nonhearing way, and we looked at each other and laughed in our own awkward hearing way.

I placed my hand on his knee, exhaled, and for the first time since we'd crossed the border looked at the spectacular landscape around me: the Pohorje mountain range rising to my right, the fallow fields of hops to my left, a modest little church and belfry dotting the top of each hillock. The sky already seemed a bit brighter.

Leaving New York

I cannot not love you.

In the end I never answered the question Aleš asked me up at Ljubljana Castle. Whether I could *really* do it, really move to this strange place and leave everything I knew behind. I didn't answer.

I went home. I told my family I was moving to another country, a country they probably hadn't heard of. I told them I was marrying in October, a writer, a poet, one they no doubt hadn't heard of either. My mother, in San Francisco, said she vaguely remembered me moaning over some Slovenian guy but hadn't taken it seriously. She'd thought he was another one of my offbeat boyfriends who would soon be on his way like all the others. My sister, also in California, expressed skepticism. My brother, who had lived in Frankfurt with his American wife for the last ten years, was thrilled. Not only would I be closer to him but I would be tantalizingly close to a war zone.

I gave notice at my job. I made arrangements for a long-term sublet of my Twenty-Fourth Street apartment. But even after all of that was done, the question still had not been answered, and because I remained stubbornly silent on the point, the void was filled by others. And so it turned out, as odd as it might seem, that the most difficult thing about leaving New York was not the leaving itself but the telling: telling people *where* I was going and hearing what they had to say about it. With every attempt to explain, a little part of the answer fell into place. With every attempt, I encountered if not horror then amazement, incomprehension, and inevitably a deep geographical confusion. For example, with a young woman at a party:

"Wow, that it so great. Congratulations on your engagement. So where exactly are you going?"

"Slovenia."

"Oh ... oh ... oh ..." (Pause)

"Yes. Slovenia!" (Pause)

"Oh, Slovenia! Wow! You're going to have such an exciting life. You'll be able to visit the Hermitage Museum, the Caspian Sea ... or is it the Dead Sea?"

With my dentist:

"So where are you moving? I can have your chart forwarded if you want. Maybe recommend someone."

"Slovenia." (Diligent scraping)

"Slovenia, huh?"

"Yup. Better do a thorough cleaning today." (More scraping)

"Now, where is Slovenia again?"

"*Pfsfybysly.*"

"You know, Hungarians make excellent false teeth, I've heard. Top of the line. If you ever need a set."

With the saleswoman at Barnes & Noble:

"I'm looking for books about a country called Slovenia, maybe some tapes on the language."

"Slovenia?"

"Yes, that's right."

"Why Slovenia?"

"I'm moving there."

"Oh, wow. Oh, my God. Oh, really? Wow. Why would you do a thing like that?"

"I'm getting married."

"Wow. Congratulations. Now what language do they speak in Slovenia? Lithuanian?"

Over time I developed strategies to deal with the conversation. Sometimes, when I felt tired or unsure or simply wanted to talk about something else, I didn't bother to tell people that I was moving at all. Or I lied about the destination and offered a different city: San Francisco, London, Anchorage, Timbuktu. Anywhere but Slovenia.

Back then, Americans, always a bit vague about the world outside their borders, had been overwhelmed by the sudden and unexpected fall of the Iron Curtain, by the strange-sounding names that had begun to appear with increasing regularity in American newspapers and evening news shows. There had been peaceful revolutions—velvet ones—in beautiful cities, and surrealist playwrights, fans of Lou Reed and Frank Zappa no less, had become presidents. Less peaceful revolutions had taken place in less beautiful cities, and less cool presidents had been lined up against the wall and shot. Large empires were breaking up into large countries, and large countries into smaller countries. Americans were discovering that what had once been rather conveniently lumped under the term the Eastern Bloc or the evil empire was actually an extremely varied and complex place made up of several regions, and these regions were made up of countries, and some of these countries were made of republics—like Kosovo, Bosnia, Slovenia, Croatia—many of whom emphatically didn't want to be lumped together anymore.

It was hard to keep track in those days.

With a bit of study, thanks in part to the saleswoman at Barnes & Noble who despite her initial confusion came through in the end with several volumes, I developed two approaches to the problem: the first historical and the second geographical. The historical approach had to do with Europe's old and now-defunct empires. In this version I explained that Slovenia, though having a communist history, never belonged to the Russian empire. Until the beginning of the twentieth century it occupied the southwest flank of the Austro-Hungarian Empire. This fact, I went on, is crucial to understanding the unique culture of the Slovenians: although they are Slavs, they are essentially Central, not Eastern, European; that they are Roman Catholic, not Orthodox or Muslim as those who had been ruled by the Ottoman Turks might be; that Slovenians are conservative and bourgeois at heart. This last was code for "not throat-slitting Balkan lunatics."

But this approach didn't work very well, maybe because Americans have a blind spot when it comes to the old European empires. They experience a strange kind of vertigo when you bring them up. Just mention to virtually any American who is not a specialist or a recent immigrant from the region the assassination of the Archduke Franz Ferdinand in Sarajevo that precipitated World War I and you will observe the same effect. First there will be a flash of recognition: yes, they know of the event; assassinations are memorable, and that one was daring and dramatic, the archduke's wife gunned down by his side—but then there will follow a moment of vagueness, historical vertigo, and the inevitable fall into confusion. What did that assassination in Sarajevo have to do with the beginning of World War I, anyway? What did Sarajevo have to do with the Ottoman Empire? What was the Ottoman Empire? Or the Prussian Empire, for that matter? Was it part of Germany? Or just Russia with a P?

I decided that it was better to stick to the straightforward geographical explanation, the jigsaw puzzle explanation. In this version I started by explaining that Slovenia is in fact far to the west of Russia, Siberia, Poland. It's even to the west of Vienna. I told them that Slovenia shares a border with Hungary to the east, Austria to the north, Croatia to the south, and Italy to the west. This last point was my ace in the hole. Yes, Italy; reassuring, isn't it? Home to Leonardo da Vinci, the Venice Biennale, Giorgio Armani. Slovenia even has a small Adriatic coast line, the sea in question being not the Caspian or the Dead Sea but the Mediterranean. And Slovenia has Alps, like Switzerland; safe, boring old Switzerland.

But this approach did not produce the desired effect either. Mention of the Mediterranean may have banished visions of snow-covered steppes, but there was still something nibbling at the edge of their consciousness, some eureka moment, some "aha, that's where you're going" realization, and I knew that one simple phrase would have furnished virtually everyone I spoke to with just such a moment. All I needed to say was the following seven words—"the northernmost republic of the former Yugoslavia"—and nobody, not even the most geographically challenged of Americans, not even the most provincial of New Yorkers, would not have known what I was talking about. Even people who kept their heads deep in the sand as far as international politics were concerned hadn't been able to entirely avoid the unrelenting stream of headlines in those days: "Croatian City of Vukovar Reduced to Rubble," "Serb Forces Overrun Muslim Villages," "Sarajevo Under Siege." I knew that if I were to utter those seven words, the necessary map would have fallen immediately into place. No more concern about harsh Siberian winters, no more excitement about as-yet undiscovered art museums, no more mix-up between the Balkans and the Baltics, between Lithuania and Slovenia.

Exit geographical confusion, enter disbelief.

"But isn't there a war going on over there?"

"Well, not in Slovenia, actually; an hour or so to the southeast."

"An hour? Those people are fucking crazy."

By which they meant that I too was fucking crazy. To even get near such a place. To marry a man from such a place. And in this case it didn't help to gravitate toward people who got the whole Yugoslav thing. Yugoslavs—who presumably got it better than anyone else—were leaving the region in droves. When I told Milena, it wasn't so much the war that bothered her but everything else I was getting myself into, the whole civilizational ball of wax. She had one doom-laden sentence to describe my future.

"He will never lift a finger."

This was a reference to her own father, who, when served a plate of food without cutlery, sat glowering throughout the entire meal, although the silverware drawer lay only steps away. And not only Milena, but Europeans in general, were far more burdened with prejudice and contempt than their more naive "oh, wow" American counterparts. When I gave notice to my French boss at the bank, he lowered his glasses to the tip of his Gallic nose, looked at me curiously, and said,

"I hope, Erica, that you are marrying the president of that country." He pronounced it *"zat countre-e-e."*

A colleague sitting in a nearby cubicle guffawed over the barrier. "She's marrying a goddamn poet."

My boss took off his glasses completely and stared at me in naked-eyed amazement. "A poet?"

The die was cast. I'd already quit. "It's a branch of literature," I explained. "You know: Rimbaud, Baudelaire..."

But it was the Austrians and Germans, former imperial rulers and would-be executioners, who responded in the most chilling fashion. Occasionally I would meet a German-speaking woman of a certain generation who, when told of my plans, would get a dreamy look in her eyes and mention a trip to Dalmatia she'd taken in the nineteen-seventies. At those times, I knew I was getting a reprieve because of the Yugo effect. She had had a memorable seaside affair with some strapping Croat. Usually, though, I didn't fare so well. Usually it was as if I'd told my Teutonic interlocutors that I'd contracted a rare and incurable disease. At one of my final farewell business dinners, I announced to a group of colleagues from a German bank that I was leaving my job, marrying, and moving to Slovenia. The announcement was met with the usual shocked silence. Finally, someone managed to spit out the standard objection.

"But isn't there a war going on over there?"

"It's an hour to the southeast," I responded with my standard demurral. "In Croatia and Bosnia."

"Ah, an hour." He fiddled with his napkin ring.

And then a blond taut-faced woman asked me in her clipped German accent a question that I hadn't fielded before: "And you will have to don the chador, no? In your new home?"

"Pardon me?"

"The burka," she explained, "the Islamic veil. Your husband will make you wear this, no?"

It was the ultimate put-down, really, delivered with typical German efficiency. In one fell swoop, she had managed to suggest that I was throwing my professional life away, moving to a backward and primitive place, and entering into an unwise and humiliating marital alliance. I didn't answer her. I couldn't. At the moment I felt too deflated to go into it all over again. That Slovenia had been part of the Austro-Hungarian Empire, that it was Roman Catholic and not Muslim, and that as far as Bosnian Muslims were concerned they were mostly secular anyway, had lived peacefully in that part of Europe for centuries, which was more than you could say for the Germans and Austrians, their neighbors to their north.

I left the restaurant as soon as I could. I despised these people, but what was really bothering me was the creeping feeling that maybe they were right. It seemed impossible that they could *all* be wrong. And besides, who was I trying to fool, anyway? If I hadn't been on a mission of love, if I hadn't been blinded by passion (like those dreamy-eyed women of a certain generation), I might have disliked Slovenia myself. I might have ticked it off as a place that I didn't need to return to. Everything I'd heard about it had turned out to be more-or-less true. Sure, the landscape was spectacular, but I'd been living in Manhattan for the last twelve years and had learned to live without landscape. The architecture in the city of Ljubljana itself, aside from the baroque and medieval city center, was appalling, little more than poured slabs of gray concrete with the occasional window hacked out of them. The weather was bad, the meat overcooked, the toilet paper came in rough little squares. The interior lighting was garish, the exterior lighting filtered through a layer of fog and coal excrescence. Loud kitsch radio was piped into every public space. People smoked incessantly. They drank hard liquor at seven in the morning standing up at tiny tables in grimy cafés. And it was true they didn't smile, and the few who did, the old ladies, for instance, hawking their beets and celery roots in the outdoor market stalls, didn't have any teeth. When they heard me speaking English, they pulled their gnarled hands from their apron pockets and held them in front of them as if what they wanted from me was mercy, or perhaps a few extra dinars.

"*Angležinja*" they cried out as I passed by.

I turned and shook my head, not English, no. "*Američanka*," I said.

"*Aaaji! Američanka! Američanka!*" they nearly wailed, overcome by a paroxysm of amazement and desire, as if they would do anything to untie the scarves under the chins, untie their apron strings, walk away from their vegetable stands, and travel with me to the land of abundance, the land of freedom, the land where everything was possible. Why on earth would anyone do the reverse?

I was doing it for love, never a sure thing, and in this case an almost absurd long shot. Who was I marrying, after all? A poet and a specialist in social thought (whatever that was), who by his own admission had spent the last ten years going to international literary and academic conferences where he scanned the roster not for brilliant or like-minded colleagues but for the single women who would be most likely to succumb to his charms in the limited space of twenty-four hours. In that brief March visit, all the young female acquaintances Aleš and I had bumped into on the streets of Ljubljana, and there were more than a few, had given me the same amused and quizzical look as if to say: "I wonder how long you'll last."

I sat on my bed with the phone in my lap. I picked up the black-and-white photograph of Aleš that I had kept propped against my lamp on the bedside table for the last year, my phantom lover, my soldier boy gone to the wars. His face rested in the cradle of his fingers and his eyes gazed unflinchingly out at his beholder: at me. On the back of the photograph, he had scribbled the words: "I cannot *not* love you."

I dialed his number. It was four in the morning in Slovenia.

"*Halo.*" That wasn't the standard telephone greeting in Slovenian. He knew it was me. "What is it?" he asked softly when I didn't speak.

"Just explain to me," I almost whimpered. By this time I was at the end of my tether; the whole project seemed utterly insane, and it was too late to change my mind. "Just explain," I swallowed deeply to regain my composure, "why there is not one person in this whole city, not one person in this whole country, not one person in this whole world, as far as I can tell, who thinks I'm doing the right thing?"

When I had calmed down, I managed to tell him about the Germans' reaction, about my French boss's reaction, about everyone's reaction. Everyone's.

"That's just the way it is," he said with a tone of resignation. "That's the way it's always been. Even before the war."

He told me about the saleswoman in Trieste who had refused to give his father a price on a cashmere sweater because she said he wouldn't, in any case, be able to afford it. So why bother telling him? When his father insisted, the woman haughtily refused, humiliating him as his son looked on. It was her way of showing him where he stood in the scheme of things. It didn't matter what he did in Yugoslavia, whether he was the mayor of Ljubljana or a marathon runner or a foreman in a factory. It didn't matter that she was a lowly Triestine sales clerk. All that mattered was that she was Italian and he Yugoslav, she West and he East, she a real European and he some inferior model.

"You can still change your mind if you want." His voice sounded mournful. I sensed that despite the roles into which we had fallen, the noble young son of socialism versus the spoiled child of the world's last superpower, he felt no pleasure at the strange reversal witnessed here, no satisfaction that I was coming to know the niggling humiliation that he, a citizen of one of the world's countless powerless nations, had experienced his entire life. It seemed to him, if anything, a matter of regret, a small tragedy even, that my optimism, my naive belief that reasonable people didn't treat each other that way, should be proved so wrong.

"You don't have to go through with it. You have a choice. Most people don't." It wasn't an accusation, just a statement of fact.

"No," I fired back angrily. "I'm not going to change my mind because of them."

"Not because of them," he said softly, "because of you. It's not going to work. It can't work. I was walking the streets of Ljubljana today, looking at the buildings, the people, the signs, trying to see it all through your eyes. You won't understand anything. You won't have a job. You won't have friends. And it's so lifeless here compared to what you know, so dull. There's only three bars, two movie theaters, a handful of restaurants. There's no place to go out. You're not going to survive."

Those three bars again. Everyone else was worried about the homicidal bloodletting going on to the south, and he was fretting about my social life.

"I will survive," I said stubbornly. "I only called because I don't understand why everyone is against it, against Slovenia, against us." A long and expensive silence ensued. "And now you too," I added petulantly.

"I'm not against us," he said. "If you want to understand why, read the memoirs of Czesław Miłosz I sent you. Did you get them?"

"I did," I answered. "Thank you. And sorry. You can go back to sleep now."

"I will," he said. I knew he would. He could sleep anywhere, anytime.

"Good morning," I whispered.

"Good night," he whispered back across the world.

I lay back on the bed and picked up the book by Czesław Miłosz, the Polish, now American, poet, Nobel Prize laureate, one more person who had been driven away by the indignities of the region and the system to which I was voluntarily going like a sheep to the slaughter, or more aptly like a pig to the kielbasa factory. Aleš had signed the inside cover of the book with another one of his sentimental bathos-filled scrawls, which for some reason I felt I could no longer live without. I scanned the opening chapter and quickly found the passage Aleš might have been referring to:

The revolving globe of the earth has become small,
and geographically speaking, there are no longer
any uncolored areas on it. In Western Europe, however, it is enough to have come from the largely un-
traveled territories in the East or North to be
regarded as a visitor from Septentrion. Standing beside the canopy bed (in Geneva), I felt both a native
and a foreigner. Undoubtedly, I would call Europe
my home, but it was a home that refused to acknowledge itself as whole; instead, as if on the
strength of some self-imposed taboo, it classified
its population into two categories: members of the
family (quarrelsome but respectable) and poor
relations.

I knew it to be true. I was starting to get a taste of it myself. In
the last few weeks, I almost felt as if I'd become one of the poor
relations. And yet, in the end, it didn't change my mind. Not the
dour pronouncements of a whole fleet of Western Europeans
would change my mind, not the scorn of a whole truckload of
Manhattan financiers, not even the beautiful and melancholy
musings of a thousand literary legends. Nothing would change
my mind.

Because in the end, I could not *not* go.

I would have followed my black-haired cradle-fingered poet
anywhere. I would have followed him to the ends of the earth. I
would have followed him to Septentrion itself.

PART TWO

Dual

Septentrion

OCTOBER 3, 1993

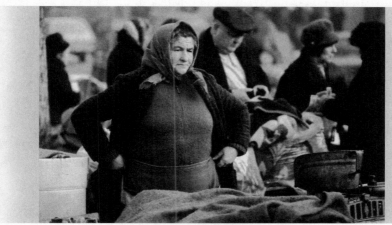

Saleswoman in the Ljubljana market

It is the day after my wedding.

I have a splitting headache, the result of a dizzying amount of wine consumed the night before. I am sitting on a couch in the living room of a small family apartment on the ground floor of a low block of housing units. I have been here before, but the place still has a somewhat foreign look to me, not exotic in the way the interior of a grass hut in Polynesia might be exotic, but still a look that speaks of exotic values.

For one thing, the apartment is impeccably clean, like a farmhouse that has been emptied of its contents for spring cleaning, walls and floors scrubbed and whitewashed, and then refilled with furniture again. For another thing, it makes the most—and I mean the most—of its limited acreage. Small apartments, I realize, are no rarity in other parts of the world; I lived in one in Manhattan. But this apartment features something as eccentric as an unheated closet off the front hallway where winter stores

are kept: rows of glass jars filled with beets and forest mushrooms, preserves made of plum and greengage, home-pickled
pickles, that sort of thing. The bathroom and toilet are in separate quarters, both tiny, and the bathroom contains a peculiar
and extremely deep half bath, the shape of which looks more
suitable for the crushing of grapes or the boiling of tripe than for
actual human bathing. The few closets in the apartment are
neatly stacked from bottom to top with an impressive amount of
fanatically ironed clothing and lace doilies, sentimental keep-
sakes, and loads of other bric-a-brac: hand-appliquéd linen tablecloths dating from the days of the Empress Maria Theresa,
favorite Mardi Gras costumes, old Scout uniforms, red-starred pioneer caps from the communist youth league.

But the most exotic thing about the apartment is simply its
location: in a provincial European capital called Ljubljana in the
newborn country of Slovenia. The country where I shall now live
through richer and through poorer, through sickness and through
health. The country where I shall give birth to whatever children
I may have, where I shall raise them to adulthood, and with any
luck, grow old and gray myself. The particular mixture of sensations I am feeling at the moment, the hangover feeling combined
with finding myself sitting alone on a couch in a strange apartment, recalls the aftermath of some of the more foolish episodes
of my party-girl youth, chapters in my life that must be firmly relegated to the past.

I am a married woman now.

Oh, yes; there's one more thing I forgot to mention, one more
element that adds to the surreal quality of the moment, not to
mention the throbbing of my head. An earsplitting siren-like
sound is coming from within the small apartment itself, its
source only a few yards away from my position on the couch. The
sound emanates from the narrow alley-like kitchen that, though
close, I cannot see from where I am sitting. The kitchen and the

source of the sound lie just beyond the tiny little breakfast nook that serves, I already know, as dinner and lunch nook as well, as ironing corner and study and family conference room all rolled up into one.

It is not a clock or a timer, not the scream of a smoke alarm.

It is not some sort of weird Balkan music.

It is the sound of ululating women. Hysterical women. Wailing, weeping, lamenting women.

"Hang on a minute," I want to call out to them. "This isn't Sarajevo. We're not mourning the dead here. We've come from a wedding, not a funeral. You haven't lost a son; you've gained a daughter." But I say nothing. I can't.

For one thing, I don't speak the language. And for another thing, I am struck momentarily dumb by the sheer earth-stopping force of the reorientation I must make. I may even be gleaning a small insight about the country to which I have come. In late June of 1991, Slovenia woke up after the surprising victory of the Ten Day War, rubbed its eyes, and looked around. The day before, it had been the perennially dull and diligent A student in a variously backward and brilliant, barren and abundant federal union made up of Montenegrin shepherds, Muslim dervishes, Zagreb coffeehouse intellectuals, Belgrade cosmopolitans. But the day after the war, Slovenia woke up alone. It looked to the west and to the north and discovered that a transformation had taken place. It wasn't the A student anymore. Far from it. It had suddenly become the poor and dangerous neighbor of a jittery European Union, the cordon sanitaire between civilization and chaos. It was all a question of context, and the context had changed dramatically and with a startling finality.

My own reorientation was only slightly less jarring. Yesterday I was the impulsive and unpredictable child in a typical middle-class Protestant American family, the one who could be relied on to get offended at the dinner table, to flounce out of the room in angry tears. But today, sitting in the living room of this small apartment, I realize that my context had also changed. Dramatically and with a startling finality. For a moment, I am able to regard myself as if from a distance, and this is what I see: a dry-eyed tight-lipped pale-haired young woman sitting nervously on a couch, feet pressed together, arms crossed over her chest. I can see that this woman has become something different from what she is accustomed to being: she is no longer so fearless, no longer as impulsive and emotional as she was yesterday. She has suddenly become the prim and cautious member of a black-haired wild-eyed clan of southern Catholic Slavs, the kind of family that finds it very hard to let go of their only son.

Otočec

OCTOBER 2, 1993

Wedding at Otočec

The wedding, for what it's worth, was a success. We pulled it off, though just barely. The weather was lovely, the meat tender to the point of falling off the bone, even the toilet paper seemed soft that day. Aleš and I had decided to get married not at one of the two most popular venues in the country—Ljubljana Castle or Lake Bled—but at a place slightly off the beaten path, a place called Otočec, which means "little island," and is located in Dolenjska, one of Slovenia's five principal regions. In terms of the country's four main axes—Vienna, Trieste, Klagenfurt, and Karlovac—it falls on the latter axis, on Karlovška, the road south-east, to Zagreb and the rest of what was once Yugoslavia. Otočec, a medieval castle straddling a tiny island that nestles in a bend of the Krka River, lies just about twenty minutes from the Croatian border. In Slovenia, no village is far from a border, nor is any village very far from Ljubljana, which lies, as a capital should, at the center of everything.

When I first laid eyes on it, three weeks before the desired date of our wedding, I knew Otočec was the perfect choice. Dolenjska has long been the poorest region in Slovenia, although locals also argue that it is the most Slovenian region in all of Slovenia. The argument is typical of a particular effort on the part of Slovenians to suggest that all other Slovenians, due to regional affiliation, political preference, or dialect, somehow lack authenticity, lack true Slovenian-ness. For its part, Dolenjska lacks the cathedral glory of Alpine Gorenjska, the Italianate allure of the Slovenian littoral, and yet—with its softly undulating hills, its ribbonlike fields each a slightly different shade of green, its humble farmhouses clustered in the valleys, its hilltop belfries—it felt to me like a secret discovery, an intimate landscape all our own. The stone castle itself—the ivy-covered walls that would be threaded with red by the time our October wedding came along, the black iron wall sconces, the romantic lancet windows—hovered magically above the green rippling reed-swept Krka. It looked like a fairy-tale setting, a picture postcard of what Americans think of as pleasing in European vistas—quaint rural hominess lorded over by a feudal castle.

Not a strip mall in sight.

We were planning a very small wedding on Saturday, October 2. We had invited only a few friends, Aleš's immediate family, and mine: my mother, my brother, Peter, from Frankfurt with his wife and two little girls, and my sister, Rachel, who was coming all the way from California with her six-month-old daughter, Nora, and would act as my matron of honor. Igor, of the kiss on Fourteenth Street, would be Aleš's best man. Yet however modest the wedding would be, however few guests, it was the crucial centerpiece of an intense propaganda campaign, a bit of agitprop, as the communists might have called it, orchestrated to convince my family that I had not gone completely around the bend this time; that the country to which I was moving was not only safe but gorgeous and soon to be prosperous, and that the man I was marrying was not only exotic but a loving companion and soon to be an adequate provider.

It would have to be an impeccably choreographed performance.

The three-star restaurant in the courtyard of the thirteenth-century castle seemed ideal for the task at hand: tastefully renovated, no communist eyesores, no garish lighting fixtures or piped-in polka music. Aleš had told me that in the ongoing denationalization process, during which it was being decided what villas and castles and national parks and other choice parcels of Slovenian land would be returned to their pre-World War II owners, an Austrian count had stepped forward and made it known that he was the rightful owner of Otočec Castle.

Walking across the pedestrian bridge that spanned the river and regarding the scene, it seemed hard to believe that the country would let go of such a gem, but to be honest I didn't care about that at the moment. I didn't have time to dwell on the challenges of economic restructuring, the effectiveness of denationalization, the benefits of shock therapy. I was focused on a far more limited canvas—a wedding—and all that mattered to me was that October and my American family would come and go long before any pretenders to the throne could make their claim stick.

Sitting at a table covered with a pristine white cloth, I gazed around at the bucolic setting. A swan floated on the water's surface, dipping its long neck down to the shallow bottom and then extending it to pluck at the narrow river's verdant banks. A waiter delivered two bowls of steaming fresh mushroom soup to our table, a salad of springy watercress, and a carafe of local red wine.

"How did you find this place?" I asked Aleš. "It's perfect."

He let out a relieved sigh. Despite his prickly Slovenian pride, or probably because of it, he had slowly but surely fallen into the trap I had set. Now he too was feeling edgy and defensive about the small troupe of Americans about to descend on what he feared was his not quite up-to-snuff homeland.

He leaned across the table to give me a kiss. When his lips touched mine, I heard a low, distant irregular rumble. I felt it traveling through the cobblestones beneath the soles of my feet. It grew in intensity for about a minute before reaching a crescendo that made the foundations of the castle quiver slightly and sent ripples across the green water of the Krka River, the single swan scooting for cover in the reeds.

We both sat up straight and steadied our wine glasses.

"What was that?"

The waiter came forward and bowed discreetly. "I am terribly sorry, madam."

I looked up at him nervously. "What *was* that?"

"It was," he made a slightly embarrassed gesture, "Karlovac. The war. The local Serbs and Croats still fight sporadically. . . ."

The situation seemed absurd: an elegant waiter in an idyllic locale apologizing to his patrons not for a late entrée or the lack of a certain wine, but for an earthquake, a tsunami, an act of god. The faint but unmistakable crackle of machine gun fire interrupted him. We sat frozen in our little tableau waiting for it to stop.

"You've got to be joking," I said.

"No, madam, regrettably, I am not."

"Do they fight on the weekends?" I wondered. "On Saturdays?"

I knew I was being crass, insensitive to the realities of war, its terrible human cost. Perhaps I was even being foolhardy; perhaps, after all, the war was too close for comfort. It was one thing for me to throw myself into the line of fire, quite another to invite my family along with all those innocent little nieces. But I put that thought out of my mind. I needed to remain focused on the goal, on the delicate balance I was trying to achieve, a balance that would be utterly undone by the report of a machine gun or the explosion of a mortar shell right in the instant I said "I do." That crucial hour's distance to the southeast would suddenly seem an awful lot closer.

"It is difficult to say, madam. Sundays are generally quiet; Croats are observant. But you never know when they'll start up. It's all rather unpredictable." He bowed once again and retreated into the kitchen with his tray tucked under his arm, his long white apron skirting the top of his polished black shoes.

Flustered, I brought a spoonful of the wild mushroom soup to my lips. It was really very good, the best thing I'd sampled at a restaurant since I'd come to Slovenia.

"What should we do?" I whispered to Aleš.

"I don't know." He shook his head.

We spoke in undertones as if spies might be lurking among the trees around the courtyard, listening in on our plans, conspiring to arrange a firefight at the key moment.

"Let's go to Novo Mesto after lunch and see if we even have the paperwork in order." He had heard that there would be some bureaucratic hurdles to overcome. What with the uncommon binary equation of a Slovenian marrying a non-Slovenian, and the confused and contradictory regulations of the new state, he didn't know what to expect. Plus Novo Mesto bureaucrats, the ones who oversaw weddings at Otočec, had a reputation as sticklers. Located next to the new border, they feared that a sudden influx of refugees and draft dodgers from Croatia (their former Yugoslav fellows in "brotherhood and unity," as the slogan went) would exacerbate the already existing problem of outsiders, mostly Gypsies, in this most authentic of Slovenian regions. And we wouldn't have much time to solve whatever problems might come up. My mother had called the night before with the good news that everyone invited had managed to purchase airline tickets for the week in question, but the tickets were nonrefundable. There was no backing out now.

As it turned out, our war with the bureaucrats in Novo Mesto temporarily eclipsed the more lethal one in Karlovac. I knew something of bureaucracy. I had recently dealt with the New York Department of Motor Vehicles; I had even spent a year abroad in France and had stood in what seemed an interminable line to get my student visa renewed. But I had only a hazy and secondhand notion of Central European bureaucracy, let alone the famed and not yet defunct communist variety. I had read Kafka's *The Castle*, which anticipated the maze, banal and surreal at once, created by Austro-Hungary's clerks run amok. I had also read Vladimir Nabokov's memoir *Speak, Memory*, which referred to *dokumenti* as the placenta of the Russian émigré community—and they were fleeing a new communist state, not rushing into the arms of an old one.

But just as I had never had a Triestine salesgirl refuse to give me a price on a cashmere sweater, so too had I never been at the mercy of paper pushers who wield their power, as the powerless almost always do, randomly and as if out of some dark need to punish whomever doesn't share in their own dull and disappointing lives. Never before had my future been determined by the bureaucrat's heavy stamp floating above an identification card. Never before had the outcome of such a hotly felt desire as mine for the perfect Slovenian wedding been decided by such a frigid arbiter. Small wonder that I felt a sense of foreboding on the morning of our trip to Otočec when Aleš asked, in an uncharacteristically stern manner, his own slim black dossier already in hand, if I was prepared, if I had all my *dokumenti* ready.

Our paper war would end up taking exactly ten days, an odd coincidence perhaps in a land made independent by a ten-day war. We made four excursions down through the harmonious symphony of greens that is the Dolenjska Valley, proving that even the loveliest of landscapes can wear on you with forced repetition. In Ljubljana we paid visits to the American Embassy, the

Slovenian Ministry of the Interior, an official translator, the notary office—to whose cashier we dispensed the then-significant sum of eleven thousand Slovenian tolars. During those ten days I maintained an uncharacteristic calm, not giving anything away to my relatives over the telephone, not warning them that they may have wasted their money on plane tickets, on fancy dress clothes and wedding gifts, not telling them that there might in the end be no festivities at all, that I might be moving to a place that bore an alarming resemblance, in its ability to control the private lives of its citizens, to a totalitarian state. To have revealed my uncertainty would have been to lose the propaganda campaign before it had even properly begun.

The bureaucrat who manned the fort at the Novo Mesto municipal office was predictably unsmiling and unhelpful, sitting behind a massive manual typewriter that in another place and time might have fetched a decent sum as a collector's item. It had been our mistake, she let us know from the beginning, and perhaps she had a point there, to have settled on such an early date without consultation with the authorities, and then she went on to find fault with each and every one of the *dokumenti* presented for her perusal.

"But *tovarišica* . . . ," Aleš protested.

Gospa would have been the standard respectful term of address for a woman in the postcommunist era. It is the frequently used Slovenian word for "ma'am," used by cashiers, taxi drivers, children, nurses, everyone; a term that I would eventually come to heartily dislike. But for some reason, Aleš chose—no doubt from some historical reflex that responded to the mood of the moment—a soon-to-be obsolete form of address: the term for female comrade.

"But *tovarišica*, that's my birth certificate."

"Yes it is," she confirmed. "But it is a Yugoslav birth certificate."

"I was born in Yugoslavia," he countered.

"Well," and here she was able to trump him not because she was right, or because her request was the least bit logical, but simply because she possessed authority and he did not, "you will need to get a new one if you want to marry."

She informed us that new Slovenian birth certificates were being issued in Ljubljana at the same office where driver's licenses were renewed, parking tickets paid, universal identification cards issued, but that there would be a wait. This requirement alone might have thrown off our timing, but in such systems there always exists a method to get around obstacles, and the method depends, not surprisingly, on whom you know: on what doctor can be called when you're about to be rolled into the operating theater, on what low-level clerk at the national airline would appreciate a small bag of coffee when you desperately need to get somewhere quick, on what official in the Ministry of Housing has just gotten engaged to a distant relative when you need a lead on a state-subsidized apartment. With the right contacts, anything can be arranged, and though undoubtedly no country has been able to achieve a system so transparent that it never matters whom you know, the former communist countries created a system where it almost never doesn't. In this particular case, Aleš's father had a neighbor named Dido who knew a man who had a wife who worked in the office that issued birth certificates. The call was made and Aleš was reborn in the nick of time.

But once that was out of the way, our comrade at the municipal office found fault with my birth certificate too, and I hadn't been born anywhere near Yugoslavia. Mine had been issued not by the wrong country, it turned out, but by the wrong office: the Department of Health rather than the Ministry of the Interior. After a long debate about whether America had a department as sinister-sounding as the Ministry of the Interior or not, and if it did, whether such a department would issue a birth certificate to a grown woman, she finally agreed to accept the document as it was, but only if it were translated by an official state-certified translator and notarized.

"No problem," Aleš whispered to me. "I have an ex-girlfriend who's an official state-certified translator."

And so it went until at last all our documents and their issuing offices, official translations, and notary seals had been deemed acceptable, at which point our tormentor threw her final card on the table, one last seemingly insurmountable barrier. By Slovenian law, a state-appointed interpreter would have to be present at the ceremony—otherwise I might not have a clue what I was getting myself into. Only one interpreter was employed in the municipality of Novo Mesto, and she was unavailable on all Saturdays in October. As marriages were conducted only on Saturdays, the first available day we could wed was the first Saturday in November.

The woman behind the counter gave Aleš a triumphant look and smiled for the first time during our many encounters. She had won. She had always known she would, and so in a way had we. Exhausted, I slumped into a plastic chair and let my face fall into my hands. And then something unexpected happened. Up until that point, Aleš had always been very correct and controlled, had always explained to me what was going on almost at the moment it occurred, but from this point onward, he stopped explaining, and more to the point, he stopped being polite. As I peeked up from behind my hands, I watched as he drew himself to his full poetic height, puffed out his slender chest, and laid into her with everything he had.

Of course, I couldn't understand a word he said, but the rhythm of the words had all the staccato impact of those distant machine guns in Karlovac. His voice went all gravelly and harsh, and his manner became scornful and superior. It wasn't the first time I'd seen him like this. Only days before I had attended an international round table about the ongoing situation in the former Yugoslavia and had been startled when Aleš—I don't re-member what triggered him: a misleading historical reference to Turkish hordes, some platitude about multiculturalism—adopted that flat contemptuous tone and in seconds obliterated his mild-mannered American and Western European colleagues. He even used a similarly imperious tone in poetry readings. He had one poem in particular that he read in what I had come to think of as his arrogant liturgical style, sending line after fiercely articulated line over his audience like wave after relentless wave onto a bar-ren shore until he reached a climax of incantational fury.

This is more or less what he did to the woman in the munic-ipal office of Novo Mesto.

To her credit she took it very well, better certainly than I would have. She stood impassively through it all, unmoving as a piece of stone. An occasional flicker of emotion passed over her face, the triumphant smile having long since departed, but it would be hard to say what the flicker signified: impatience, bemusement, concern. When Aleš was through, she wordlessly passed a large black rotary telephone over the counter. He dug his tiny address book out of his jacket pocket—he had one for local contacts that he always carried with him and one for international contacts that he kept in a desk drawer at home—thumbed through it, and placed a call. He spoke briefly to the person who answered on the other end—six or seven sentences at most. His tone was clipped and respectful, although it still carried the red rim of his rage. He stopped talking, listened briefly, replaced the receiver, and pushed the phone back across the counter.

"Hvala," he said coldly, with a disdainful smile, more of a sneer, really. But the word at least I recognized, a small triumph for me. It meant "thank you."

Then he waited. Then we all waited for whatever it was he was waiting for. From my plastic chair I surveyed the gray office once again, taking an inventory of the Slovenian flag hanging from a pole in the corner, the great big book of rules and regulations that lay next to the black rotary telephone on the counter that had been consulted several times during the proceedings as if there were no higher authority, the faded square on the wall where a picture had once hung: no doubt a portrait of President Josip Broz Tito, the hero of Yugoslavia and of a past now so thoroughly shunned that Slovenia was trying to erase all mention of it from the record books.

Finally, what we were waiting for came. A slim dark-suited man sauntered briskly through the double doors. He patted Aleš collegially on the back and shook his hand warmly. He had an exchange under his breath with the staff and even, to my immense surprise, paused in front of me and said in buoyant accented English, "Congratulations! Ha-ha. Welcome to Novo Mesto. How do you like it here?"

I stood up and stepped forward. The woman who had so tirelessly tormented us the past ten days came out from behind the counter—this was also a first—and shamelessly pumped both of our hands. She beamed at Aleš and said something which he later translated for me.

"At last! We have found a common language."

I still didn't speak that language. It was, I inferred, the language of whom you knew, and naively, perhaps, I hoped I never would. It went against the egalitarian American spirit. On our way home that day, once the date and hour for the nuptials were definitely set, Aleš told me what he had said during his decisive harangue. When I realized what it was, I didn't know how I should feel: horrified at just how high up the ladder one needed to reach to get a simple wedding ceremony performed, or thrilled that my future husband had such a long reach. But however I felt about it, it got the job done, and it had a recognizable dramaturgical punch. It had all the joyful hubris of the climactic scene in a Hollywood movie, when the underdog good guy finally takes down the bad guy with some unexpected and monumentally unrealistic maneuver. This is how Aleš paraphrased the speech to me as we zipped back up to Ljubljana in the now familiar cocoon of the little gray Clio:

"I came here as an ordinary citizen of the new republic of Slovenia in order to avail myself of the services of the state. But I inform you now, comrade, that I am *not* in fact an ordinary citizen of this new republic. I am a poet laureate, I am a recipient of the prestigious Prešeren Award, and here in my pocket I have the telephone number of the president of this republic, and I am going to call him right now, that is if you will be so kind as to let me use your telephone" (this was in the era before cell phones made such scenes that much more elegant) "and tell him about the lowly Novo Mesto employee who is preventing me from marrying my foreign bride, about the lowly Novo Mesto clerk who is determined that my bride's family will come from America to this new republic and see that it is nothing more than a pathetic little state run by pathetic little mindless bureaucrats who extract fees while not providing any services to speak of, who do not know the meaning of democracy: government for the people, of the people, by the people. . . ."

"Amen," I rejoiced, glad to see American rhetoric put to good use for a change.

And, of course, the one positive feature of bureaucratic wars, as opposed to flesh-and-blood wars like the one going on in Karlovac, is that once they are over, once the bureaucrat's seal hits the vellum, they are almost immediately forgotten. One's humanity remains intact. They leave no scars, no embedded shrapnel, no destroyed lives—if you win them, that is, and on this occasion we had.

And so our wedding took place as planned on Saturday afternoon, October 2, 1993. The choreography and the setting were flawless: the rolling hills of Dolenjska, the little island of Otočec, the feudal castle and its courtyard shot with red ivy, the single swan drifting peacefully from bank to bank. My brother, who arrived with his family from Frankfurt and had been reading up more closely on the ongoing war, seemed almost disappointed on the road down to Otočec as he gazed out the window at the bucolic farmsteads, the pastoral meadows, the prosperous two-story houses lining the village lanes, most of them built during a decade of Saturdays by their dull and steadfast owners. He scanned the narrow lanes for telltale bullet holes ripping through the plaster, for burned-out rooftops, for any sign of war at all. But the only martial presence he detected was the military precision with which the typical Slovenian housewife arranged the rows of cabbage and lettuce in her thriving vegetable garden.

The guns in Karlovac remained silent on the day of our wedding, and the only memory of the bureaucratic proxy war we had waged could be found in the text of the ceremony itself, translated by the official state interpreter brought in from another municipality for the occasion.

> The couple swears to respect each other, trust each other and help each other.
>
> Each spouse is free to decide about the birth of children.
>
> Each spouse is free to choose his/her own work and career.
>
> The couple will collectively decide on where they will live.
>
> Each spouse will support the family to the extent that he/she is able.
>
> A spouse who does not have financial means, who is through no fault of his/her own unemployed or incapable of working, has the right to be supported by the other spouse to the extent the latter is able.

The Slovenians in attendance slouched low in their chairs, mortified by the lack of romance in the text, by the socialist plunk of the words, hearing them as if for the first time only because they were also falling on the ears of outsiders. But in fact the outsiders were charmed, as outsiders so often are. My mother, a liberal feminist lawyer, gushed after the ceremony, "How wonderful. How sensible. Why, I almost expected the magistrate to include a schedule for who does the dishes each night of the week."

"I know," I gushed back at her. "It's an amazingly egalitarian system. Slovenia has kept everything that is good from socialism and gotten rid of the rest."

When had I learned to lie so shamelessly? When I was cherry-picking from the available data about Slovenia for all my friends and colleagues back in New York? When I way chanting my mantra about the war being an hour to the southeast? I happily told my mother about the yearlong paid maternity leave each woman gets when she has a baby, about the cheerful and inexpensive state-run day care centers, about the nationalized health care system that provides free medical services and pharmaceutical drugs to everyone. All true, but in this, my new age of censorship, what I failed to tell my mother was Milena's tart one-liner regarding domestic life behind what was once the Iron Curtain ("He'll never lift a finger"), or that the few foreigners I'd met in Slovenia crossed the country's nearest border the moment they thought they might need some medical attention, let alone a root canal. And chief among the things I didn't tell her was that we wouldn't be having this marvelously egalitarian wedding at all if Aleš didn't happen to be acquainted, however distantly, with the president of the country.

I had mastered the art of agitprop.

But in the end, none of that really mattered. None of it, not the unseemly scramble to arrange the wedding, not the white lies to mask the insecurity of the vulnerable little state, not the genuinely tenuous position Slovenia occupied in the newly emerging Europe, nor even the genuinely tenuous position of Aleš and me as a couple—none of it cast a shadow over the happiness of that day. Real life with its small fears, its nuances of gray, its never-ending uncertainties withdrew for a short while, because however cynical and harsh this world can be, however much we tend to emphasize our differences ("Those people are fucking crazy"), there are certain human events that transcend the specificities of place, transcend the specificities of culture and history and language and political system; certain milestones that are so universal that whatever the bureaucrats might say, they need no interpreter. And this was one of them.

When Aleš and I signed the register, and the stamp hit the vellum, and our stolid female comrade solemnly intoned, "This marriage is now legally valid," no translation was needed. We all knew what she meant. And though nowhere in the pragmatic socialist version of the ceremony does it say that the groom may kiss the bride, Aleš kissed me anyway. He didn't need instructions. And when my sister's little daughter beamed at Aleš's mother, she plucked the child up into her arms, took her into a corner where the two communed happily in what language I do not know.

Pavel's toast

And when Aleš's father lifted his glass above the collected company and said—well, half of the gathered company had no idea what he said. Aleš, moved by the brilliant success of the day, by its emotion, and giddy from all the wine, forgot to translate. But our hearts expanded with joy all the same. In some crazy way, it sounded even better because we didn't understand what he said, didn't know what exact words the man was using to honor his son and the wife brought over from America. It was like the difference between reading a book and seeing a movie. We had to supply our own words just as we supply images when we read, and not specific words or specific images either, but some never completely defined notion of what the perfect words or the perfect images might be if perfection actually existed.

That was our fairy tale in Otočec.

Ljubljana
OCTOBER 3, 1993

Mija and baby Nora

The next day, Sunday, we dropped my family off at the airport. They waved and smiled and boarded airplanes that took them back to their familiar homes. Then Aleš took me back to my unfamiliar home, to my unfamiliar family, to the occupants of that small Ljubljana apartment, and suddenly the meaning of words mattered again. Reality returned, and with it the realization that if I am going to make it here, I will have to get to know and understand these people, this new family of mine, this limited cast of characters that now populates my life. Some unarticulated dream of perfection will not be enough.

First the ululating women: Mija and Polona Debeljak.

Mija, my mother-in-law, was born Marija Mohar in a remote village called Loški Potok that occupies a pretty green valley in Notranjska, a region not far from Dolenjska and the Croatian border. When Mija was a girl of less than twenty, she left her village, as did countless others in those days, and went to Ljubljana with a young husband in tow and a dream of building a better life for herself. There she took a single room in a small house on the edge of town, a room with no electricity or running water, and looked for work as a domestic servant. Now thirty years later, she is a young and energetic fifty, her children have both finished high school and gone on to college if not graduate school, she has central heating, and the only home she cleans is her own. The evolution of her life, from village to city, from bare room to modest urban apartment, from a washboard dunked into a cold river to a centrifugal washing machine, is the typical story of her generation of Yugoslavs, even though to Americans she might well appear poor.

Mija is graced with thick brown hair, a heart-shaped face, and heavy-lidded blue-gray eyes. She wears an old cotton T-shirt and a batik wraparound skirt inside the apartment. These are her house clothes. She wears her city clothes when she goes to market and to mass. She wears shoes outside the apartment, slippers inside, as do guests, such as me, who are furnished with a pair of guest slippers upon entering. She laughs and cries easily and seems not to understand what it means to relax or lie down or do nothing at all. Mija was a war baby, conceived while her father was in Loški Potok for a rare conjugal visit. Otherwise he spent most of the war years hiding out from both sides in the civil conflict that consumed Slovenia and the rest of Yugoslavia during World War II—a vicious little war that had far deeper consequences in these lands than the wider European one, and some argue it planted the seeds for the war that is going on right now. When Mija's father came home after everything was over, he must have forgotten that long-ago visit. He spotted a little girl sitting on the ceramic stove in the corner of the cinderblock house, the last one in the valley, tossed his chin in her direction, and inquired of his wife, "Čigava je ona?" Who does that one belong to?

Family legend, but I believe it. I've only been in this country a month now, and I already know how essential and inescapable the notion of belonging is, not just in the narrow sense of paternity but in the wider sense of clan, village, nation, the world all around. I need only open my mouth and order coffee in my rudimentary Slovenian to cause the waitress to shake her head, look off into the middle distance, and remark to no one in particular, "*Tale pa ni naša.*" This one's not ours.

Polona Debeljak, my sister-in-law, is a tall, willowy brunette with impossibly high cheek bones. She is twenty-four years old, single, a college student studying what is known here as pedagogy. She lives at home with her parents, commonplace in Ljubljana and the rest of the former Yugoslavia and indeed in all former communist countries where not very long ago a two-room apartment was considered a privilege that you had to wait half of your professional life for, and once you got the apartment you put your name on another list and waited five more years to have a phone installed. And yet despite the material deprivation, young people of Polona's generation are spoiled beyond reason by their hardworking rural parents. Not only do these young people wear shoes all year round and eat bananas and drink coffee instead of chicory, luxuries unknown to the generation raised in the brutally poor postwar villages of Yugoslavia, but they are as lazy as their parents are industrious. They loll around a good deal, they smoke hashish, read Lacanian philosophy, listen to pop music, have their clothes regularly laundered for them (their whites boiled at a hundred degrees Celsius and their underpants ironed and folded), and usually take at least a decade to get an ordinary bachelor's degree. Understandably, many of this younger generation are reluctant to sacrifice these privileges for anything as risky as a marriage or a career or children of their own.

Polona

But I like Polona; I like her very much. She is lovely and warm and enthusiastic. She speaks serviceable English, a monumental plus where I'm concerned. I see in her my most likely ally in this, my new home, which says a lot because she is the one who started all the howling and weeping in the first place.

Then there is Pavel, my father-in-law. He emerges from the little alley-like kitchen where he has been trying, with little success, to quiet the womenfolk. I can hear Aleš's low urgent voice in the kitchen amidst the higher hysterical tones of his mother and sister. Pavel has either been instructed or chosen of his own volition to come and sit beside me in the living room. Or perhaps he simply couldn't take it anymore. He is a man of few words and even fewer overtly expressed emotions, a man who views the telephone as an instrument to be used solely in emergency situations, and emergencies are rare. When his wife went into labor with Aleš, they were still living in that tiny unheated room on the outskirts of Ljubljana, and he didn't have a phone with which to place a call. When his wife went into labor with Polona, they were living in this apartment already, and on that occasion he lay down for a few minutes to conquer his sudden bout of dizziness and then got up and walked the few blocks to the communal garage and fetched the car. He did not pick up the telephone.

Like Mija, Pavel was born in Loški Potok. He is one of five brothers. Three other siblings died in infancy. He has an identical twin named Peter who also married a Marija from the village and moved to Ljubljana. I think of the quartet as a nonsinging precursor to Peter, Paul, and Mary, although, of course, they would have to be called Peter, Paul, and two Marys, and their foundations would not be folk but the devout Catholicism prevalent in great swaths of rural Slovenia, where every other girl is baptized Marija. Pavel's father spent the war years in Dachau, punishment for lending a cart to a partisan brigade that operated in the forests around Loški Potok. When the war was over, his father took a single step outside the prison gates, and another, and then proceeded to walk the nearly three hundred miles back to his home in that pretty green Notranjska valley. Pavel has an astonishingly good set of strong straight teeth and a head of thick steel-gray hair, although for him the main measure of a man is neither his hair nor his teeth but his automobile, even a machine as modest as an Italian Fičo or an East German Trabant, virtual ashtrays on wheels.

For him, function is all, aesthetics nothing. Pavel is a Volkswagen man himself. I have nothing whatsoever in common with him.

He sits down on the couch beside me and puts his hand very close to mine without touching it. He doesn't look at me but instead chooses a spot at the edge of the carpet to focus on. I choose a spot next to his, and together we wait for the crying to subside.

After what seems like a very long while, Aleš emerges from the kitchen. Seeing him at this moment is like catching sight of a bright ring of color tossed into the wild gray water. He is quite literally the only thing I have to hold on to, the only thing that is *mine* here. He steps into the breakfast nook and instinctively—it is the survival instinct—my eyes catch hold of his slate-blue ones and hang on tight. Mija and Polona step out of the kitchen behind him, both looking somewhat shamed, their faces having slid into a state of soft focus after the release of such torrential emotion. Polona is still crying, though silently. Once you open those faucets it's hard to shut them. That is something I must keep in mind now that the wedding is over, now that real life has begun.

Aleš was born, aptly enough, on December 25, 1961, and like Jesus before him, to a young, devout, and humble woman named Marija who was married to a good and selfless man who would walk to the ends of the earth for her. Also like Jesus he arrived into a world of extremely straightened conditions, not a manger exactly, but into that single room that lacked heat and running water, and into a country that lacked bananas and coffee and hard currency and washing detergent.

But there, I am afraid, the similarities end. For while Aleš was a talented and precocious student who grew to possess much of the charisma and rhetorical skills of the savior, he most emphatically lacks His modesty. This is something I already vaguely knew before I married him, but the startling show of emotion by the women in his family and the showdown in Novo Mesto, among other things, have slowly made me realize the extent to which he occupies the starring role not only in my life but in the life of the Debeljak family and in circles beyond. He is a celebrity in his country, loved and reviled in equal measure: wunderkind, former national youth judo champion (of Yugoslavia), poet laureate (of Slovenia), womanizer (no national limits in this sport), pasha, and demigod. When we come to the family apartment for our frequent lunches, the main meal of the day in Slovenia, he promptly lies down on the couch and dozes, his sister hovers above him, his mother moves about the kitchen preparing his favorite dishes, his father reads aloud from newspaper clippings that have come out about him recently, and I sit uneasily on a nearby chair and wait for my cue.

In short: he is the sun around which all of our lives orbit.

Now this glowing planet, this new husband of mine, takes a few steps forward and stands in front of where I am sitting beside his father. He holds out his hand toward me.

"Come on," he says in English, "let's go."

I reluctantly let go of his gaze and look past him toward his mother and sister. The women, it seems, are willing to release him. Tears leap up to my own throbbing eyes. Now it looks as if I may start to cry along with every other female in the family. Pavel, sensing this, gives my knee a reassuring pat, stands up, and takes three long strides to the recently abandoned kitchen. Mija rushes forward and takes his place beside me.

"*Sori! Sori*," she says. She squeezes me around my waist and lays her head briefly on my shoulder. She has gone to the trouble of learning a few English words but always combines them with pats and caresses and gestures just to be absolutely sure she's getting her point across.

Polona regards me from the breakfast nook, face still wet. "Have fun tomorrow," she whispers through quavering tear-stained lips.

Yes, fun. I must try to keep that in mind too.

Life begins tomorrow. Aleš and I are not going on a honeymoon just yet, which is a shame, really, because that would be another way to defer real life, ordinary life, or more to the point ordinary Slovenian life, something I haven't a clue about and haven't much experienced during the excitement and tension of the past month of wedding preparations. Aleš begins lecturing at the university the next day, and I am registered to attend the first session of a five-day-per-week, four-hour-per-day course in the labyrinthine Slovenian language. The government of this new country, I am discovering, has a complex attitude toward foreigners, a love-hate relationship, you might say, something to do with the hot war going on to the south and the cool embrace of the European Union beckoning from up north. On the one hand I am the amazing *Američanka! Američanka!* On the other hand I am not allowed to work, something that the now long-forgotten Mr. Klemenčič overlooked when he called me up at five in the morning to offer me a job at the Ministry of Finance. Not only are the authorities reluctant to issue marriage certificates but they are not handing out work permits either, not even to the foreign wives of their treasured national poets.

So school will be my job. That is the fun Polona is referring to.

"Let's go," says Aleš again. "Let's go home."

Proletarska Cesta

OCTOBER 4, 1993

Workers in Ljubljana

This is the plan.

First breakfast, then walk into town, then language school.

Aleš smears honey on a piece of untoasted bread and drops a teabag into hot water, these being the outer limits of his culinary skills. He looks grim, as he often does in the hours before noon. It is true that he can sleep anywhere, anytime, but getting up is an altogether different matter. I, on the other hand, am rather chipper in the morning, a classic marital mismatch.

The kitchen we occupy is a miniscule closet-sized kitchen— camp refrigerator, two electric burners, no oven, a cupboard for shoes and guest slippers, a telephone with a long cord, and a fax machine suspended from the wall beside the front door. The kitchen itself is located in a studio apartment in a dilapidated eleven-story building at number 2, Proletarska Street, at the corner of Zaloška, a broad avenue. The building, while not terribly old, looks tired, its facade peeling away in great mournful sheets. It has two interior elevators. One brings you to odd-numbered floors, the other to even-numbered floors.

We are on an odd-numbered floor: the ninth.

However dilapidated or peculiar it may be, the apartment is a luxury. Most Slovenian newlyweds, because of the persistent housing shortage, begin their married life with one or another set of in-laws, either in the cramped confines of a city apartment or in one of those prosperous two-story dwellings in the suburbs and villages around Ljubljana, generally not palatial country spreads as they might appear to the Western eye, but two- and even three-unit homes where extended families live together.

The Debeljaks do not pay rent on the Proletarska apartment. It is a family asset, purchased during the economic liberalization of the eighties with scarce family funds squirreled away over the years: cash on the barrelhead. Ljubljanska Banka is not, as it turns out, in the mortgage business.

There are two kinds of tea in Slovenia, or so the language indicates: black caffeinated tea, which is called "real tea" or "Russian tea"—*ruski čaj*—and all other teas, from green to ginseng to rosehips to the chamomile gathered in the nearby forests and laid out on yesterday's newspapers to dry. The latter are known under the umbrella term "fruit tea" and are drunk in massive quantities with lemon and honey to prevent colds and other ailments. Honey is revered in Slovenia; it is believed to have strong counteractive powers, warding off anything from a cold to a cold sore to throat cancer. There is even, Aleš has informed me, a museum of honey and beekeepers in the nearby town of Radovljica that we may visit some weekend.

Aleš drinks Russian tea in the morning and fruit tea in the afternoon. I am a coffee drinker and am on my own in this endeavor.

I move about the small kitchen trying to be as inconspicuous as possible. I have learned from experience not to ask how Aleš slept, if anything is wrong, if he is annoyed with me. I remain studiously silent and set about making myself a Turkish coffee, which is the only kind of coffee they drink around here as far as I can tell. It is sometimes said that the real border between Western Europe and the Balkans could be drawn along an imaginary line, on one side of which people drink espresso and cappuccino and macchiato (Italians, Spaniards, the French) and on the other side of which they drink Turkish coffee (the Ottoman hordes). Another way to define this same border would be to draw a second imaginary line, similar to the first, only this one would divide the people who maintain the Oriental practice of wearing slippers within the inner sanctum of the home from the people on the other side: the barbarous Occidentals who wear shoes or socks or flip-flops or nothing at all on their feet regardless of whether they're inside or outside, in the bedroom or the barroom.

By either measure, Slovenia, in 1993, falls squarely in the Balkans.

The kitchen at Proletarska 2 is sparsely equipped. Most food of any real nutritional value enters the apartment in made-in-Yugoslavia casseroles that ply their way back and forth—empty in one direction, full in the other—between the family apartment on Gotska Street and Aleš's Proletarska studio. The night before, we returned from the Gotska apartment with our arms laden: me carrying a basket of freshly laundered and ironed clothes, Aleš, a shallow cardboard box that held one casserole containing *sarma* (rolled cabbage leaves stuffed with meat and rice), a second casserole containing *ričet* (a thick barley soup with chunks of pork sausage in it), a jar of beets, a jar of pickles, a plastic container with homemade beef broth, four pieces of apple strudel wrapped in brown paper, and a bag of impeccably cleaned and dried lettuce from Mija's vegetable garden. Before we left, the still somewhat tearful Mija instructed me, using a series of elaborate gestures and the occasional visual aid, to add potatoes to the *ričet*, and it could likely be stretched to two meals.

The kitchen, although it contains little else, does contain a *džezva*, a small handled copper pot, the kind that were once hammered out by turbaned men in the covered markets of Sarajevo and more recently manufactured in the communist factories of Yugoslavia and Bulgaria. Turkish coffee is made in such a pot. First you fill the *džezva* with water and bring it to a rolling boil. Then you remove the *džezva* from the burner and drop two heaping spoonfuls of coffee grounds and one heaping spoonful of sugar directly into the hot water.

Stir vigorously.

Put the *džezva* back onto the burner and bring it to a rolling boil once again, pulling it off just at the moment when the furious black foam threatens to spill over the rim and make a mess on the stove top. Pour the thick dark liquid into a cup and wait a moment or so for the grounds to settle to the bottom. Add milk if you care for it.

Do *not* stir.

After you finish drinking it you will find a thick layer of grounds at the bottom of your cup. If you do not, it means that you have drunk them or that they are spread like soggy poppy seeds across your lips. This happens more often than you might think. All you need to do is forget momentarily where you are and gulp down the turgid goop as you might the more watery stuff that is served by the gallon in New York City diners.

I do not know when I will be trusted with the actual care and feeding of Mija's son, but for now Turkish coffee, both making it and drinking it, is test enough of my survival abilities in this world that lacks tumble dryers and drip coffee machines and elevators that stop on all floors.

After I drink my coffee, I slip into the bathroom to touch up my face and gather my wits.

The bathroom is the only private space in the apartment, with the exception of the tiny balcony, which, being one of nearly a hundred other tiny balconies clinging to the sagging flanks of Proletarska 2, cannot be considered truly private. Our balcony looks out, along with the others, onto the Moste industrial zone and the gaudy chimney stack of the coal burning *toplarna*. In the foreground the Ljubljanica River winds its way under a concrete bridge toward castle hill, and a small farmers market huddles warily beneath the dun-colored apartment blocks. In Ljubljana, unlike Manhattan, balconies are not luxury items but necessities. The balcony is an extension of the imaginary rural space that young people like Mija and Pavel lugged with them from their distant villages. It is used not for cocktail parties or for sun-bathing or the occasional clandestine cigarette (cigarettes being anything but clandestine), but for the storage of apples and po-tatoes and other root vegetables during the winter months, and during the spring and summer for the drying of clothes on fold-ing racks in preparation for their inevitable scalding under the housewife's iron.

I do not know how to iron. I do not make apple strudel.

I close the door of the bathroom, lower the toilet seat, and sit on it. Last night was my first night as a married woman in this apartment. The night before last we spent in the wedding suite of the Otočec Castle. We slept in a room that had an armoire as big as this bathroom, a bathroom as big as the whole studio, and a view onto the reed-swept surface of the green Krka River: a vi-sion so romantic that it temporarily banished all memory of the *toplarna* and the adjacent Moste industrial zone. Last night, after we unpacked Mija's bounty, Aleš had pressed me up against the fax machine in the kitchen.

"You're my lawful wedded wife," he murmured into my ear.

"I know," I protested weakly, the edge of the telephone receiver gouging my lower back, "but I have a headache."

"This is the phone you used to call me on, remember?"

He pulled back a bit and scanned my face, his melancholy eyes doing their playful dance. He was referring to all of the hundreds of phone calls made over the months since we'd parted, first after the "I think I'm falling in love with you at the Veselka Diner" incident, and then after New Year's at the Cuban restaurant in the West Village when our philosopher-waiter had assured us that it, or we, had only just begun. Aleš was referring to all the midnight calls placed from Twenty-Fourth Street that found him here at six in the morning, in this unimagined little cell on a street called Proletarska, many of the calls conveying not worries or plans but long-distance long-frustrated desire. I noticed the phone when I first entered the apartment. It was next to the front door, after all, just above the little slipper cabinet, opposite the electric burner, the first thing you saw when you walked in. I'd been surprised to see that it wasn't cordless.

He kissed my eyelids.

"Now we don't need to call anymore."

"Oh, my head . . ."

He let out a heavy sigh. "This is what everyone warns you about: the drought after the wedding night." But soon he relented. He guided me to the narrow bed in the main room and laid me down on it. He made me a cup of fruit tea, laced with curative honey. He placed a cool compress over my eyes, and then settled in for the night on the floor beside me. His first night as a married man in this apartment, his first night as a guardian on the perimeter of this, my alien camp.

Ten hours later, head clear at last, I look around the tiny bathroom. Half of it is filled with the same sort of odd deep half-bath that I have seen in Aleš's family apartment. The toilet is odder still. It has a high inner shelf upon which one can examine, if one wishes, what one's body has just produced, on dry land as it were, before yanking the chain on the tank and flushing it down. Slovenia's most famous export—a Lacanian philosopher, predictably enough—wrote somewhere that you can analyze national character by the design of the toilet: the wasteful prudish Americans with their ten-gallon bowls, the earthy strong-thighed Turks with their minimalist holes in the floor, the pragmatic water-saving Slovenians with that gruesome inspection shelf. But whether it is economics or national character that dictates reality (or whether economics actually *is* character) is beside the point to me right now. What is the point—the main point, the only point—is that this apartment, its tiny balcony, its *džezva*-equipped kitchen, its bizarre bathroom fixtures, is home.

Outrageous, impossible, but true.

I know it is true. The proof is right here in front of my eyes, arranged on a narrow plastic shelf affixed to the wall between the toilet and the sink: all of my toiletries, those miniature pastel-colored bottles of liquids and creams, purchased at places like Bloomingdales and Bergdorf's and B. Altman's. There they stand, lined up like fanciful soldiers on a bleak field, and next to them Aleš's far more plainly appointed army. I shipped some larger items separately via Austria Air Cargo: an Oriental throw rug, an antique mirror, a selection of books and posters and framed prints, but they remain in the boxes where I packed them, stacked somewhere in the Debeljak's basement storage room next to the skis and the bicycles and empty glass mason jars. There's no room for them here.

"Are you ready to go?" Aleš knocks on the door.

I stand up from the closed toilet seat, turn, and glance at my reflection in the mirror. I brush a few specks of coffee from my lips. It is the same person looking back at me from the mirror, only the context, the background, has undergone a radical shift.

"Are you OK in there?"

"Yes, I am," I call back, "I really am."

I lay a finger on the tapered tip of one of the little bottles. Like a talisman: for luck, a blessing. Then I turn around and give the chain a decisive yank, open the door, and step, the apartment being so small, directly into Aleš's arms.

In the hallway, we summon the odd-numbered elevator. The hallway at Proletarska, unlike the rest of this fluorescent-lit country, is bathed in a mawkish purplish light and smells vaguely of sauerkraut. A neighboring door opens a crack and a pair of eyes gazes out into the dim light. The door slams shut.

The elevator doesn't come.

We walk down the stairs to the eighth floor and summon the even-numbered elevator. It also does not come.

We walk down the stairs to the lobby and out onto Proletarska Street and the bright white fog that shrouds Ljubljana on autumn mornings, sometimes clearing in the late morning to reveal the ring of snow-covered Alps that glitters along the city's northern border, and sometimes never clearing, leaving the city in a sunless limbo for days on end. In the center of Ljubljana, the new Slovenian street-naming authorities have gone through the ritual postcommunist post-Yugoslav cleansing of street names. The main drag, for example, that was once called Titova Cesta—Tito Street—is now called Slovenska Cesta, though for the time being everyone, including the Slovenian street-naming authorities, still calls it Titova. But my street, Proletarska Street—a stone's throw from the Cultural Center of the Spanish Republican Fighters and

Ho Chi Minh alley—has not been cleansed of its working-class moniker, perhaps because it is so obviously a proletarian street in a proletarian neighborhood, and as a consequence, no Western officials are likely to visit any time soon, sniffing out signs of lingering Marxism.

The neighborhood, called Moste, meaning bridge, provides a home to many Bosnian and Slovenian proletarians and an increasing number of refugees from the war-torn south. Moste is nothing if not a convenient neighborhood. It was designed that way. The Yugoslav socialist model—which was called self-management to distinguish it from its Soviet counterpart—strived to create urban clusters where workers would have everything they needed within walking distance. So from the doorway of my new apartment building, I have easy access to a nursery school, a primary school, a technical high school for the print trade, an outdoor vegetable market, a self-service market, a pharmacy, a paper-shredding factory, a sausage factory, an animal-feed factory, a curtain factory, and a paint factory, not to mention a small brigade of weary apartment buildings that look exactly like mine.

Happily I am across the street from a national health clinic, although without citizenship I do not possess a national identity card, and without a national identity card it is not clear that I have access to the virtually free national healthcare system, not to mention a host of other state-sponsored services. I am also an easy walk from the Ljubljanska Banka Moste branch office—though I have discovered that foreigners, even those with bank accounts and Slovenian husbands, are not allowed to have ATM cards, which were recently introduced here and are considered something of a novelty item for the exclusive use of citizens. The hope is that Aleš, performing the usual bureaucratic ablutions, will manage to rectify these and other as yet unencountered problems.

Last night Aleš parked the Clio in the lot in front of the Mercator self-service market, but we will not drive today. Aleš will show me the way to walk to school, and perhaps later I will graduate to a bicycle. I am definitely not ready for the car yet. Back in New York, I paid a fee, had an instructor for one hour, took a driver's test on the wide and nearly unpopulated streets of Staten Island, and was issued my first driver's license. In Slovenia it costs a small fortune to get a similar *dokument*: would-be license-holders have to drive with an instructor for nearly thirty hours at an extortionate rate. Yet despite all the practice, or because of it, the drivers here seem half-crazed, oblivious to the rules of the road, heedless to the safety of pedestrians. Not only does Slovenia vie for the top suicide rate among European countries, it also occupies one of the top spots in vehicular fatalities per capita. Most of these deaths take place on the winding back roads of the country, but nevertheless city driving is an art all its own. Tiny exhaust-spewing cars—Fičos, Yugos, Citröen Deux Chevaux— barrel along the city's narrow streets at whatever speeds they can muster, passing like maniacs, maneuvering up one-way cobblestone lanes in the wrong direction. Occasionally they have to swerve impatiently around an old woman laboriously pushing a green vegetable cart to market, or a horse-drawn wagon piled high with a teetering load of straw. Cars are parked helter-skelter throughout the town, pointing in all possible directions, on all possible surfaces—sidewalks, crosswalks, the occasional grassy square—two tires on the curb, two tires off. With only one Staten Island under my belt, I am unprepared for this particular form of madness.

So we walk.

We walk past Mercator, past Ljubljanska Banka, past the Eli flower shop where days before I selected an ivory and yellow bouquet of miniature roses. We cross the pedestrian bridge over the Ljubljanica River and turn to the right, keeping to the banks of the slow-moving green river. This is the prettiest way into the center of town, and crucially for me the most straightforward. You cannot get lost. Just keep the river on your right, always on your right. Walk past one railroad bridge, another pedestrian bridge, a span for two-way automobile traffic, Plečnik's sluice gates that control the flow of the river (before they were built, the Ljubljanica regularly flooded its banks, deluging the old part of the city), the Austro-Hungarian Dragon Bridge, the arcades of Plečnik's main market, and then Plečnik's Three Bridges.

Plečnik, Plečnik, Plečnik.

Like Prešeren, Jože Plečnik, the prewar Catholic architect, is an icon in this town. He fell out of favor during the communist years and much of his urban planning was regrettably left undone, but nevertheless, his unifying mark on the city—the elegant pillars, the alcoved walkways, the series of bridges, the rows of art deco streetlamps—is unmistakable.

In many ways, Ljubljana looks like a typical Austrian town, which is to say like a typical Central European town: pastel spires of baroque churches, antiquated Maria-Theresa-yellow administration buildings, cobblestone squares adorned with marble statuary, a meandering river that flows though the town under a series of ornamented bridges, an austere castle squatting on a low plateau, the art nouveau touches of the early twentieth century. Here and there one catches a glimpse of the recent communist past: the Stalinist apartment blocks on the outskirts of town, the abandoned Yugoslav army barracks, a socialist-realist public sculpture featuring a group of muscular workers lugging some massive hunk of machinery. And, of course, there is the language itself, the street signs and the store signs, words with no obvious reference to Latin or Germanic or Anglo-Saxon languages: *lekarna, krojač, bolnica*.

But what strikes me as strangest of all is not the political, not the architectural, not even the linguistic elements, all of which I had half braced myself for, but the agrarian element. As Aleš and I walk hand in hand toward the center of Ljubljana, the river always to our right and on the opposite bank a complex of modern hospital buildings (where, Aleš tells me, President Josip Broz Tito breathed his last in 1980, setting off the chain of events that led to the current Yugoslav wars of secession), I am bowled over by an unexpected odor. It is an incongruous smell, an odor that one does not normally encounter in a city. It is the stink of fresh fertilizer, the stench of cow dung, the rank smell of farm. How can that be?

I turn away from the river on my right and gaze across the street. We are walking past a structure that looks suspiciously like a barn. I spy a grid of small individual farm plots beside the railroad tracks: tall bean poles reaching up into the foggy morning sky, a puff of black smoke emanating from the chimney of a ramshackle garden shack, row upon row of cabbage. I sense the shuffling of warm cows within, their lowing, their excrement steaming in the darkness. Aleš glances in the direction I am looking and tells me, as if there is nothing at all out of the ordinary about a barn located in the vicinity of the city's commercial center, that the vegetable patches are called *njive* and that his mother maintains two of them, one in town and one at the summer hut they keep in Logatec. She never buys produce from Mercator or the outdoor markets. If anything, she has a surplus, and what she can't use in the growing months she jars or pickles or freezes for winter.

An old woman with a scarf tied beneath her chin sweeps the walk in front of the barnlike structure. Slovenia is a nation obsessively concerned with the outer appearance of their modest homes, the walkways and gates and gardens, and so women sweeping sidewalks is an extremely common sight. This particular woman pauses in her work and stares across the street at me. I give a faint smile, awkwardly raising my hand in an aborted wave. The instant I do it, I know that she has instantly identified me as not ours, not *naša*. Besides Aleš and I and the sweeping woman, the only other people on the quay are a clutch of blue-jacketed factory workers on a mid-morning break. They lean laconically against an iron fence, smoking cigarettes, gazing bareheaded and motionless across the misty water. The scene is as still as a painting. It is Monday morning, the start of the work week, and yet there is no rush, no hustle to work, no beeping of horns, no yellow cabs, no fast-walking out-of-sorts pedestrians. I am struck by the sudden realization that here on this spot, in this out-of-the-way capital, a bucolic and feudal society is colliding, on a rather delayed schedule, with the late twentieth century.

Aleš and I walk together across Plečnik's Three Bridges and enter Prešeren Square just as the fog lifts. A sudden warm glow blasts its way through the whiteness and pours into the circular square. A tall statue of the gesturing romantic poet dominates the square. True enough, he holds not a sword but a book sculpted from darkest marble in one hand, the weighty pages resting between his cold dead fingers. The poet looks toward the delicate alabaster face of a woman that has been carved into a niche in the facade of a brightly-patterned secessionist building across the square. Her lovely patrician profile turns away from the poet, snubbing him. It is none other than the haughty Julia. Aleš turns me round and points me in the direction of the school, Filozofska Fakulteta, where my Slovenian language classes will be held.

"Do you want me to come with you?"

I pretend to think about it for a moment, but I have gathered enough experience in my short time here to guess the effect that a living Slovenian poet might have on living Slovenian language teachers. I would prefer to start school as an ordinary student of the Slovenian language, whatever that may be.

"No. I'd rather go alone."

"OK," he says. "Will you find your way back?"

"No problem. Just follow the river. Three Bridges, the market, Dragon Bridge, the sluice gates, the railroad bridge, then our bridge."

"OK." He seems reluctant to let me go. "Do you have the key?"

I rummage through my bag and pull the key from it, holding it out to him like a child.

"Ninth floor."

"Ninth floor," I nod.

"Proletarska 2."

"Proletarska 2. Moste. Ljubljana."

"We'll meet at home for a late lunch."

"*Sarma*," I say, rolling the *r* like a native.

A look of sudden alarm travels across his face. "I can't believe we're doing this," he says.

"It's all right. It's just a language lesson. It's just lunch."

Thus begins day one of our ordinary Slovenian life

Filozofska Fakulteta

Plečnik's Three Bridges

Moments later, I step into the entry hall of Filozofska Fakulteta—the faculty of philosophy, the local version of the college of humanities—and find it filled to the gills with a crowd of milling foreign students. There are far more people here than I imagined there would be. This pleases me, thrills me, in fact. I had been secretly hoping that school would provide not only much-needed language skills but a much-needed social life as well. It looks promising.

Though I can't help but wonder who these people are, and why they have enrolled to learn a language—an incredibly difficult language, as I have been repeatedly warned—that is spoken by only two million people on the globe, a language that, if you climb into a car and drive two or three hours in any direction, becomes completely useless. Despite the immense effort that will go into learning it, the Slovenian language, in virtually all places and situations on the planet except for this one, becomes an appendage with no discernible function.

Weaving my way through the waiting bodies, I listen in on the various languages being spoken, trying to figure out what, as a practical matter, brought these people to Slovenia, how long they might be staying, and if any of them is remotely like me. After a short walk up and down the lobby, I conclude that our numbers could be divided into several subcategories in none of which I comfortably belong.

First of all, there are the scholarly elite: the Slavicists, speakers of Slavic languages, Poles, Czechs, Slovaks, Russians, who are here to enjoy the relatively warm climate of Slovenian autumn, the bright white fog that sometimes clears and sometimes doesn't, and while they're at it to tuck another Slavic language under their belts. These guys are untouchable, in a league entirely their own, not likely social targets.

Then there is a crew of assorted Western Europeans who neither speak another Slavic language nor seem much interested in speaking this one, but by some accident of fate, some unexpected twist in the ordinary flow of their lives, have been dropped into the main entry hall of Filozofska Fakulteta in the city of Ljubljana. A Belgian doctor named Xavier, formerly with Médecins Sans Frontières, who fell in love with a Slovenian woman while on walkabout and wound up married to her. The spouse of the French ambassador, aptly named France, whose husband has entered the sunset years of his diplomatic career, a phase characterized by the shift from assignments in vibrant hubs like Washington, Moscow, and London to assignments in the rinky-dink capitals of the new countries that are appearing on the map of late-twentieth-century Europe like a sudden and persistent rash. There is an Austrian general who tells me that he will be advising the Slovenian military, though I infer by a number of factors—his advanced age, his being stuck in a four-hour-per-day language school, and above all the miniscule, verging on nonexistent, state of the Slovenian military—that his superiors have let him out to graze in southern pastures. And then there is Andre, a young British fellow, seemingly out of place, who informs me in his broad Midlands accent that not only is he a Slovenian citizen but that both his parents are Slovenian.

"Then you already speak the language," I say. "What are you doing here?"

"My parents never spoke Slovenian to me. Not a word."

"Really? Why not?"

He shrugs. "They were angry at the commies, I guess. At Tito. He took away the family's assets, their houses and businesses. My mother and father have been living in England for nearly fifty years now. Never once came back here for a holiday. Never spoke a single word of the language to me or my sister. Never learned English all that well themselves. But now with the recent changes —independence, capitalism, denationalization of government property—they've come back home to reclaim the family jewels. Or we've come back home," he adds uncertainly.

Like that Austrian count for Castle Otočec.

It doesn't take me long to figure out that the only students who are really enthusiastic about being here, and moreover who know exactly why they have come, are my fellow Americans. They have a purpose, it turns out, and it is a higher purpose than love or reclaiming a lost patrimony. They are missionaries. They have come to convert the godless communist masses.

"But aren't most Slovenians Catholic?" I query the young fresh-faced Baptist woman who hails from Virginia.

"Yes, they are," she responds, nodding her blond head vigorously. "That's what we're finding out. It is so interesting." She appears entirely untroubled by the notion of American Christian missionaries arriving in droves to introduce Jesus to a country of devout Roman Catholics, many of whom, in relatively easygoing communist Slovenia, spent the last fifty years attending mass every Sunday, getting their children baptized and confirmed, bringing ham and hard boiled eggs and horseradish to be blessed on Easter Sunday by the local parish priest. It beats Africa, I guess.

There is one last faction comprised of about nine or ten students: the women tall and surly and sexy, the men also tall and with a startling abundance of hair on both heads and faces. They stand apart from the others, not mingling with their fellow students, not swapping stories about what they're doing here in this obscure and unpronounceable capital city. They lean against the back wall of the hall, smoking cigarettes and regarding the gathered company with a mixture of bemusement and contempt. If the Slavic scholars are the smart geeks and the rest of us are the clueless nerds, these guys are quite literally too cool for school. They are the ex-Yugoslavs. They don't need to be here; this was their former country after all. They are practically locals, townies amidst a throng of gawping outsiders.

More to the point, they don't want to be here.

There had been a brief window when non-Slovenian Yugoslavs residing in the former republic of Slovenia, which became an independent nation-state unexpectedly and virtually overnight before the other Yugoslav wars of secession had properly begun, could have opted for Slovenian national citizenship. No questions asked, or at least not very many. But some didn't hear about the open window, or they weren't ready just yet to give up their Yugoslav passports no matter how long they'd lived in Slovenia, no matter what kind of job they had. Like the sign painters working on the Austrian autobahn, they preferred to wait and see how things would turn out. Maybe the situation would get better. Maybe the politicians and the warring militias would come to their senses. Maybe Yugoslavia would emerge from the chaos that had engulfed it, regain its former glory, and they would be able to return home to the places from which they'd come, to the villages and cities of Croatia, Bosnia, and Serbia, to family and friends and the remembered haunts of childhood. And they wouldn't have to apply for a visa to do it.

Then again, when they didn't exercise the brief option to become officially Slovenian, they may not have been making rational wait-and-see calculations. They may have just instinctively held on to their old *dokumenti*, to their Yugoslav papers, the way I would hold on to my American ones in a similar situation, or indeed in the situation I am in. It's hard to give up a passport. It's like giving up an identity. It's like burning a bridge.

Then time passed, the window closed, the situation did not get better but instead got much, much worse. To be deported to the south now is more than just an inconvenience; it can be life-threatening, especially if you are a young man and fit for proscription in the military. At the same time, the requirements for Slovenian citizenship suddenly got more stringent, starting with the necessity to pass a rigorous test in the Slovenian language, a language that up until recently many former Yugoslavs looked at as little more than a minority tongue, an amusing and provincial dialect.

Now three female teachers of this minority tongue step up onto a small platform at the front of the hall. One of them calls the disparate group to order and makes an announcement in English, our lingua franca for now. The three teachers also seem taken aback by the size of the turnout, by the sudden interest of so many people in Prešeren's language of shepherds and milk-maids. And like me, they must first tackle the task of figuring out who we are, of dividing us into categories, though their criteria is not geographical or degrees of Yugoslav cool but mastery of languages, especially Slavic languages, knowledge of basic grammatical structures, and the amount and variety of Slovenians words and phrases that we have managed to pick up along our way to the lobby of Filozofska Fakulteta.

They distribute questionnaires.

These are the words I managed to pick up along the way and that I write down in the empty boxes and columns of the questionnaire.

Dober dan: Good day.

Kako si?: How are you?

Dober večer: Good evening.

Lahko noč: Good night.

Hvala lepa: Thank you very much.

Nasvidenje: Good-bye.

Vino, kavo, mleko, ričet, sarma, džezva—though that last one—who knew?—is not a Slovenian word at all but comes from the south where the little copper pot itself comes from, the word being a Turkish borrowing in Serbo-Croatian, once an official language in these parts but now, in a fit of defensive nationalism, being vigorously erased like all those Yugoslav birth certificates.

These are the words I managed to pick up along the way but do not write down:

Pička (variant: *pizda*): cunt.

This word is used with such frequency and variety as to lose much of its meaning and ability to shock. It is used to start sentences, to end sentences, as a stopgap in the middle of sentences. It is used to express a wide array of both positive and negative emotions: disgust, disbelief, dismay, admiration, anger, amazement, awe. Used in the diminutive, *pičkica*, it can mean a hot chick, as in, *"Kakšna pičkica!"* What a babe! Or, it can refer to any girls, as in, "There were a lot of *pičkice* at that party last night."

Combined with your mother, as in *"pička ti materna,"* it creates the classic Mediterranean insult, a turn of phrase so common that it is abbreviated to *p.m.* when used in movie subtitles. Combined with the *ija* it makes *pičkarija* or *pizdarija*, which translates into something like "mess" or "chaos." There is a good deal of disagreement, I have found, among Slovenian men and women alike, as to whether the word is offensive or not. With the typical tin ear of the foreigner, not to mention the foreigner who has learned much of her vocabulary in bed, I cannot seem to summon the feminist outrage to condemn the word. To me it has a sweet and sexy sound. It sounds onomatopoetically like "peach."

Kurac: dick, prick, cock.

On the grammatical and expressive levels, the word has a similar function as *pička*, beginning and ending sentences, expressing disgust, disbelief, dismay, anger, amazement, awe. In this masculine Balkan culture it is rarely used in the diminutive, though it is employed in a number of set phrases, such as, *"Kurc te gleda,"* meaning "my dick is looking at you," and translating into something like "go to hell," or, *"Imam poln kurac,"* meaning "I have a full dick," and translating into something like "I've had enough of this, I'm fed up."

Južnjak: southerner.

This word refers to all former Yugoslavs—Croats, Bosnians, Serbs, Macedonians, Montenegrins, Kosovo Albanians—other than Slovenians. I have been told that it is a completely neutral and objective term, not in the least bit derogatory, merely descriptive and geographical.

Bosanc: Bosnian.

This word also refers to all former Yugoslavs—Croats, Bosnians, Serbs, Macedonians, Montenegrins, Kosovo Albanians—other than Slovenians. Like *južnjak*, it is a neutral term, or so I have been assured, although the fact that all former Yugoslavs except Slovenians should be lumped together by Slovenians under the classification of "Bosnian" makes one wonder.

Čefur: Bosnian, southerner.

Yet another term for all former Yugoslavs other than Slovenians, this one unambiguously derogatory, especially when used in a phrase such as *"Raus čefuri!"* These two words—deliberately echoing the World War II racial epithet *"Juden Raus!"* Jews Out!—are spray painted on the walls and cement bridges of my proletarian neighborhood.

Šiptar: Albanian.

This refers exclusively to Kosovo Albanians, who are numerous in Slovenia and the other former republics of Yugoslavia, usually working as ice cream vendors or sellers of fruit and vegetables imported from Italy and Spain (one rung lower on the market hierarchy than the old women who push their home-grown products to market along the streets of Ljubljana), or, as the Slovenian locals rightly or wrongly complain, as drug mafia. As to whether the term *šiptar* is derogatory or not, the question, when I have asked it, has been met with mystification, as if Albanians belong to some entirely separate human category in which such notions no longer apply.

Zamorček: the little one from across the sea.

This term, in contrast to the previous ones, designates not the known and despised foreigner—Albanians and other southerners—but the unknown foreigner, the mysterious foreigner: blacks, moors, Africans. The turbaned *zamorček* with the gleaming whites of his eyes and his full red lips is both an exotic and frequent figure in Central Europe, a fact that makes Americans uncomfortable. He appears on the logo of Julius Meinl, a chain of Austrian grocery stores, on boxes of imported coffee, on sugar packets in Ljubljana cafés. He also appears in the classic Slovenian story of exile, *Lepa Vida*, in which, in a reversal of the usual tale of subordination, a moor comes and lures away a young Slovenian wife and mother named Vida and forces her into bondage as a wet nurse in his land across the sea.

The contemporary unturbaned black, on the other hand, is an extremely unusual sight on the streets of Ljubljana. Briefly, during Tito's reign at the head of the nonaligned movement, Slovenia's universities hosted many dark-skinned students from other nonaligned countries, but this is no longer the case. Indeed, there is only one dark-skinned student in the otherwise surprisingly large group at Filozofska Fakulteta. But whatever its origins, I like the term *zamorček*. I like it much more than all those words for former Yugoslavs, and I hope it is not, as I suspect they are, insulting. After all, were it not for the color of my skin, for the fact that I can slip virtually unnoticed (as long as I keep my mouth shut) through a crowd of Slovenians, the word *zamorček*, the little one from across the sea, would be a very apt description of me.

I do not know whether I would have been placed in a more advanced class if I had been allowed to write down the unexpurgated list of the words I managed to pick up along the way. I doubt it.

Many Slovenians, and especially the lexicographers and language specialists among them, argue that most such vulgarities, like the word *džezva*, are borrowings from the language that was once called Serbo-Croatian and is now called Serbian, Croatian, or Bosnian depending on whom you happen to be talking to at a given moment. There are also many Slovenians, the Yugonostalgic ones, as they are coming to be called, who argue that the juiciest and most expressive words, the words that give the language flair and personality, come precisely from the southern dictionaries; but these Slovenians generally do not find work as language teachers. What is indisputable is that the parsing of language—what expressions come from Ottoman times and what from Yugoslav, what word is a bastardized German word for which a perfectly good Slovenian equivalent exists, what is a newfangled English word for which, if there is no equivalent, one should be invented—is a passionate pastime here.

The three teachers retreat into an adjoining room to sort the questionnaires. When they return, I, with my knowledge of French and my smattering of permissible Slovenian words, am assigned, along with the most of the Western Europeans and the few grammatically able Americans, to the intermediate group. The single dark-skinned African and the three Asians, whose mother tongues are light years away from Slovenian, and to make matters worse, have not necessarily mastered English, which will be the language of instruction for the time being, are kicked down to the remedial program along with the Americans who do not know the difference between a direct and an indirect object, knowledge that is crucial when learning a language with six grammatical cases.

The former Yugoslavs or southerners (if I may call them that) are assigned, along with the Slavic scholars, to the advanced group. I am sorry to see them go. They are not real foreigners, real outsiders, like the rest of us. They are somehow more authentic, and I have the feeling that if I could just get to know them, they—unlike the trio of instructors, who are likely to teach us children's ditties, the names of indigenous plants, the Slovenian national anthem (a drinking song written by none other than the ubiquitous France Prešeren)—would be an excellent source of local information, of the inside dope.

But, alas, I am unlikely to get to know them. Not only have they been assigned to a different class, but they see me as just another American, just another person on a holy mission.

Klub Drama

Narrow lanes of Ljubljana

"Do you want to go out tonight? V *life*?"

Aleš and I have just finished our lunch of reheated *sarma*. He is sipping a cup of fruit tea with lemon and honey; I am drinking Turkish coffee. One wall of the studio apartment, the one that gives on to the balcony, is a single great pane of glass covered with the slats of Venetian blinds and beside it the doorway out to the balcony. The door is ajar, and the afternoon sun streams through the blinds. Aleš and I occupy two armchairs, lazing like two cats in our individual pools of autumn warmth.

"What do you mean *v life*?"

V *life*, he explains, is one of the sillier recent borrowings from English. It just means to go out, to party, to have fun, suggesting that life is lived fuller if one does it with an English word. Such coinages are flooding Slovenia right now: *ful kul* for totally cool, *ful sufer* for totally suffering. Nobody really knows who starts them, but once in circulation, they spread, much to the chagrin of the panicky grammarians who are trying to put Slovenian on the map before it goes the way of Irish and Inuit, with all the speed and heat of an uncontrolled wildfire.

"Sure, I've love to go out to life," I say. "I've been waiting to sample Ljubljana's legendary three bars for a while now. Though I must say: I dread crossing that hallway again today. Our neighbor, you know."

When I emerged from the elevator earlier in the afternoon—the odd-numbered elevator had actually been working for a change—that same neighbor opened his door a crack, peered wordlessly at me as I fumbled with the keys, and then slammed the door shut again. No greeting. No acknowledgement.

"What's with him anyway?"

"That's just the way Slovenian neighbors are," Aleš says. "Better get used to it."

Then, and this was his and everyone else's way of explaining things that had better be gotten used to, things that just are the way they are, he tells a joke. Jokes—racial jokes, ethnic jokes, sexist jokes—are common currency around here. Nearly everybody trades in them. Joke-telling is a necessary social skill, used to break awkward silences, and sometimes to compete in all-night joke marathons. The vast majority of jokes in circulation illustrate the different nature of each of the former Yugoslav peoples. The Bosnian character, for example, in the universe of Yugoslav jokes, is good-natured, stupid, and omnisexual. So you have the joke about the Bosnian who when asked whether he'd rather be beautiful or stupid, answers that he'd rather be stupid.

"Why stupid?" his questioner persists.

"Because," the Bosnian responds with irrefutable logic, "beauty doesn't last."

Or the one about the Bosnian who is asked if he would fuck a gorilla for five hundred German marks. German marks are still how anything of real value is denominated in this region, the Slovenian tolar being too new to resonate with any real meaning, and the Yugoslav dinar, since the war and subsequent hyperin-flation, having more zeroes on it than Italian lira.

"I would," responds the Bosnian amiably, "I would. But I don't have five hundred German marks."

Macedonians, in Yugoslav jokes, are said to be lazy by nature, hence the joke about the Macedonian who slaps his wife's ass on his way to work and discovers that it is still shaking when he comes home: not because his wife's ass is so fat, but because his work day is so short. Even the high-achieving, relatively straight-laced Slovenians do not get off the hook entirely. There is one joke, for example, about a Serbian prostitute who, until her en-counter with a Slovenian customer, had never heard the word penis before. When the job's done, she concludes that a penis is pretty much the same thing as her Serbian customer's *kurac*—only smaller.

Internal jokes about the character of Slovenians tend to be less racy and more pastoral. The joke Aleš tells to explain the be-havior of our neighbor goes like this. A fairy comes to a farm-house and informs the peasant who lives there—in Slovenian the word for "farmer" and "peasant," *kmet*, is one and the same—that she will fulfill any wish he has. She will give him more grain in his silo, more milk from his cow, more coins in his purse, the only condition being that whatever he wishes for, his neighbor will get twice as much of it as he. In other words, his neighbor will get the wish times two.

The peasant scratches his head and ponders the thing a while. Finally he answers. "Poke out one of my eyes," he instructs the fairy.

One eye, two peasants, three bars.

I always knew it had to be an understatement. In a country that consumes as much alcohol as this one, per capita alcohol consumption in Slovenia being yet another statistical list topper, it would have to be. But it is true enough that there are only three bars in Ljubljana regularly frequented by the city's young and sophisticated *kulturati*, as its writers, editors, playwrights, filmmakers, and their hangers-on are collectively known. They are:

ŠKUC, an art gallery-bar located in the medieval pedestrian zone that has no chairs, plays loud music, and caters to the black-clad postcommunist postfascist postpunk set.

KUD, an art gallery-bar located in the Trnovo district that has no chairs, plays loud music, and caters to the black-clad postcommunist postfascist postpunk set, although it differs from ŠKUC in that it has a small theater adjacent to it offering occasional poetry readings, musical performances, plays, and even puppet shows.

Klub Drama, located on Slovenska aka Tito Street next to the National Theater. Klub Drama has the dilapidated decor of a turn-of-the-century Austrian coffee house, unflattering fluorescent lighting, plays innocuous music at relatively low volume, and caters to the literary set. It has lots of chairs.

We go to Drama.

The advantage, or disadvantage, depending on your point of view, of three bars in a city of three hundred thousand people, as opposed to three hundred thousand bars in a city of ten million, is that you inevitably run into people you know. Indeed, in certain circles and on certain nights, everybody knows everybody else. There literally are no strangers. The true stranger, the authentic factor x, does not exist as a category.

People living in Ljubljana have developed various techniques for dealing with the claustrophobic social situation. One of them, as Aleš had so cheerfully informed me back at Marion's restaurant on our first date, is suicide. But there is also an array of less extreme social practices that have evolved over the years. For example, the use of the word *živijo* (pronounced zhou-yo), which is used at least as frequently as *pička*, and not being a vulgarity, I might have written down on my language questionnaire if I had had a clue how to spell it.

Živijo is the Slovenian version of *ciao*, a casual greeting that can be used night or day, coming or going, or just passing by. It serves multiple functions depending on the tone of voice: "hello," "goodbye," "long time no see," "I see you and acknowledge you but don't have time to talk to you right now," or "I can't stand the sight of you but don't want to give you the satisfaction of ignoring you." It can be said curtly with an almost dismissive nod if the two exchanging greetings have already seen each other several times that same day and expect to see each other several times more. It can be muttered lazily, almost soundlessly, eyes at half-mast, more of a stifled yawn than the deliberate articulation of a word, to those one expects to see, those who are always there, hunched over a glass at Drama, burning through their umpteenth cigarette. Or it can be roared out with real gusto, with life-gobbling pleasure, like the Yugoslav toast *živeli*! To life!

Ljubljana dwellers are also necessarily adept, I have had occasion to notice with Aleš, in their dealings with ex-lovers, ex-wives, current lovers, current wives all mixing together at the same bar, the same gallery opening, the same film debut. These encounters almost have the feeling of a stage play in which all the actors pretend not to know what they know, what line comes next, who bedded whom yesterday, who will be bedding whom tomorrow. Such a system would wreak emotional havoc in New York, where people assiduously and without much effort avoid the places where they might with a current fling run into an ex-fling. To make matters even more awkward, a kind of infidelity is still practiced in this part of the world that as far as I know is virtually extinct, or at least has gone underground, in the feminist West. The kind where great, larger-than-life men can't be bothered to get a divorce because they are Catholic, or simply because they want to have their cake and eat it too, and so maintain one apartment on one side of town with a wife and two teenage daughters, and another apartment on the other side of town with a big-breasted mistress and an infant son. Sometimes the great man goes out with his wife, sometimes with his mistress. In either case he meets the same people, and they all nod to the couple and say the same word: *živijo*.

I enter this society like a breath of fresh air, or some might say like a boot to the solar plexus. Nobody knows what to make of me, what to say to me, how to deal with me. I am a real stranger, the authentic factor x, and nobody has any idea how to solve for it.

This is when the notion of affiliation—*Čigava je ona*? Who does that one belong to?—comes in handy. The first level of identification is possession. I am no longer Johnson, not Debeljak, but Debeljakova: the female possession of Debeljak. This is another usage, the attachment of the feminine possessive *-ova* to married women's surnames, that I should abhor. Slovenian feminists do. They either don't marry—for all its Catholicism, common-law marriage is extremely frequent in Slovenia—or they drop the *-ova*, or they adopt laughably long combined names, two multiple-syllable Slavic surnames strung together with a hyphen that don't fit on a business card let alone on a doorbell buzzer. But I am in the throes of romance, in the throes of the exotic, and I want to be the female possession of Debeljak. That's why I came here, after all. I may not be ready for the Islamic veil, but wearing the name Debeljakova seems harmless enough. It reminds me of the Russian patronymics, and the most romantic heroine of all: Anna Karenina, the female possession of Karenin. Then again, her end on the Moscow train tracks might stand as a reminder of the danger of possession in its more extreme forms.

Aleš, courteous and attentive as he has been since I arrived in Slovenia, fills in the blanks on my side. They may not know anything about me, but I will know plenty about them. Aleš steers me into the club, holding my elbow, his lips pressed against my ear.

"That's Niko Grafenauer," he whispers. "He was an anticommunist dissident in the seventies and eighties, editor of the magazine *Nova Revija*, very good poet, womanizer, big drinker." The man in question looks the part. He stands at the bar, deep in serious conversation with another man, freshly filled glass and freshly lit cigarette in hand, hair a mane of wavy gray, eyes a yellowish pickled hue shot through with bright red veins. But handsome nonetheless, features chiseled and ruined at once, the wandering eye of the libertine, already visibly drunk. He seizes my hand when introduced—he has heard about the new *američanka* in town—pulls me to him and breathes sweet rancid words into my ear, saying something I don't understand but don't really need to. I feel certain he has propositioned me in some way.

We move on.

"That's Uroš Zupan. He just published his first book of poetry, extremely talented guy." Uroš is more the wispy-haired absent-minded type, drifting through the bar, composing verses in his head.

"That's Jure Potokar, poet and translator from English." There is a saying that if you throw a stone in Slovenia it will strike a poet, and now I know why. Jure is so thin and so tall that he has to bend over when introduced to me, the little one from across the sea. Aleš tells me that he met Jure at Filozofska Fakulteta, where both sat out their Yugoslav military service. Jure failed the weight requirement. Aleš had a kidney injury that stopped his judo career and had to undergo surgery. I know the scar well, have run my fingers along the heavy gutter of that wound, dipped them into the indentations to the side and below it, where stitches and a drainage hole were made as if by an industrial riveter rather then a needle. The upshot was that there were very few men in the otherwise entirely female freshman class of the university, all other Slovenian men of the same age being off in southern republics digging trenches and shouldering rifles. And thus Aleš's life of poetry and womanizing was effectively launched.

As for the women, Aleš and I have developed a system for them as well, one that involves no whispered asides. I am not even sure why we do it. Perhaps Aleš wants to include me in everything, to make me as well-informed as all the other actors in the small stage play of Ljubljana's social life. Or perhaps he is such a raving egotist that it is the kind of information he cannot resist imparting. Or perhaps it is simply love. We are one now. We share everything. But whatever the reason, whenever we meet a young woman in the street or in a café or at Klub Drama, I send a questioning glance to Aleš and he responds with an answering glance: "Yes, I have been with her," or "No, never got around to that one."

When I meet the laughing Nela I get an affirmative glance. So too with the sullen Alenka who looks as if she must have had her heart set on being the female possession of Debeljak herself.

But when I meet the beautiful Tanja Gvozdenovič—half Serb, half Slovenian, fierce black eyes, blood-red lips in a field of almost Kabuki white—Aleš responds to my questioning glance with a nervous negative as if to say, "This one's out of my league."

I rejoice.

If she hasn't been his, then she'll be mine. Not only is she beautiful, but she knows everybody, and seems eager to take me under her wing. She is similar, in basic profile, to Aleš's sister Polona: twenty-six years old, still lives with her mother in a village called Medvode on the outskirts of Ljubljana, her Bosnian Serb father having died some years ago. She is officially enrolled as a student at Ekonomska Fakulteta, and though she continues to enjoy student privileges—steep discounts on public transportation, cheap lunches in city cafeterias, easy access to health care—she is never seen handling anything as pedestrian as a textbook or a spiral notepad or any other materials that might in some way be associated with the activity of study

Tanja

But Tanja is far from idle. She sews her own eccentric wardrobe: capes and matching hats and wide swirling skirts. She bakes delicious cakes without benefit of a recipe. She can light a campfire anywhere any time with any fuel and scornfully rejects those who even flirt (as I secretly do) with the notion of lighter fluid. But her principle activity, what fills her jobless school-less days, are *obiski*—visits—a word that in Slovenia implies a whole shifting network of spontaneous afternoon socializing, providing assistance when needed, meandering conversations, the long slow consumption of Turkish coffee, fruit tea, and as afternoon turns to night, other more potent beverages. Tanja moves in a range of social circles—musicians, photographers, foreigners, students—and brings people together whom she thinks need to be brought together. She is resourceful. If the destination of her visit lies outside the public bus routes, she hitchhikes and invariably makes a useful contact in whatever car happens to pull to the side of road to pick her up. She is generous. If foreign back-packers ask for the location of the nearest youth hostel, she in-vites them to sleep at Medvode and makes a friend for life. She can stay up all night long without showing much strain, which turns out to be a common trait in this country where parties never seem to end even after they have staggered into a state of deep and despondent inebriation.

But I know none of this when I meet Tanja. All I know is that she walks me around Drama, teaching me amusing Slovenian phrases (a nonexistent word, for example, for female hippopota-mus), introducing me to people such as Vitaly Osmačko, a Russ-ian singer of Gypsy music, and clapping with exuberance when we try to communicate with each other in halting Slovenian. He knows no English and I, no Russian.

"At last," she exclaims, "the two superpowers are speaking to each other. And in Slovenian, no less."

Hours later, when midnight has come and gone, a crash res-onates through the small rooms of the brightly lit club. Everyone looks up from their drinks and toward the sound. It was an im-pressively loud thud, as if some extremely large and heavy object had fallen a good distance without actually breaking. It turns out to be Niko Grafenauer's companion. He has plummeted to the floor with all the massive weight of an unfeeling and unconscious and slightly overweight adult male who has been ritually soaked in alcohol. The man lies motionless on the linoleum floor, stretched out beside the bar stool like a pale dead fish on a filthy cigarette-butt-strewn shore. A smile lingers around the corner of his lips, the only indication that he survived the fall.

"Jeez," I marvel to Aleš and Tanja, "I wonder how he's going to get home tonight."

They turn to me with a curious look, as if they don't quite understand what I'm getting at, what I could possibly be concerned about. Soon I understand why. A group of men crouch down around the body. Laboriously, with a great deal of huffing and puffing and slurred words of encouragement, they scoop up the heavy shapeless mass. They get him more or less to his feet, balancing the weight of his torso over wobbly coltish legs. They prop him up against the bar, catching their breath, I figure, before they escort him outside and into the fresh night air where he might just manage to come around. But once he is poised against the bar, the barman places a tall glass in front of him and fills it to the rim with wine. He decants nearly half a bottle of the blood-red liquid into what is essentially a beer stein. Niko tenderly wedges a lit cigarette between his friend's fingers. The man's eyes flutter open, and soon, perhaps stimulated by the nicotine, he is standing on his own again with only a slight buckle and sway now and then. He picks up the heavy glass in front of him and guides it very slowly to his lips. He doesn't spill a drop. Home is out of the question.

Life, the party, goes on.

Loški Potok

The house behind the little fence

The time has come to meet the extended family, the country cousins, the relatives in Loški Potok.

It turns out, to my dismay, that being the female possession of Debeljak is not always enough to solve for x. It cannot be avoided; we are more than just the sum of two. Wider circles of affiliation exist, and sooner or later I must be incorporated into them. I already got an inkling of this when I occasionally met older Slovenians, rural types, not from Ljubljana, and I found that my definition of myself, Debeljakova, wife of the poet Aleš, no longer sufficed.

"Debeljak." They would ponder the surname. "Where is your husband's family from?"

"Loški Potok," I dutifully answered, though I already knew that Loški Potok is composed of seven distinct settlements, and that during World War II the residents of the seven settlements were pretty much evenly divided against one another: communist-leaning partisans and resisters of the German occupation against the so-called home guard, known as *belogardisti* in the Slovenian littoral, or clerics in Ljubljana because of the support they received from the Catholic Church, but above all as traitors to the partisans who massacred them by the thousands after the end of the war and disposed of their bodies in shallow mass graves, traitors because their anticommunism had trumped their hatred of the anti-Slav foreign occupiers, traitors because they had collaborated with Germans and Italians against their own people.

This is the main divide even in contemporary Slovenia: red versus white, left versus right, communist versus fascist, partisan versus home guard. Both sides are stained by original sin, the collaborators for collaborating, the partisans for the unforgivable postwar massacres. With the fall of communism, however, the divide has grown if possible even deeper and more bitter, the right-wing sympathizers of the old home guard having been emboldened by the failure of the global communist project, the left-wing inheritors of the communist past taking most of the influential government positions after independence. The split is like a cancer. It poisons politics and social discourse and makes the recent historical milestone of the Ten Day War seem like an afterthought, like just another chapter in an ongoing and never-ending fraternal struggle. In this one regard, Loški Potok, evenly divided against itself, is like the country in miniature.

"What settlement in Loški potok?"

"I have no idea."

"What were they called *po domače*?"

"I don't know." I don't even understand the question. What are they asking me: red or white? partisan or home guard? I know *domače* comes from the word home, *dom*, so it must mean something like "home name."

Mija informs me that we can only visit the Loški Potok relatives on Sunday. Every other day is a work day.

Most farms in Slovenia in 1993 are so-called mixed farms. The name is deceptive. "Mixed" doesn't mean diversified crops or growing methods. It simply means that the farmers in question mix the rigors and fresh air of agricultural work with the rigors and routine of factory work or some other paying job. Mixing the two activities was the only way for Slovenian villagers to survive in the decades after World War II, and often even that was not enough. Many, like Mija and Pavel, ended up leaving their villages and going to the larger towns and cities of Slovenia and Yugoslavia in order to make better lives for themselves, in order to escape the grueling menial work of village life and its scarce rewards. Many more, mostly men but also women, went as far as Germany and Austria in the fifties and sixties and seventies to work as *gastarbeiter*, guest workers, physical laborers in a foreign country. This army of migrant labor missed out on a regular domestic life, on their children's childhood, and tended to be more beaten down than enlightened by their travels, but they did earn a pile of hard currency with which to support their families and even build a new house or barn back in their home villages.

If I think Pavel's city work hours are cruel—he is a foreman in a small factory that makes welded metal fittings for both military and civilian use, domestic consumption and export to places such as Western-boycotted Iran—they are a breeze compared to the hours worked by mixed farmers in the villages. In 1993, well after the fall of communism and the turn toward the West, most Slovenian city dwellers begin work at six in the morning and stop at two in the afternoon, coming home for a three o'clock lunch, the principal meal of the day. These are the hours at factories, offices, and many other jobs, which explains why the country's cheerful and inexpensive day care centers open their doors to their squalling charges at five in the morning. By early afternoon, most parents have already picked up their children (or more likely their child, as the current national birth rate in Slovenian languishes at 1.2 children per woman, not enough to replenish the small nation of two million, Slovenia ironically being on the verge of breeding itself out of existence at the same point in history when it fought itself into existence). Perhaps socialism's early work schedule also provides the reason for the determined idleness of the younger generation, for the *kulturati*'s habit of whiling away the nocturnal hours at ŠKUC and KUD and Klub Drama: they are exacting their revenge for a childhood of being dropped off at the school doors at five-thirty in the morning.

And yet, incredibly, those who stayed behind in the villages get up for work even earlier. Pavel and his twin brother Peter moved to Ljubljana when their were under twenty, but the two elder Debeljak brothers, Mirko and Ludvig remained in Loški Potok, while the youngest of the quintet defected to the capitalist West in the 1960s where, free or not, his standard of living isn't all that superior to his brothers in the communist East, and his existence, cut off from village and family, is a good deal lonelier. But at least it can be hoped that he got to lie in bed a little longer in the morning. For in Loški Potok and other Slovenian villages, men, women, and sometimes even children rise before dawn, at around four in the morning, to milk the cows, shovel shit from the barn, pile it in the compost heap, and do whatever other chores are needed before the men depart for their factories, the women for the offices and stores where they work, and the children for school.

Then home for a hot lunch at three (cooked, who knows when, by the women).

Bucket of Turkish coffee.

Afternoon chores.

Homework.

Bed.

Saturdays are dedicated to large jobs: the clearing of meadows along the edge of the forests, the construction of barns and additions to houses, the slaughtering of pigs for sausage.

Sunday: mass and visits. But no sleeping in. The cows don't take the day off.

First we will visit the eldest Debeljak brother, Mirko, and his wife, Ivanka. Then we will go to Ludvig's, the second eldest Debeljak brother. Then to look at Mija's little abandoned house, the last one in the village, and pay a visit to her next-door neighbors.

Then up to a little village above the valley called Gora, which means mountain, to visit Mirko and Ivanka's daughter, Miri, and her family. Miri is yet another nickname for Marija. Not only do many Slovenian villages have literal names like Hill, Middle Village, Lower Village, Saturday Market Village, but most Slovenian farmers still name at least one of their daughters Marija.

We bring along a gang of translators: Mija and Pavel to translate from the local Notranjska dialect into standard Slovenian, Aleš and Polona to translate from Slovenian into English and back again. There are more than fifty recorded dialects in Slovenia, which means that amazingly I don't actually need to drive two or three hours or cross a border in order not to be able to speak or understand the local language. I need only go to Loški Potok or to Prekmurje, the region that straddles Hungary and boasts a dialect that *nobody* in Slovenia can understand. Yet another strategy to counter the claustrophobic smallness of the place: the division of what is quite obviously a finite territory into an infinite number of smaller mutually incomprehensible parts.

As we enter the village of Loški Potok, which is, like most Slovenian villages, a compact, well-tended cluster of uniform square cinderblock houses and barns with a church and grave-yard at the center, Mija warns me to pace myself as far as food and drink is concerned. I will be expected to eat at every house, both savory food and sweets, and to drink schnapps as well. To decline is an insult.

Mirko covertly studies me as I bravely hurl a shot of home-made apple brandy down my throat. It is a curious thing, it seems, to have an American woman standing in one's kitchen, drinking one's home-made apple brandy.

Mirko, only five years Pavel's senior, is an old man already. A tough and wiry and energetic old man, but an old man all the same. He stands at the head of the small kitchen table with a shot glass in his hand, a smoldering cigarette tucked between his yellowed fingers. From what I can make out, he has only two or three nicotine-stained teeth in his mouth. His face is etched with deep furrows. His gnarled hands are permanently stained by tree sap and soil and tractor fuel. He could easily be Pavel's father, though I know he is not. All of Aleš's grandparents are dead, none of them having made it within spitting distance of the age of seventy. The different in Mirko and Pavel's appearance distills the essential difference between city life and village life: the hours worked over a lifetime, the hours not slept.

After the schnapps, Ivanka gives me a tour of the farm. Ivanka is also old beyond her years, looking far more worn than the brown-haired, light-stepped Mija. Ivanka's hair is a brittle gray-white. Her back is beginning to curve into a hump, the beginnings of unprevented and untreated osteoporosis. But like her husband, Mirko, she is tough and capable. Work, sixteen hours a day of it, is the only life these two know.

Polona—she is called Palwana in the local dialect—accompanies us to translate. Ivanka first shows off the six lowing and shifting animals in the cinderblock barn, eyeballs turning nervously in their heads as we strangers enter: two cows for milking and breeding, two bulls for slaughter, and two new calves. Ivanka and Mirko assist at the births of the calves, reaching their arms up all the way up to their shoulders into the enormous birthing females. The place has the same pungent nose-wrinkling smell, a mingling of acidic urine and fresh-cut hay, that I recognize from the barns I walk past in Ljubljana. But nevertheless it is remarkably clean, walls scrubbed and whitewashed, excrement scraped from the cement floors with the sharp edge of a shovel several times each day.

Slovenian farmers are nothing if not *pridni*, a word which means industrious, diligent, hard-working. *Priden*, I have learned early and repeatedly, is the most favored of all Slovenian adjectives. It perfectly expresses the aspect of the Slovenian soul that yearns for the north, for Teutonic efficiency, for all that is Habsburgian, conservative, bourgeois, orderly. Its flip side, of course, is the wild primitive south. Babies who sleep through the night are *pridni*. Women who don't scream while giving birth are *pridne*. Men who take out the garbage are *pridni*. Housewives who hang their laundry out to dry, or put out a pot of geraniums on the balcony rail, are *pridne*. Foreign students who master the six cases of the Slovenian language are *pridni*. The only people in this industrious society who are not *pridni*, as far as I can tell, are the southern laborers working twelve-hour days on all the construction sites around the country: the new *gastarbeiter* of Slovenia. They, I am often told, are lazy.

Ivanka shows me the chicken house next. It holds some twenty or thirty squawking hens and a couple of roosters. The preponderance of mixed farms has numerous benefits, if not for the hard-working farmers themselves then for Slovenians in general. It gives the landscape its bucolic appearance, a charming balance between nature and cultivation, a combination of elements in pleasing harmony: compact flower-filled villages topped by church belfries, well-tended pale-green meadows and fields on their outskirts, mown regularly to provide feed for the cattle, the meadows and fields surrounded in turn by running brooks and abundant forests that, were it not for the labors of the mixed farmers, would have long since overrun the meadowlands. Likewise, the mixed farmers supply Slovenians with unfathomably fresh produce: eggs with sturdy shells and bright yellow yolks the likes of which ordinary Americans have not seen for more than a generation, firm pale potatoes with a clean, sharp, unmushy flavor, small crisp apples so tasty that you can almost hear them being snapped from the branch of a nearby apple tree as you sink your teeth into them. And the farm women know the ancient skill of walking the forests and meadows, gathering fresh chamomile for tea, bay leaves for soups and stews, blueberries and lilac blossoms and the pale fresh new-grown tips of pine branches to distill the different-flavored syrup bases for the juice they drink year round.

Ivanka then shows me the pigpen, which houses one enormous bright pink pig that is scheduled to be made into pork roasts and blood sausage and crunchy lard in a couple of weeks' time. In the corner is the feed trough where virtually all the refuse from the house winds up. That is another benefit of Slovenia's rural legacy: the resistance, at least among the older generation of Slovenians, to consumerism and waste, the tendency to save everything, throw out nothing that has a potential use in the household economy. Potato peels tossed into the feed trough, cotton T-shirts ripped into strips to tie up tomato plants, old whiskey bottles used to decant the season's newly brewed schnapps and sweet home-made syrups. Store-bought juice and its excessive packaging: who needs it?

"That pig is really pink," I remark. I am like a novice driver who cannot recognize the make of the car or how many horsepower it has, but can at least name its color. Polona translates to Ivanka, Ivanka explains, Polona laughs.

"It's sunburn," Polona says. "They left it out too long in the sun yesterday."

I didn't know pigs could get sunburn. I didn't know cows only give milk when they are pregnant or nursing a calf, although when you think about it, it makes sense. I didn't even know that potatoes grow underground, in the soil, and not on bushes or trees, that the potatoes themselves are the seeds for next year's crop. I gaze at the sturdy Ivanka, her sharp features, hooked nose, and long teeth, her faded work apron tied around her waist.

"Do you ever go on vacation?" I ask her through Polona.

She snorts. Then she pauses mid-step, pondering a moment, trying perhaps to recall some long-ago trip. Then she remembers:

"I was at the seaside once, in Piran," she says softly. "That was a long time ago."

The Adriatic lies only an hour away as the crow flies, although that means little in this remote valley.

"But you could go," I insist. "You could get the neighbors to milk your cows."

She lets out a high whoop of laughter when Polona translates this to her. "The neighbors."

And then I remember: "Poke out one of my eyes."

The older generations of villagers don't go on annual vacations, and especially not summer vacations. Their lives hew to the natural cycles. They rise and set with the sun. When it is summer, they do not think of beaches and bikinis, lounging on the warm sand, lazily flipping the pages of a book. Summer is the season of heavy work leading up to the autumn harvest and slaughter. Winter, when nature is in repose, gives the villagers, and especially the women, their sole opportunity for relative ease. Winter is the season when the fields need no weeding, the orchards no tending, the flower boxes no watering. Even the words Slovenians use to discuss natural processes reflect the lingering affinity between people and nature. Plants and seeds and bulbs *počivati*, they rest, during the winter, as do the women who tend them. They *roditi*, give birth, in the spring. The word for a young fruit, *plod*, is the same as the word for a human embryo.

Ivanka shows us the *mlekarna*, evidence that, after all, neighbors do cooperate on some projects. It is a little dairy house containing a stainless steel vat to which the villagers bring the milk produced by their two or three or four cows. Each day when the sun goes down, Ivanka sits in the booth and collects the milk that her neighbors bring to her in tall aluminum containers slung high on their shoulders, carried through the narrow nameless lanes of the village. They pour the warm grayish-white liquid into the stainless steel refrigerated vat and Ivanka records the incoming amounts in her ledger. They chat a while, swapping items of village gossip. Periodically, Ljubljanska Mlekarna, the Slovenian milk company, comes to pick up the collected milk from the village dairy, and Ivanka disburses the appropriate sums, less a cut, to her fellow farmers.

Back in the kitchen we eat and talk and drink some more. I am not pacing myself, I fear. We still have three or four visits to go. Mirko and Ivanka's son Janko joins us. He is Aleš's age, unmarried, and lives at home. On the way down in the car, Mija explained why he will probably never marry. There is, it turns out, such a thing as being too *priden*.

"No woman will marry him," she said. "That's the biggest and cleanest farm in the village, and Ivanka is the hardest-working farmwoman. They keep more cows and chickens and pigs than anyone else in the seven settlements. Any woman who marries Janko will have to work as hard as Ivanka, and no woman wants to work that hard."

"That's ridiculous," I said, Polona sitting between us translating. "She'd be marrying the man, not the family."

When Polona translated that, Mija let out a little *hmph* and looked out the window at the passing scenery, the lush yellow-red forests. Polona grinned and poked me in the ribs. But now, in this kitchen, on this farm, I am beginning to understand.

Just as it is time to leave and move on to our next house, our next *obisk*, I remember what it was that I had wanted to ask Mirko.

"What were you called *po domače?*"

Mija and Pavel in 1960

Polona translates, and Mirko looks up at me in sharp surprise, his icy eyes turning a paler shade of blue, going a bit misty even.

"We Debeljak boys, the five of us, were called *pri kadečih*—the smoking ones—not because of this," he holds up his lit cigarette, "but because our kitchen chimney wasn't any good. It belched black smoke."

Then in a sudden fit of reminiscence, he tells the story of how Pavel, the brightest of the five boys, was accepted into a vocational trade school outside of the valley, up over the hill, past

Gora, in the direction of Ljubljana. He was fourteen at the time. In those days, after the war, the children wore no shoes in the spring and summer and fall, wearing them only in the winter when it was too cold to go barefoot. That way the leather didn't get too worn throughout the year and the shoes could be passed on to a younger brother. But the year Pavel was fourteen he received a new pair of shoes in September and Mirko drove him over the hill in a horse-drawn cart to the town where the vocational high school was located, some thirty miles away. Pavel attended classes the first day and slept in the dormitory that night. But on the second day he put on his new shoes and took a step outside, and then another step, and then walked, like his father had walked from Dachau after the war, all the way back over the hill, past Gora, and down the steep slope into that pretty green Notranjska valley. Those were the days when people still used their feet as a means of transportation.

The boy missed his mother.

Mirko waggles his finger. "We took him back to school the next day. Blisters and all."

As a result of this education, Pavel ended up getting a good job in Ljubljana and eventually became a factory foreman. Mirko went to Germany for five years, leaving Ivanka alone to care for the two children and the farm, while he earned enough money to build a new house with a better chimney.

"What about Mija? What was she *po domače*?"

"Ah, Mija," Mirko sighs and smiles and shakes his head softly. He looks at Pavel and speaks as if the two were alone at the table.

"Do you remember the time when Mija came into the kitchen, before you two were married, before you went to Bosnia for your military service? Do you remember how all five of us brothers were sitting around the kitchen table? Mija—seventeen, maybe— fresh, young, sweet, just a girl still, came flouncing into the kitchen. She sat right down on her young man's lap, kissed her young man right smack on his lips." He guffaws. "Only it was the wrong young man. It was Peter, not Pavel. And she didn't know it, and we all did. How she flew out of his lap when we told her so." Mirko puts his head back and laughs loud and long. "The wrong twin! She kissed the wrong twin." He stops laughing and looks at me. "She was Mija *iz ogradca*. Mija from behind the little fence, because her house at the end of the village had such a low fence around it." Then he turns to Aleš. "And she still is," he says, raising an admonishing finger. "The other day a bunch of fellows were down at the tavern having a drink, and you were up there on the television screen, some conversation, some talk about poetry or politics, or nationalism or Yugoslavia, or who knows what."

Aleš, generally a big talker both on screen and off, has been relatively quiet today, not certain of how I would take his rural connections, not certain of how they would take me.

"And one of the fellows looks up at you on the screen and says that you look familiar to him. He knows your face from somewhere. 'Who is that?' asks the fellow. Then somebody else says, 'That's Mija's boy. Mija, from behind the little fence.'"

There was a certain comfort in it. I had left New York only a few months before, and my departure had been like a drowned body slipping beneath the waves of a cold sea. The anonymous waters closed over my head the instant I was gone. I was completely forgotten. I might never have been there at all. I had no home name, no village name, was not called anything *po domače*. My address had been a long stream of cool forgettable numbers: 240 East Twenty-Fourth Street, number 5E. A slot that anybody could fit into. No doubt somebody already did.

Mija left Loški Potok over thirty years ago, and she is still known by her village name, and her famous son with the American wife is known as Mija's boy, Mija from behind the little fence. At that moment the Mija in question, the girl who kissed the wrong twin so long ago, stands up abruptly, shaking off the spell of nostalgia that has fallen over the kitchen.

"Let's go, she says matter-of-factly, brushing the crumbs from her lap, or, we'll never finish."

There are still four houses to go. *Obiski* are hard work.

Bijelo Dugme

Graffiti on the banks of the Ljubljanica

We are working on verbs.

Still confined to the present tense, the goal is to expand our meager vocabularies, our menu of potential action. Xavier and Andre and the other Western Europeans, in response to this call for action, have declared open battle on the American evangelicals. Gita, the businesslike instructor of the intermediate group, resolutely ignores the culture wars bubbling up in her classroom and tries to focus on the matter at hand. She gives us an assignment during the break to prepare ten sentences using ten different verbs describing what we typically do at home. After the break we file back into the classroom, and one of the Americans in the front row volunteers to go first.

"I drink Coca-Cola and eat a hamburger," he painstakingly reads from his notebook. He speaks haltingly. He pronounces "Coca-Cola" and "hamburger" with a stubborn American accent, not lilting upward on the *a*'s in Coca-Cola, not rolling the *r*'s in hamburger (the word being another English borrowing), indeed not moving his lips much at all.

Gita chides him for his lazy American mouth, urging him to enunciate each sound and syllable: *ham-bur-ger*. She grimaces exaggeratedly as she says the three syllables, demonstrating the more muscular Slovenian pronunciation.

"I open a bottle of wine and light a cigarette," Andre carefully articulates. And yet despite his more robust European mouth, his authentic Slovenian roots, the very un-American-ness of the sentence, he is unable to rid himself of the broad flat plains of his British accent.

"I read the Bible," says a young evangelical with flawless God-given pronunciation.

"*Zelo dobro*," says Gita, very good. She is referring, the nonevangelicals in the class assume, to the pronunciation of the word rather than the action itself.

"I buy a porn magazine and lie down in bed," says Xavier. It is the most complex sentence thus far, and Xavier delivers it with aplomb.

Gita praises his pronunciation but notes that, like the Bible, a porn magazine is a feminine singular noun, and functioning here as a direct object would be in the accusative case, therefore with the ending *-o*: *pornsko revijo*.

Gita nods to the next student in the row.

"I pray," comes the ardent voice of an evangelical.

And the next one.

"I have sex with my girlfriend," says an eccentric middle-aged Swiss man who has just joined the class and seems to have gotten right into the spirit of things.

Gita sighs. He has completely botched the sixth case ending for girlfriend, and she points out that *seksati* is a reflexive verb, requiring the reflexive pronoun *se*. We haven't done reflexive verbs yet, so perhaps he had better find something else to occupy his time at home. Gita slams her notebook shut, an indication that the lesson is over, and dismisses us a full ten minutes early.

When I get home to the Proletarska apartment, the phone is ringing. The phone is my nemesis these days. Telephonic communication transmits only words, and generally only foreign words at that. No facial expressions help to convey their meaning, no body language, no embarrassed shrugs or cute smirks in place of apologies for not being able to understand, not being able to communicate. Naturally most of the incoming calls are for Aleš, and many of the people who call insist on leaving messages with the wildly unreliable secretary who answers. When Aleš comes home for lunch, I deliver a series of vague and indeterminate messages, not much more precise than smoke signals.

"A man with a low voice called," I tell my new husband.

He puts down his bag and kisses me. "Did he leave a name?"

"Yes," I confirm, "he did."

"What," Aleš probes, "was the name he left?"

From the kitchen I carry out bowls of steaming *obara*, a hearty soup with flour dumplings prepared by Mija, and lay them carefully on the table between the bed-couch and one of the armchairs. I go back to get spoons and the bread basket. Only when I sit down do I answer.

"It was Zarko or Darko or Zdravko."

Aleš picks up his spoon. He is persistent. He will try to narrow it down further, though he has little to go on.

"Was he speaking Slovenian or Serbo-Croatian?"

I give an embarrassed shrug and a cute smirk. I'm only just beginning to hear the difference between the two languages. All the same, I always answer the phone when it rings. It's my job to keep trying; my only job. And today it pays off. The person on the other end speaks words I understand: English words. The call, unbelievably, is for me. It's Tina calling from New York. She wants me to give her the inside scoop on what's going on in Sarajevo, what people are saying around here, what's the mood on the ground. The besieged Bosnian capital city has caught the world's imagination, and I live a mere five hours away from it, a shorter distance than between Los Angeles and San Francisco.

After the Ten Day War in 1991, the Yugoslav leadership, never all that passionate or proprietary about homogenous Slovenia with its miniscule Serbian minority, revised its military goals. The defeat in Slovenia had been a bit embarrassing; nearly a thousand Yugoslav National Army soldiers had been taken prisoner and truckloads of arms and ammunition seized by the small but well-organized and highly motivated Slovenian territorial guard. After the war was over, a flock of angry Serbian and Montenegrin mothers arrived in Slovenia to pick up their prisoner-of-war sons and take them home to southern kitchens. For its part, the Yugoslav leadership stopped speaking of preserving Yugoslavia within its previous borders but instead of preserving it wherever Serbs lived, or for that matter, wherever dead Serbs lay buried. Thus the notion of Greater Serbia was born. (The joke currently making the rounds about the Serbian nationalist program goes like this: "How does a Serb define pacifism?" "Serbia from here to the Pacific Ocean."

In their defense, the young Yugoslav army conscripts had never really known what or who they were fighting in Slovenia, or even that the military action was a real war and not some sort of extended ten-day exercise. In those early days, even the Belgrade architects of war were irresolute and confused, dropping contradictory messages from Yugoslav army airplanes onto the streets of Ljubljana. On some of the flyers were written the words: "We invite you to peace and cooperation." And on others: "All resistance will be crushed."

But after the debacle in Slovenia, they quickly became less confused and more resolute: no more blather about peace and cooperation, no more pamphlets raining down from airplanes. Bullets and mortars and cluster bombs had a more immediate and demoralizing effect. After Slovenia, the Yugoslav National Army, which was quickly becoming an all-Serb army, turned its attention first on Croatia, where a sizable Serbian minority lived in a rugged and inhospitable region called Krajina, and then, along with its proxies and local paramilitaries, on the unfortunate Bosnia, the landlocked republic that had almost an equal number of Bosnian Muslims, Serbs, and Croats and that stood to lose the most from the collapse of Yugoslavia.

The siege of Sarajevo began on April 5, 1992, and although October 1993, the month of my wedding in Otočec, was neither the worst nor the most eventful month of the siege that would end up lasting four years, the longest in modern European warfare, it was nevertheless the month when the world sat up and took notice. Serb paramilitary units and weekend snipers kept the city under pretty much constant shelling. The Bosnian Serb paramilitary used the resulting chaos as an excuse to insist on the closing of the ostensibly UN-controlled Sarajevo Airport and to halt all evacuations from the city, including medical evacuations, including, as it happened, the evacuation of a four-month-old baby boy who had been found by a sniper's bullet as he lay sleeping in his pram. Perhaps even more crucially, as far as Western news organizations were concerned, October was the month of the Sarajevo Film Festival, and not only was the Bosnian Serb paramilitary not allowing anyone out, it was also not allowing anyone in. As a result, Vanessa Redgrave and Daniel Day Lewis were cooling their heels in Ancona, Italy, waiting for permission to land at the Sarajevo Airport and making occasional press conferences about the injustice and barbarity of it all.

So Tina calls her friend in the former Yugoslavia to find out what's going on.

"I have no idea," I say, standing in the kitchen of the Proletarska studio. "No one talks about it here. It's as if it's not happening, as if it were on the other side of the world, or on some other planet. It's as if Slovenia had nothing to do with Yugoslavia."

The largest-circulation Slovenian daily does feature the war as its top story nearly every day, but then so too do most other papers in the world. Aleš writes a column for the left-wing biweekly *Razgledi* and lately has been writing mostly about the war in Bosnia, and the world and Slovenia's response to it or lack thereof. Stories from the battlefields appear on the news show each evening, but we don't have a television, and even if we did, I wouldn't be able to understand them. I could read about the war in the *Herald Tribune*, three copies of which are delivered two days after printing to the Union Hotel, where most international travelers stay. But what really boggles the mind, what I am trying to explain to Tina and figure out for myself, is that ordinary Slovenian people don't seem to talk about it much. The people I meet make almost no mention of the war, and when I do they seem strangely subdued, disconnected from the fate of their former country. They *tsk-tsk* over the headlines, shake their heads quietly, but there is no real outcry, no shared outrage, no collective mourning, and strangest of all, no sense of "there but for the grace of God go I."

Of course, segments of society—government agencies and refugee centers—unavoidably have to deal with the consequences of the war. The Slovenian Writers Union and PEN chapter send packages of food, money, and material to any ex-Yugoslav writer of any ethnic persuasion who is in need. But even its solidarity has limits. When a group of ex-Yugoslav writers got together with the idea of creating an ex-Yugoslav writers' union, the Slovenian organization was aghast. They don't want to be part of an ex-Yugoslav writers' union. They want their own writers' union, a Slovenian writers' union. The hell with disenfranchised, passport-less, and writers' union-less Serbian dissidents, the few that there are.

Perhaps Slovenia is suffering from a severe case of survivor's guilt. Exacerbating the complex, Slovenia, having been the first republic to secede, is often blamed for the carnage that followed: the carnage that is going on right now, day and night, month after sickening month. Or perhaps Slovenians are just anxious to get on with their non-Yugoslav story, to get on with being Western, to turn their backs on their wild bearded Balkan uncle and embrace their dull bourgeois Austrian aunt.

In either case, the irony is not lost on me when Tina brings me up to date on the latest outrages of the Serb militias operating around Sarajevo, the latest disgrace of the United Nations Protection Forces, Vanessa Redgrave's most recent statement.

"Sorry," I apologize to Tina for my ignorance. "What information I get I get by osmosis. For what it's worth, I'm going to see a Sarajevan pop band called Bijelo Dugme tonight. Aleš says it was huge in the 1980s."

Tina, my expert on all things Yugoslav, has heard of the band. Its main songwriter was Goran Bregović, a rising star who is now a darling of the Hollywood movie industry.

"But I don't think he lives in Sarajevo anymore," says Tina. "I think he got out."

He did. So too did the other three Bijelo Dugme band members, Aleš informs me on the way to KUD that evening. Goran Bregović lives in Paris, where he is making a brilliant career as a writer of movie soundtracks. The Sarajevo street—the *raja*, as it is called—

has taken mournful note that Bregović failed to forcefully condemn the war in his former country and the siege of his former hometown.

"Is he a Serb?" I ask.

These are the kind of questions that non-Yugoslavs are constantly asking Yugoslavs, and that Yugoslavs dismiss because, though it may seem to, the answer does not quite capture the essence of identity and belonging, does not fully explain why people do what they do, why they decide to stay or to leave, to fight or die trying. The question contains a single finite element—blood, ethnicity—and ignores a host of others: the possibility of mixed loyalties, the possibility of exercising individual will against the will of the group, the possibility of making choices, of quixotically upholding some abstract moral principle in the face of more immediate contingencies. It also ignores, of course, the very madness of war, the dynamism of ongoing events, the justifications it produces, the new stories it writes, and how the stories themselves change identity and belonging.

"I don't know if he's a Serb," answers Aleš, "or if I knew once, I don't remember anymore."

A second band member, Ipe Ivandić, the drummer, left Sarajevo when the war began and went to live in Belgrade, where he would later commit suicide. Željko Bebek, the lead singer, went to Zagreb. Thus Bijelo Dugme, the rock band, itself a sort of nuclear family, suffered the same fate as countless other Yugoslav families of mixed ethnicities: members scattered to different republics now at war with each other, to countries outside of Yugoslavia, mutual recriminations, the loss of an idyllic childhood never to be regained. Only Željko Bebek will perform at KUD tonight.

"How can a lead singer perform all by himself?" I ask. "What's to lead?"

"I don't know," Aleš shrugs, pulling the Clio up onto the sidewalk on the curb across from KUD, two tires on the curb, two tires off.

"Is this a real parking place?"

"I'm not sure."

Ambiguity, it seems, is a condition to which I will have to grow accustomed.

Toward midnight, the hundred-strong clientele of KUD files down a dark hallway and into a cramped and musty theater for the evening's main entertainment. We carry our drinks and cigarettes with us. Holding our drinks in one hand and our cigarettes between our lips, we push down the backs of the creaky wooden chairs in the old provincial theater and sit on the bare unupholstered seats.

Before long, the star attraction walks out onto the small curtainless stage at the front of the hall. The audience grows quiet and expectant. Željko Bebek, a middle-aged pop star, looks decidedly past his prime, a parody of what he might have been in better days. He has the standard heavy-metal hairstyle: a mane of long frizzy curls flipped back over skinny shoulders. His pencil-thin legs are jammed into skintight denim pants, his narrow torso draped by a black leather motorcycle jacket. He comes on stage alone: no band, no guest artist, no family. In one hand he carries a microphone, and in the other a boom box of sorts. He kneels down and plugs his microphone into the boom box and slides a tape into the cassette holder. A stage hand comes on stage with another cord and helps him to connect his contraption to KUD's crackling sound system.

"This is pathetic," I whisper to Aleš.

Aleš doesn't answer. He just looks on sadly. The rest of the audience, ranging in age from about twenty to seventy, also gazes silently toward the stage. There is no noise at all in the theater now, save for the low buzz coming through the speakers from Bebek's boom box. The tape will be the singer's only instrumental accompaniment. The concert is going to fall well below the technical standards of an American high school garage band. I slide down in my wooden seat and look down at my knees, embarrassed for the man's exposure. He has lost everything: his band, his city, his country. Why would he come to perform in this place that doesn't even care about Yugoslavia anymore? That seems to feel so little solidarity for its southern brethren as their villages are burned, their women raped, their families scattered? Did he come for money, some pittance? Or for nostalgia? Because he can't quite let go of his former glory in this former country? Can't quite let go of his idyllic childhood?

Whatever he came for, I can't wait until it's over, until we can get back to the bar, get another drink, and go on not talking about it.

Bebek looks out over his audience, holding up a hand against the stage lights.

"*Zdravo,*" he says. It is the standard Yugoslav greeting, the equivalent of *živijo*.

He kneels down and presses the play button. The solemn sounds of an organ, the first almost churchly chords of a ballad, pour out of the speakers and fill the small room, drowning out the buzz. Bebek lowers his head and whispers a woman's name into the microphone.

"Selma ..."

A near holy reverie descends on the darkened space; a chill, a hush. The crowd holds its collective breath. The song begins very slowly, more like talking than singing, more like a prayer than an anthem. Bebek is addressing a woman, Selma. I look around me at all the faces in the darkness and see that everyone else is addressing her too. Everyone else is mouthing the words along with the singer. Everybody in the theater, from the youngest members of the audience who had hardly been born when Bijelo Dugme was popular to the gray-haired poets who lay claim to a higher sort of culture, from the cute blue-jeans clad *pičkice* to the stumbling drunks who can barely remember their own names— everybody closes their eyes and sings the words of the ballad, articulating each and every syllable, intoning each and every sigh.

And when the climactic refrain finally comes, a fervent plea to the girl named Selma who is leaving her local Sarajevan boy and getting on a train to travel, the place explodes. The audience jumps to its feet and wails along with Bebek. There is no hesitation, no need for them to search for lyrics. The words have been grafted onto the collective soul of all those gathered in that tiny hall.

"*Selma, zdravo, Selma! Putuj Selma! Ne naginji se kroz prozor!*"

"What does it mean?" I whisper to Aleš.

"He's telling her to go ahead and leave, to go ahead and travel. The last words are lifted directly from the standard warning sticker in European train compartments. You know, that warning about not leaning out the window."

Bebek at KUD after the concert

In its agony and its irony and its final acceptance that people leave and there's not much you can do about it, no way you can protect them where they're going, no way to keep them from leaning out the window, no way to protect yourself if you stay, the chorus perfectly reflects the mood of the crumbling Yugoslavia, and the departing Selma stands as the perfect metaphor for Sarajevo's fate. Sarajevo as tragic love story: a girl leaving her beloved boy behind, the boy watching her go, the knowledge that nothing will ever be the same again.

Outside when the concert is over, I corner Aleš.

"But no one ever talks about the war here. They pretend it's not happening. No one says anything."

"What can we say?" he sighs. "What good would it do? She's gone. Selma's gone. She's not coming back." He spreads his hands in front of him and leans his head back against the wall. "Gone," he repeats hollowly.

The next day after school, I don't go home right away. I stop at a little record store I have noticed in the center of town and buy Bijelo Dugme's record. I play it for Tanja when she comes to visit, to see where my digs are and spend the afternoon drinking fruit tea.

She too falls into a post-Yugoslav swoon. She too knows all the words. She writes them down for me.

Day of the Dead

NOVEMBER 1, 1993

Žale Cemetery

When a new country comes into being, its leaders face a series of tasks ranging from the monumental to the symbolic to the banal. A flag must be designed, a currency issued, a color decided on for the cover of its passports: red like the old Yugoslav passports, or blue like the American, or white like UN passports for stateless people. Missions must be established in foreign countries, ambassadors appointed, consulates opened, a niche in the world carved out for the new state.

The leaders of the country must also decide on matters as quotidian as a schedule of annual national holidays, something that, because it is soon taken for granted, represents symbolism at its deepest and most foundational. The leaders must determine which new holidays need to be established, which ones from the former system can be safely gotten rid of, and which ones can simply be dressed up in a new acceptable guise. Holidays that were pagan in pre-Christian times, Catholic in prewar times, and secular in the postwar communist years can now be draped in religious vestments once again.

The first step in this process is uncontroversial. The people living in the newly formed state will get at least one new holiday, some variant of an independence day. When Slovenia was born into the family of nations, the new country, in what was either a spasm of insecurity, or the sophisticated postmodern recognition that one can only exist when captured in the gaze of the other, or simply the desire for more work-free days, established not one but two independence days. The first, celebrated on June 25 and called Day of Nationhood, commemorates the day when Slovenia unilaterally declared its independence, the day that was followed by pamphlets raining down from the sky—"All resistance will be crushed"—and the Ten Day War. The second, celebrated on December 26, is called Independence Day or sometimes Recognition Day and commemorates the day when Slovenia was granted recognition by the United Nations, caught and accepted, however reluctantly, in the multilateral gaze of the outside world.

"OK. We see you. You exist."

Whatever one's ideology and convictions, subtracting holidays is always a more controversial process than adding new ones. Slovenia avoided the controversy by keeping virtually all of its old holidays, even those with a distinctly Marxist flavor. May 1, for example, the international day of labor, celebrated by nearly all Western countries except the United States, was too firmly embedded in the culture to be jettisoned because of the minor matter of switching from a communist to a capitalist economic system. Nor could April 27, the day the partisan resistance or the Liberation Front was founded, and the symbolic armistice of World War II, be done away with, although the right-leaning home guard sympathizers would have liked nothing more than to strip the communist partisans of any heroism in ending the war in Yugoslavia. But they could not.

They could not for the simple and awkward reason that Yugoslavia was the only European country to have liberated itself from Nazi Germany without the aid of either the Americans or the Russians. Although this fact has been a legitimate source of national pride for the last five decades, it considerably complicates the present picture and not least the postcommunist reckoning with history. After 1989, other East European countries—Poland, Czechoslovakia, Hungary, as well as the Baltic states—had the luxury of rejecting communism as an entirely alien system, an external virus with which they had been infected against their will. These countries could claim, accurately or not, that the heroic resistors of World War II had become the heroic dissidents of the Cold War and finally the heroic founders of the late-twentieth-century postcommunist democratic states. The statues of Lenin came crashing down, the statues of local heroes rose up to take their place in the city squares. These countries got to throw out the baby *and* the bath water too. No historical contradictions, no shades of moral gray, all of which makes for easy textbook writing.

But Yugoslavia was not occupied by a foreign force after World War II. Indeed it split, publicly and acrimoniously, with the Soviet Union shortly after the war. Its communist revolution was homegrown, its people liberated, not by Marshall Plan-bearing Americans or raping and looting Russians, but by local Yugoslav heroes. Thus the mathematics of postcommunist historical revisionism doesn't add up. The heroic resisters of World War II *were* the communists. They *were* the founders of the Yugoslav state, and some of their ideological followers participated in the founding of Slovenia as well. If you strip them of their heroism, you may end up with no heroes at all. You may have a nation founded by phantoms or, worse still, by Nazi collaborators. You may have a country filled with government buildings that have lots of large faded squares on the walls—the traces of fallen heroes—and no consensus on who should rise up to take their place. You run the risk of not just revising history, but of erasing it altogether.

So, as a compromise, the World War II armistice is not removed from the calendar of holidays. Instead, its name is changed from the Day of the National Liberation Front (that is, of the communist partisans) to the vaguer Resistance Day as if to say: somebody resisted, though we no longer remember who exactly it was. The day of culture, Prešeren Day, celebrated rather morosely on the day of the poet's death rather than his birth, remains firmly in place. A host of Catholic holidays—Easter Monday, the Feast Day of the Assumption, and Christmas, which, under the godless communists, had been an ordinary work day— is reinstated. Indeed, December, in the new Slovenia, becomes a parade of gift-giving figures and gift-giving days that promises to satisfy everyone: the secular (Grandfather Cold still pays a visit on New Year's Eve), the mildly religious (Father Christmas on December 24), and the deeply religious ever mindful of the underlying church calendar (Saint Miklavž comes on December 6, his saint's day). Above all, it promises to satisfy the emerging commercial class, ever mindful of the potential profits to be reaped in the new system.

The one holiday that is massively celebrated without controversy or discussion or much profiteering, perhaps because it so easily segues from pagan to secular to Christian, or because it is so well-suited to Slovenia's slightly morbid national character, well-suited to its high rates of suicide and vehicular fatalities and alcoholism, is November 1. All Saints' Day. The Day of the Dead.

It is no minor holiday, no child's play, no mere dress-up like Halloween. During the week prior to November 1, when schools and some government institutes get a full week off, the nation's flower shops change their inventory en masse. Gone are roses and baby's breath and other delicate life-affirming floral species. In their place come chrysanthemums and lilies and hardy varieties that have a better chance of surviving on the cold and windswept surfaces of graves. A throng of long-lasting wind-resistant candles housed in multicolored plastic containers crowds the pavement in front of these and other shops. Throughout the week prior to the holiday, flocks of women can be observed, mostly older women with dark scarves tied beneath their chins, descending like vultures onto the autumn streets of Ljubljana. They walk or ride on bicycles. They carry, either in their hands or in the baskets of their bicycles, a small bag filled with a gardening trowel, a hoe, and some new plantings. They are heading not toward the *njive* for the last gardening session of the season but toward Žale, the city's main cemetery designed by none other than Jože Plečnik. Their task is to tend to the graves, to tend to the dead. It is a passionate national pastime.

On the afternoon of November 1, Aleš and I also take a walk to Žale, albeit a leisurely one without a trowel. We will visit two graves: one in the old part of the cemetery and one in the new. The first is that of Aleš's bourgeois and childless great aunt Slavica Rozman, the first of the family to live in Ljubljana, and a grave that Aleš's mother assiduously tends to and pays the rent on, not only out of filial duty but also because of her wish that she and her own children will have access to such a valuable piece of real estate in the afterlife. I know of aunt Slavica Rozman only through the embroidered linen at the Gotska Street apartment, white thread on white linen, elaborate figures of peacocks and flowers and vines, always featuring the entwined initials RS, always impeccably ironed.

The second grave is that of Boštjan Seliškar, a boyhood and very close college friend of Aleš, a young poet who committed suicide when he was just twenty years old. His method was carbon monoxide fumes in a closed garage, though I have been

informed that hanging is the method of choice for Slovenian sui-
cides—not a lily-livered bunch—chiefly because the materials
are easy to come by and its outcome is the most certain.

Approaching Žale from the Moste side, it strikes me that
Ljubljana has not yet decided what it wants to be: a European
capital city or a semiurban favela. For around Plečnik's classical
arches that mark the entrance to the cemetery and might function in another city as the culmination of a grand urban avenue,
a Champs Elysées or a Via Veneto, spreads a hodge-podge of
ramshackle vegetables plots, garden shacks with makeshift
rooftops of corrugated steel, beanpoles poking up here and there,
an overturned wheelbarrow. It is an odd sight: this shanty town
in the shadow of an elegant Old World graveyard.

Passing through the arches and into the cemetery itself, I see
within the marble walls an echo of the inglorious fields outside.
There is such great industry here. Women bend over nearly every
grave plot: hoeing, planting, weeding. There are bags of topsoil
and seed scattered on the walkways, boxes of sturdy perennials
waiting to be set in the ground. At the end of each narrow pathway stands a graceful stone water fountain where the bereaved
women collect water in ewers to sprinkle on the flowers they
plant above the dead.

"Wow." I survey the scene.

"Wow what?" asks Aleš.

"It's so different from American cemeteries. American cemeteries are more like golf courses. Vast and grassy and empty. Lots
of rolling green hills. You have to drive to the graves in a car and
you're given a little map to guide you. Even so, you usually get
lost and there's nobody there to ask where you are, to ask where
you're going."

"I guess that's one way to look at the afterlife," he shrugs.

As we walk slowly along, hand in hand, he tells me about
southern cemeteries where the dead are even more demanding

than they are here, where relatives come to visit carrying freshly bought button-down shirts with the pins still in them, leaving them on the grave as an offering in case the worms start nibbling away at the shirt of the corpse below. They bring bottles of slivovitz and shot glasses. They light a cigarette and place it carefully atop the gravestone, so the dearly departed can enjoy a posthumous puff.

As we walk and talk and look at our surroundings, it occurs to me that a visitor to Ljubljana, who had only a single day and wanted to learn about the country's convoluted history, could do worse than a visit to Žale. For written on all the gravestones, both the ornate ones and those that lack even a name, is the story of the last hundred years. Etched onto all that marble are the strands of a people that have lived in three multiethnic states during the last century, fought in three wars, and labored under four or five distinct government systems: one imperial monarchy (Austro-Hungary), one federal monarchy (the Kingdom of Yugoslavia), two Fascist occupying powers (first Italian and then German), one communist federation (the Socialist Federation of the Republic of Yugoslavia—shortened to SFRJ on the graffiti around town), and now an independent capitalist democracy.

In the oldest section of the cemetery there are German imperial names carved into pompous family tombs. On nearly every gravestone one can find evidence of that particular Austro-Hungarian obsession with titles: rector, postmaster, mayor, chief engineer, customs clerk, head butcher. A little farther along, one spots, amidst all the Roman Catholic prayers and incantations— REST IN PEACE and GONE TO JESUS—words in the Cyrillic script of the Eastern Orthodox Church and, alongside the foreign symbols, the yellowed photograph of a florid Serbian patriarch staring out from an oval setting. Midway through the old part of cemetery, to the right of the main walkway, lies a special enclosure for enemy Italian soldiers who perished on Slovenian soil during

World War I and whose remains were neither sent back home nor properly identified. Their nameless markers bear the simple description: MILITARE ITALIANI. These foes of the extinguished Austro-Hungarian Empire remain forever exiled from their homeland and, lying in a graveyard within a graveyard, from the rest of Žale's tenants as well. Still more enemies of Slovenia, German soldiers who fell during World War II, are buried a stone's throw away from the Italians.

And then, of course, there is the enormous constellation of red communist stars, monuments to the victims of fascism, to the fallen partisans, and rising up beside them now in this brave new post-1989 era, a crop of fresh clean white monuments dedicated to the victims of communism, the fallen home guard, the *belogardisti*. It is a competition that doesn't end even with death.

"I could use a map now," sighs Aleš.

We have been walking up and down the rows of the newer and flatter part of the cemetery for the better part of a half hour. Here the tablets tend to be simpler and lower. There are fewer landmarks jutting up from the field of graves, fewer grand crucifixes, although here and there a jagged thunderbolt or a wild starburst exceeds the bounds of a kitschy tomb. Now in the throes of our search we no longer hold hands or even walk together, but fan away from each other, eyes downcast, carefully reading the name on each and every stone. We cannot find Boštjan's grave.

"I thought it was the second row from the wall," Aleš says.

"Look at this one," I call out to him.

It is the Ložar men: one dead in Slovenia, one in America, another in Argentina. The motherland and the two most common destinations of twentieth-century Slovenian migration: Cleveland and Buenos Aires. And there is another one, a Ljubljana family, mother, father, infant daughter, who all perished on the same day in 1945 a single week before the liberation. And then there are those few, those very few, untended graves, dark and bare and wild. I wonder who lies buried in them, forgetting momentarily the name I am supposed to be looking for. The answer is probably the obvious one. Whoever it is, his family has scattered now, nobody left behind with a trowel or a hoe or a pack of matches.

"I found it," Aleš calls out to me from the third row closest to the wall.

Bojan Seliškar. January 22, 1962–March 31, 1983.

His grave is one of the obsessively tended ones. It is blanketed from edge to edge with mums and candles. He was an only child survived by both parents. We kneel down, push some candles aside, making room for the one we brought. Aleš pulls his lighter from his pocket, lights the candle, then lights a cigarette: for himself, not Boštjan.

On the way out, we stroll past aunt Slavica's grave, which lies at the end of a row in the old part, in the shadow of a towering pine tree. There is a figure bent over the grave.

"Živijo," I call out, happy to see someone I know. It's Mija.

Pavel is standing nearby, handing her the tools when she needs them, sweeping the dirt off the walk. Mija doesn't drive, so she either travels by bus or by bike or with Pavel. She has her driver's license, spent the thirty costly hours with an instructor and passed her test, but the first time she drove to Loški Potok she accidentally plowed the car into a stream with the two children in the back street. No harm done; Aleš and Polona recall the event with pleasure, but it spooked Mija, and she never drove again. Now Mija is planting a clump of low cypress bushes. She wears latex surgical gloves and has a streak of dirt across one cheek. She scowls up at the towering pine tree.

"There's not enough sun here for flowers," she complains.

They've been at it all day, it turns out, having just returned from Loški Potok, where they weeded and planted flowers on the graves down there. I kneel down beside her and help her tamp down the soil around the plants. While I do, I try to project myself forward in time, wondering if I will be able to take Mija's place in this familial endeavor, this seasonal tending of vegetable plots and children and the dead, year in and year out. I doubt it.

It's not just that I'm from a different country and a different culture. It's generational. I don't think even Polona, a local girl with a fresh memory of these traditions, will have her mother's wherewithal and energy. It feels, here in Žale with all these older women and their spades and their soft bent backs, their husbands hovering nearby, like the end of an era.

Later that same evening, Aleš and I step out of the doors of Proletarska 2 and walk toward the Mercator self-service market to get in the Clio. We are going out to Drama: *v life*.

The night is cold and I glance up to see if there are any stars in the sky, if it is clear, if tomorrow is likely to be foggy or not.

"Look at that," I point toward the horizon.

Whatever starlight there may be is being eclipsed by a strange and diffuse yellow glow hanging over the northwest side of town. It looks like some otherworldly radiance. Or like a sickly yellow industrial leak. Or, less ominously, like the lights from a huge outdoor concert, though oddly I can hear no music.

"What is that?"

Aleš gives me one of the looks he often does when I cannot get my bearings in his small town. When I first got here, I actually thought it was much bigger than it was, because of the disorienting curve of the river and all the bridges crossing over it, the confusion of the winding cobblestone streets, the tunnel that runs under castle hill. Driving to Drama the first night, we crossed two bridges and went through the tunnel and, when we finally got there, I felt as if we'd arrived in a completely different neighborhood. But then Aleš pointed out that Drama was actually on Tito Street. We had just approached it from the other side. There is, in the end, only one destination neighborhood in Ljubljana.

"That's where we were today," he says. "That's Žale."

And so it is. The strange yellow glow is nothing more sinister than the light shed by thousands and thousands of candles lit once a year to honor the dead.

Medvode

NOVEMBER 14, 1993

Ljubljana in the snow

Saturday morning.

A strangely muffled hush as we lie long in our narrow bed together. No cars passing along the ordinarily crowded Zaloška Street. No voices rising up to the ninth floor from the green market below the balcony, although Saturday morning is generally its busiest time. By Saturday afternoon the market is a ghost town. I look at the clock; it is not yet noon.

The phone rings. Aleš doesn't stir.

I stand up from the bed, peering quickly though the slats of the Venetian blinds as I pass into the kitchen to the ringing telephone and the *džezva* for my morning coffee. There is no market today, I see, or not much of one. A heavy white blanket of snow covers the square. Only the hardiest of vendors have come and opened their tables, their hands protected by moth-eaten fingerless gloves—fingerless so they can count out the money—and their greens, what few there are, wrapped in woolen blankets.

The year's first snow. My first in Ljubljana.

Tanja is on the telephone.

"Come to Medvode," she says. "We'll make snowmen."

Medvode means "between the waters." It is a little bedroom set-tlement lying at the confluence of the Sava and Sora rivers, twenty minutes outside Ljubljana. It is a straight shot from the city along the old road toward Škofja Loka and Gorenjska. We zoom along in the little gray Clio, the road already neatly plowed. The bare branches of the trees along the roadside show off their glittering sleeves of frost. As we motor past, it appears as if the meadows and pastures on each side of us are spinning, the snow, sparkling and untouched, radiating outward, virgin white fields all the way to the foothills of the Polhograjski Dolomites on the left, and the Kamnik Alps on the right, the high mountain world of Gorjenjska rising up in front of us.

Tanja is ready and waiting when we pull the Clio into the park-ing area of the squat cinderblock apartment building on the high banks of the Sora River. The sound of shovels against asphalt fills the air as the *pridni* apartment dwellers rush to outdo each other in the clearing of paths and stairways and terraces. Above the snow, several meters up along the outer wall of the building, I see a line drawn with chalk and a date next it. Tanja notices me look-ing and informs me that was the highest the Sora ever flooded. It must have been some flood.

Tanja has pulled a wooden sled out of the cellar door that opens below the flood line. It is loaded with supplies: red and black felt, scissors to cut it, a carrot, several hats and swatches of fabric to dress up our creations. She instructs us to cut the felt before we leave—she doesn't want to take the scissors along— so we have to come up with some concept of what we want our creations to look like. It is the first time I've seen Tanja in pants.

She wears one of her trademark homemade hats, fashioned like a medieval squire's cap, pulled down over her thick black curls.

Tanja's mother, Nina, and her older brother, Mladen, lean out the second-floor kitchen window and observe their kinswoman as she commandeers the visitors from Ljubljana, instructing them in the rules and regulations of snowman construction.

"Are you coming with us?" Aleš asks, looking up at them with a wave.

They grin and shake their heads. "No thanks."

"So," Tanja holds out the little sewing scissors to us as if she were throwing down a gauntlet, "will it be a traditional snowman, or will you do something different?"

Aleš's eyes glitter at the challenge.

"Mine," he takes the scissors from Tanja, "will not be traditional. It will be a snowman, or should I say a snowwoman, the likes of which Medvode has never seen."

He kneels down beside the sled and begins to busily cut shapes from the felt. He obviously has a vision.

"I guess I'll make a traditional snowman," I murmur. My hands remain at my sides. I have no idea what shapes of felt or supplies I will need. "I've never made a snowman before," I admit.

It's not that I haven't experienced snow before. I moved from the snowless California coast to New York when I was twenty, but in Manhattan we did our resolute best to remain as oblivious as possible to the passing of the seasons and to nature in all its manifest forms. Central Park was as wild and untrammeled as it got.

Amazed, Tanja looks first at Aleš as if to say, "Where did you find this creature?" and then up at Nina and Mladen in the window.

"She's never made a snowman before," she says in Slovenian.

They laugh and shrug. Who knew?

Then she puts her arm around my shoulders and looks down at Aleš, who has finished cutting his felt patches and is now rifling through the hats and scarves she has laid out. He scorn-fully tosses aside a carrot. She narrows her eyes.

"Never mind," she says. "We'll do it together. A traditional snowman. A big fat *babuška*."

She leans over the supplies, grabs a hat and a scarf, and then as an afterthought picks up the discarded carrot. She shakes it at Aleš.

"This is war."

In the end, after much cold wetness has seeped into my unsuit-able shoes and down the neck of my unsuitable coat, after much back and forth and laughing on the wooden sled (plastic bobs are still a decade away), after the wanton destruction of one of those pristine Medvode meadows radiating out toward the pine-covered foothills, our two creations could not be more different.

Aleš has made a modernist odalisque, a tribute to a particu-lar sort of womanhood. The shapes he so decisively cut from the felt in front of Tanja's apartment block were: one black triangle for the pubic mound, three small red circles for nipples and belly button, two black almonds for lascivious slanting eyes, and one full red voluptuous mouth. He plants a saucy gray homburg hat upon her cold bald head, and she is done. Statuesque, with swelling hips and breasts, and a pedestal in place of legs. Aleš has always been a self-confessed breast enthusiast, not a leg man. Igor of the kiss on Fourteenth Street once noted, long ago in New York City while admiring my legs in a miniskirt as Aleš and I were on the way out the door, that Aleš would probably be sat-isfied with a woman with no legs at all, just two breasts on a pedestal; and now that is pretty much what he has rendered from this coldest of building materials. But she is beautiful, no ques-tion about it, and Medvode has certainly not seen the likes of her before.

Tanja's and my creation, though a tribute to a very different sort of womanhood, is beautiful too. Made of three rotund balls of snow, she is far more corpulent than Aleš's little vixen, and yet paradoxically, Tanja and I, in the service of a less exploitable female image, have exploited the virgin field far more mercilessly than Aleš, the rolling accumulation of our massive orbs ravaging the purity of the meadow and exposing great patches of damp brown grass beneath the whiteness. Our snow woman, unlike Aleš's limbless beauty, has great doughy white arms. She has a carrot for a nose and a floppy red rimmed hat. The only thing she is missing, and this due to an oversight on Tanja's supply cart, is an apron tied round her heavy waist. Otherwise she is the spitting image of one of the women in Ljubljana's market squares.

The snowwomen

Stepping into the foyer of Tanja's apartment, I am shocked to discover no discernible difference in air temperature between inside and out. The building lacks central heating, a not unusual state of affairs in Slovenia in 1993 and certainly not a sign of poverty or hardship, still less a reason for complaint. Only the living room is heated, by a tall wood-burning ceramic stove in the corner that needs to be loaded and stoked from time to time. The door between kitchen and living room remains open, at least while cooking is underway; otherwise all the doors in the two bedroom apartment are kept firmly shut to prevent the passage of cold air into warm rooms, warm air into cold. A basket of fuel and small kindling nestles between the ceramic stove and the couch. Aleš, shoes and parka off, guest slippers on, assumes the pasha position on the couch, his eyes drifting slowly closed, weary after his exertions with his snowwoman. I step into the un-heated bathroom for a pee and can hardly get up again, the cheeks of my bare bottom adhering momentarily to the frigid toi-let seat.

In the kitchen, I join Nina and Mladen and Tanja at the table. Lunch is being prepared. The smell of cheese *burek*, a savory Bosnian pastry, fills the small warm room. Nina Gvozdenovič, Tanja's mother, is a solid woman with broad smiling cheeks who spends her weekends—and often enough her weekday after-noons and evenings as well—tromping across the meadows, through the forests, and up and down the hills and mountains of this little country. She is a member of the Slovenian Moun-taineering Association. She collects dandelion for salad in the spring, wild berries in the summer, wild porcini and chanterelle mushrooms from the tangled forest floor in the fall. Mladen is black-haired and alabaster-skinned like his sister, as handsome as Tanja is beautiful. Their father, a Bosnian Serb who went to medical school in Slovenia and had a medical practice in Med-vode, died of natural causes before the beginning of Yugoslavia's disintegration. Families of mixed Yugoslav ethnicities are quite common in Slovenia and indeed throughout Yugoslavia, al-though in Slovenia the husband is invariably southern and the woman invariably Slovenian, never the other way around. More evidence of the mysterious Yugo effect.

I am on a mission to force Slovenians to talk about them-selves, about the changing conditions of their world, how they feel about the war down south, their recent communist past, their new independence. Tanja is normally an excellent interlocutor on such themes. While many Slovenians blithely behave as if these last few years of their existence were nothing more than business as usual and that they had always been, even as small children, sufficiently sophisticated not to buy into the communist pioneer camps and the cult of Tito, Tanja happily shows me the sentimental poems she and her classmates wrote for the Marshall. She tells me about the bombastic parades that took place when Tito came to town, how all the children got the day off school, and how, with pioneer caps poised jauntily on their little heads, they lined the street where the motorcade was scheduled to come by, and when it did come by, how they hurled flowers by their stems toward the black cabriolet where the old man sat next to his wife, Jovanka, both of them waving like royalty. She told me how inordinately proud she was, how boastful to her friends, the day her floral projectile hit the mark, making it all the way into the great leader's car, falling onto the floorboards where it would be trampled under his and Jovanka's feet. She told me how she and all the other Yugoslav school children wept the day Tito died in 1980.

But I cannot, alas, talk to her about the war in Bosnia because her aunt and uncle are Bosnian Serbs, the bad guys in my lexicon, which perhaps shows why such lexicons should be avoided. Living in the Krajina region of Bosnia in a small village called Titovi Drvar—Titovi Drvar because it was required that one settlement in each Yugoslav republic be named after the great man, and in Bosnia, it happened to be Drvar—they are right in the thick of it.

(And indeed, before it is all over, the couple will be part of the largest single ethnic expulsion of the war: the expulsion of Croatian and Bosnian Serbs from Krajina to Serbia proper during Operation Storm in 1995, a military campaign allegedly planned and sponsored by American advisors and carried out by the Croatian Army in gratuitously brutal fashion. Eventually Tanja's aunt and uncle would come back to their little village of Drvar, no longer Titovi, as part of the UNPROFOR refugee return program. They would find their family house, built and fitted out over a decade of Saturdays, looted of everything including the electric cable from inside the cinderblock walls, and although international agencies would provide some limited assistance—the loan of three chickens and one fat Austrian cow named Angelika with an UNPRO-FOR tag stapled to her ear, a strange and almost mystical creature when compared to the scrawny cows to which Bosnian farmers were accustomed—nothing would ever be quite the same again.)

So I avoid the subject of the war in Bosnia and the siege of Sarajevo and instead ask them about the Ten Day War—what they were doing during those warm days in June 1991.

"Hmm." Tanja's mother, Nina, rubs her chin and thinks. "What were we doing?"

Mladen also draws a blank at first. He remembers, as all Slovenians do, the festivities of the night before, on the twenty-fifth, when President Milan Kučan made a rousing speech about the troubles that were certain to come, but told his fellow Slovenians that tonight of all nights was the time to dream. That night Slovenians took to the streets in large numbers and raucously celebrated their independence. The next day fliers fell from the skies and tanks rolled into town. Aleš had told me how his father Pavel shook him awake early on the morning of the twenty-sixth as he slept on the living room couch in the Gotska Street apartment, much as he is sleeping now, and whispered into his ear, "It's war."

"There was the day they bombed the airport," Tanja remembers suddenly.

The small Ljubljana airport, from which my family had flown after my wedding a little over a month before, was situated quite near Medvode, also in the shadow of the Kamnik Alps.

"Oh, yes," says Nina, her eyes lighting up, "the day they bombed the airport."

"That morning, I think it was the third day of the war," recalls Tanja, "the radio announced that the Yugoslav air force was planning to bomb the airport that day, and inhabitants of nearby settlements should take appropriate measures to protect themselves. We didn't know what measures they meant. So we decided to go into the forest, to have a picnic."

"A picnic," Mladen scoffs. "You two women were terrified. You panicked. You packed up all the nonperishable food in the house, put all the canned goods in a wicker basket."

"Nonsense," said Tanja sharply. "We took liver pâté in a tin, some canned tuna, and brown bread. There wasn't much else to take."

"You rifled through all the drawers," he insisted, "searching for all the foreign currency in the house. Austrian shillings. Germans marks. You thought we'd have to hike over the mountains into Austria. You thought we were escaping."

"That's absurd." Tanja stares at her brother in disbelief. "We didn't have any dinars that day, so we just grabbed whatever money there was in case we might need it."

And it is true that in a place as small as Slovenia inhabitants tend to keep a small collection of the currencies of neighboring countries—in those days marks, shillings, and lire—so it isn't necessary to stop at an exchange office every time you hop across the border for this or that.

"And a blanket," Mladen says, to bolster his case. "You brought a blanket because you thought we might have to sleep in the woods. You thought we wouldn't be able to return to our own beds. That they'd be bombed to smithereens."

"Now you're really being stupid," Tanja fumes. "Who doesn't bring a blanket on a picnic, I'd like to know."

"Children, children," Nina quiets them.

But whatever their motivation, terror or pleasure, going into the forest was without a doubt an excellent and time-tested strategy. Slovenia has more forest per capita than any other country in Europe. At the moment it also has more bears, as Bosnia's ursine population has been migrating northward through the forests to get away from the ungodly human racket down there. But bears or no bears, the forest was precisely the secret weapon with which the partisans managed to sabotage the efforts of the much better armed and equipped Italian and then German occupying armies during World War II. The Italian army had gone so far as to erect a fence around the entire perimeter of Ljubljana, rendering it the largest prison camp in Europe, enclosing its population, imposing a curfew, and shooting on sight any locals who broke it. And yet despite the fenced-up capital, the partisans managed to launch raids and undermine enemy efforts from the shelter of the surrounding forests. They built an extensive network of camps, arms depots, and supply lines, even medical facilities and surgery hospitals, all under the dense cover of the trees. In the winter they holed up in tree houses built high in the conifers. Only when betrayed by local woodsmen or hunters were enemy forces able to smoke them out of their hiding places and shoot them down in the snow.

That's how well the partisans mastered the forests, and Nina mastered the forests at least as well as any partisan. With her knowledge of the paths and byways of Gorenjska, not to mention of the local edible fauna, she could probably survive in the forest for months, although that of course would hardly be necessary in a war that lasted only a few days more than a week. But while it is a matter of historical record how the partisan resistance defeated the Italian fascists and German Nazis in the nineteen-forties, it remains somewhat obscure as to how the tiny Slovenian territorial guard pulled it off again fifty years later, how they managed to defeat the Yugoslav National Army, which was the third-largest standing army in Europe at the time, a formidable fighting force.

The aboveboard interpretation relies on two main factors: on one side, the canny and well-executed strategy of the fledgling Slovenian state and its territorial guard, and on the other, the Yugoslav National Army side, indecisiveness at the highest echelons of power and utter pandemonium at the lowest. The Slovenian territorial guard had had the foresight to keep and even stockpile small arms even after the federal government had ordered the disarmament of the militias of the individual Yugoslav republics—its Croatian counterpart, in contrast, had obediently disarmed, an error it would pay dearly for later. And the Slovenians went the extra mile, secretly procuring antiaircraft and antitank systems on the international arms markets. When push came to shove, the Slovenian state wrong-footed the Yugoslav leadership by announcing independence one day earlier then expected and forcing their opponents to play catch-up. And then when the war actually began, they pursued a disciplined strategy of taking control of border crossings, army barracks, and other strategic points. On the second day of action they shot down two Yugoslav helicopters, killing all the occupants, one ironically being a Slovenian conscript, one of their own. Ours: *naš*.

On the Yugoslav side, the top brass wavered in those early days, fearing a negative international reaction if they responded with brute force, and at the same time underestimating the determination of the Slovenians, never dreaming, for example, that they would actually dare to shoot down a Yugoslav aircraft. Meanwhile, on the ground virtually all Slovenian, Croatian, and

Bosnian soldiers and officers in the army promptly went AWOL once the action began, leaving their Serb and Montenegrin fellow soldiers to try to sort things out in what had overnight turned into a foreign land. Within the civilian population of Slovenia, there was no substantial fifth column of local Serbs on which the Yugoslav army could rely. These are the basic ingredients of the aboveboard interpretation.

The below-board interpretation invariably involves some kind of secret deal in which Slovenia said to the federal government of Yugoslavia, "Leave us alone, you don't care about us anyway, and we'll let you retreat to Croatia, which you do care about, and you can wreak whatever havoc there you like." Without such a cynical deal, the skeptics say, the Yugoslav army would have rolled right over the lightly armed Slovenian territorial guard like a bug.

As for the Gvozdenovič family, their strategy during the third day of that short war was one of retreat and relaxation. The family walked several kilometers out of Medvode and into the forest before settling on a pleasant low-lying mountain meadow. Once they had consumed the tin of pâté, the canned tuna, and the loaf of brown bread, Tanja lay down on the blanket, pulled a book from her basket, flipped through the pages awhile, and then dozed as the sun climbed high in the sky. Nina took the empty basket and waded into the nearby vegetation, where to her delight she discovered an abundance of unpicked blueberries and spent the afternoon hours filling the basket to overflowing. Mladen sat on a tree stump in the middle of the meadow and stared at a sky that remained clear and blue throughout the day, empty save for the occasional passing cloud, silent save for the buzzing of summer insects and the chirping of birds overhead.

The calm of their day, however, should in no way suggest that the Ten Day War was just a cute little make-believe war for the independence of a cute little make-believe country. For beyond the

horizon of the meadow, beyond the tops of the high leafy decid-
uous trees, the sky was considerably less placid. The Yugoslav air
force did attack the airport as promised. They damaged four passenger planes in the Adria fleet and obliterated several cars
parked at the abandoned airport lot. In one of those cars, two
Austrian journalists burned to death. The planes then swung
around to the north, to Strihovec, near the Austrian border, and
dropped cluster bombs on a column of foreign trucks waiting for
the border to open so that they could leave the country. Another
column of trucks in Medvedjek in the center of the country was
also hit. Some ten truck drivers, mostly foreign, perished that day.

At dusk, the meadow still calm and silent, Nina and Mladen
and Tanja Gvozdenovič decided to walk home to Medvode. Nina
picked up her basket of blueberries, Tanja folded up the blanket,
Mladen gathered up the refuse from their picnic. Walking along
the pathway home, Nina let out a sigh of pure satisfaction. It was
just the sort of day that she enjoyed above all others, and now
that her children were grown they rarely took the time to enjoy
such outings with her.

"What a wonderful day," she said to them. "We must do it
again some time."

The Bureau for Foreigners

Slovenia for Slovenians

At the end of November, Aleš and I decide to take one more stab at approaching the new state as ordinary applicants.

I still do not have a long-term residence permit or a work permit, and my second tourist visa, the one stamped on my passport when I entered the country a second time, will soon expire. Everything we've heard suggests that marriage to a Slovenian citizen does not confer any special benefits, that essentially I have the same status as any other foreign refugee. I will first need to apply for a temporary residence permit and then wait one or maybe even two years before I can apply for some more permanent status. But this is just what we've heard through the grapevine.

"Let's go the proper office and find out," I suggest. My egalitarian American spirit, the one that believes in the straightforward and honest approach, still burns strongly within me, still determines my strategy for dealing with the outside world, with the powers that be. I am, after all, in Slovenia for legitimate reasons.

I have nothing to hide. I am not engaged in any criminal activity. I married for love, not for the citizenship privileges that marriage could but apparently doesn't offer. My motives are pure. Surely that should count for something.

Aleš looks skeptical.

"All right," he says, "we'll give it a try."

Waiting in a socialist country, or in a recently socialist country, for that matter, carries wholly different implications than it does in a capitalist country. If you take away the maxim "Time is money," which of course was anathema in planned economies, then the activity of human waiting becomes utterly transformed. With no value attached to time, no notion of something better to do, waiting becomes amorphous, meaningless, and measureless, something akin to Buddhist meditation.

So, for example, when I call my new hairdresser—her name is Meta, and she is currently the most fashionable hairdresser in Ljubljana—and ask for an appointment, she says, "Sure, come on in."

So I come on in. I take her at her word. And though I have no appointment per se, no specific time for my haircut, three o'clock or three-thirty, I imagine she has time for me. Why else would she tell me to come on in? When I get to the salon, the receptionist nods—she's expecting me—and instructs me to sit down and wait. Meta knows I'm there; she also nods and smiles at me. So I sit. And I wait. And I wait some more. I can see Meta cutting a woman's hair. I can see another woman with a towel around her head sitting in the chair next to Meta's current customer, clearly next in line. I can see many other women sitting and waiting like me, flipping through fashion magazines or just staring into space and doing nothing at all. I see other hairdressers working as well.

After a while, I do what I have seen none of the other women do so far. I get up and approach Meta.

"How much longer will it be?" I whisper.

She squeezes me warmly, smiles, tousles my hair. I desperately need a haircut.

"Don't worry, *draga*, I'll get to you soon."

Chastised, I return to my chair. She's so nice, calling me darling. She said soon, whatever that means. Besides, what else can I do? Storm out? Cut my hair by myself? Demand a specific time in a culture that hardly has a concept of what an appointment is? Waiting, and worse not knowing for how long, is unspeakable torture for me, but there's no way around it. I cultivate the habit of bringing reading material, and lots of it, wherever I go.

When Aleš and I enter the Bureau for Foreigners, we are also confronted with a room filled with waiting people. There are some crucial differences here, however. Nobody sits. There are no chairs. Nobody flips through fashion magazines. Indeed, it might be unkind to say so, but nobody looks as if they take advantage of the most fashionable hairdresser in Ljubljana.

Here in the Bureau of Foreigners, the lines splay loosely out of control. The place is too crammed, the service too slow, the air too rank with hopelessness for anything as frivolous as a fashion magazine. Most of the applicants in this office hold not magazines but booklets with blood-red covers, the telltale Yugoslav passports. They are refugees and *gastarbeiter* and all manner of long-term residents from the former Yugoslav republics who failed to take advantage of that briefly open window during which time they could have obtained Slovenian citizenship and avoided this place altogether.

(Some years later there will be an international scandal about Slovenia's version of Argentina's vanished ones, the disappeared, as they were called. In Argentina the totalitarian government dumped its victims from airplanes into the sea, never to be seen again. In the new democratic Slovenia, the disappeared suffered a more insidious bureaucratic fate. They were simply wiped from the state rolls, all the years of working toward a pension eliminated, their existence on paper obliterated. They became known as the *izbrisani*, the erased.)

At just before ten in the morning, Aleš and I enter the line marked RESIDENCE PERMITS, EXTENSIONS AND ISSUANCE. We wait. I read. Aleš disappears from time to time to stand outside and stare at the river and smoke a cigarette, or even to run an errand. This was my idea, after all. The man in front of me, a small dark-haired fellow with rounded shoulders and a sallow complexion, reads nothing, speaks to no one, hardly looks around at all. He just steps forward from time to time when the space in front of him opens.

And so we wait.

It is just after noon when the little man finally steps behind the ad hoc barrier to speak to the female official there. Aleš is back beside me, and he eavesdrops on their conversation. Even I, by now, have graduated to the level where I can tell that the man is speaking Serbo-Croatian and the official is speaking Slovenian. Or perhaps I infer it from context, from the red passport he carries in his hand. She is speaking sharply, saying something to him with an overtly condescending tone. Aleš suddenly looks at me with wide eyes, as if he's been punched.

"Oh, no," he cries, an expression of despair on his face.

"What?"

He rushes to the back of the line and reads from a piece of paper that has been folded in half and taped to the wall below the larger sign marked RESIDENCE PERMITS, EXTENSIONS AND ISSUANCE. He strides quickly back to me.

"We're waiting in the wrong line," he says.

I sag. It's been over two hours, nearly a hundred pages read. I look at the other lines in the place. They all contain at least twenty to twenty-five people—another two hours at least. Time may not be money, but I am finding other ways to measure it.

"How can that be?"

"That little paper taped to the wall," he says. "They're not issuing residence permits from this line today. We're supposed to be standing over there, in that line."

He points to one of the long lines extending back from a glass-windowed front counter. The small round-shouldered man emerges from behind the barrier and goes over to take his place at the end of the line that Aleš has just indicated.

Aleš and I watch his figure as it crosses the room, then we look at each other, and without speaking, step behind the ad hoc barrier and face the female official who just berated the little man. I place my American passport on the desk in front of her.

"I think I've been waiting in the wrong line," I say in English.

She picks up the passport and leafs through it, pausing at the two tourist visas, one already expired, one about to expire. I wonder if she has the power to deport me.

"I need a residence visa," I say. "I'm married to a Slovenian."

I deposit my marriage certificate on the desk next to the passport and nod back toward Aleš, who stands one step behind me. She picks up the marriage certificate and studies it for a moment. I have certainly waited long enough to come in, until the very last minute, in fact. I have been married nearly two months already, and my tourist visa expires tomorrow.

She looks up at me. She has a neat little hairdo and a pinched face above her navy blue jacket. She doesn't look like a very happy person. I don't imagine she likes her job. I wouldn't like it either. In her position I might also be callous. I might also snap at people, look down on them, almost forget they're human; there are so many of them waiting out there in those endless lines. I might also chide them for not reading the temporarily posted sign, either because they didn't notice it or because they don't know the language. But for some reason she doesn't treat me that way. Instead, the woman stands up and steps out from behind her desk. She hands my marriage license back to me and picks up my blue passport and holds it high above her neatly coiffed head.

"I'm terribly sorry for the misunderstanding," she says in excellent English. "Please follow me."

So we follow her. We follow her as she walks past the line we have just been standing in, and then past the line we should have been standing in, and past the little dark man with the rounded shoulders who is at the end of it. He watches us dolefully as we pass by. We follow her to the head of that line and right up to the glassed-in counter, and all the while that we are following her, she holds my blue American passport above her head, parting the sea of red Yugoslav passports. She has a quick whispered consultation with her colleague behind the glass, who then interrupts his current transaction in order to issue me my first residence permit. It takes less than five minutes.

She hands my passport back to me. Aleš pulls out his wallet to pay the fee.

I mutter my muffled thanks—my cheeks are burning—and then walk as quickly as I can toward the door. I can see the river twinkling off in the distance, light blue and silver as it catches the winter sun. I fix my eyes on the glittering water, averting them from all the eyes in the office as they watch me leave, and especially from the eyes of the man who has been standing in front of me throughout the long morning.

Then we are outside. We are done. Free.

"That was awful." I stand in the cold air, gasping, practically crying. Aleš lights a cigarette and looks out at the river.

175

"Well," he shrugs, "it's over. For a while anyway."

The residence permit has a six month expiry date.

I have the feeling that I have betrayed all my vaunted American principles and that, worse, I would do it again in a heartbeat just to avoid waiting in that dreadful place for one more minute.

"Awful," I repeat the word.

At that moment an elderly gentleman approaches us. He knows Aleš. I infer that he is an acquaintance of the family or someone from the university. He speaks English well, and he quickly picks up on the emotions of the moment.

"It's nothing," Aleš says, dismissing his concern, nodding his head toward the office building behind us. "We were waiting in line all morning. That's all. For a residence permit for my American wife. It was a long wait." His voice tapers off.

The gentleman looks at me in surprise.

"You had to wait with them?"

"What do you mean, *them*?" The sound of my own voice surprises me. It is harsh, even rude.

"The others," he says.

"I'm a foreigner too," I remind him. "What do you think, that they can have two lines, one for good foreigners and one for bad?"

He leans in toward me kindly. He is patient, pedantic, willing to explain the facts of life to me. Yes, he can understand how I feel, brought up in a different world as I was. He can understand my naiveté, my idealism. Americans are charming that way. But there are some things I don't understand, and I will have to if I am to live here.

"They're a different race," he says to me, "like a breed of savage dogs." He thrusts his thumb in the direction of some imagined south.

"How else do you think such things can go on down there? The things we hear about every day?"

THE BUREAU FOR FOREIGNERS

I know what he's talking about. He is talking about neighbors killing neighbors, men raping women and young girls, raping them systematically, repeatedly, so that the land where such a thing happened can never be considered home again, deliberately impregnating them so that their own blood, their own bodies, their own children become the enemy, so that life itself, even the ability to create it, is forever poisoned. He is talking about the weekend snipers in the hills above Sarajevo who kill human beings for sport, for the fun of it. He is talking about the massacres that target not one but hundreds and even thousands in these increasingly brutal Yugoslav wars.

I don't know the answer to his question, how it could be happening. And I have often wondered about it myself. But I do know that it is not because different blood runs in their veins, that it is not because they are a race of savage dogs. Or else there have been many races of savage dogs in human history.

And I also know that he is a fool to think he is somehow above it all. Were he to walk across the border to Austria, he would be treated exactly the same way as *they* are treated in the Slovenian Bureau of Foreigners. He would have to wait in the line for the bad foreigners, in the line for the dirty and lazy Slavs, for the Balkan killers, the savage dogs.

Every nation has its southerner.

Fužine

JANUARY 14, 1994

At *home*

It is nearly midnight. I am lying on the couch-bed in the Prole-tarska apartment reading a book. Aleš is working at his desk in front of the window, banging away with his two index fingers on the computer keyboard.

I am reading Ivo Andrić's *Bosnian Chronicle*. Aleš has put me on a strict diet of literature from Yugoslavia and the other former communist countries. It is a rich harvest of irony and under-statement and despair. Occasionally I pick up a contemporary American novel just to remember my roots, my native optimism, to eat some empty calories, as it were.

Ivo Andrić was Yugoslavia's first Nobel Prize winner and pre-sumably its last; if the war keeps on going the way it is now, there will be no such thing as Yugoslavia. He was born in Bosnia, served as Yugoslavia's prewar ambassador to Germany in the era when it was common for *kulturati* to serve as *diplomati*, and during the war was put under house arrest by the Germans in occupied Belgrade. It was during this time of enforced isolation that he wrote his famous *Bosnian Trilogy*, which some now view as anti-Oriental, these days meaning anti-Bosnian and anti-Muslim. In any case, Andrić never returned to Bosnia.

"Was he an ethnic Serb?" I ask Aleš, thinking in terms of the contemporary conflict, although Andrić didn't live to see it.

Aleš turns from his desk in front of the window and sends me a look that says, "Not that again. Not that ethnic-this, ethnic-that stuff."

"Let's just say Yugoslav," he answers, and returns to his work.

I am reading a passage about another diplomat, a French one, posted in the Ottoman Bosnian town of Travnik during the brief period of Napoleonic rule in this part of Europe. The diminutive French emperor had conquered Slovenia and other parts of the southern Austrian empire, renamed them the Illyrian provinces (using the old Roman name), and sent his representatives fanning out into Ottoman territory. Interestingly enough, Slovenia recalls the short-lived Illyrian period—it didn't last much more than a decade before the Habsburgs reconquered the southern provinces—as a time of liberation and national awakening. For the first time in their history, Slovenians were allowed to have Slovenian language schools, and the culture blossomed. But the tale I am reading now is a darker one. The French diplomat, Napoleon's representative, along with his entourage, is taking a tortuous route through the narrows streets of the almost medieval settlement of Travnik. His destination is the residence of the Ottoman vizier, where he has his first official reception, and he proceeds through the town under a hail of yellow spittle and muttered curses and venomous insults shouted by the xenophobic locals. It is a vividly written scene, and just as I reach its climax, the peak of the foreign consul's humiliation, a powerful explosion rips through the night outside our window, providing a sort of external exclamation point to the chilling literary depiction.

I sit up on the edge of the bed, putting the book face down against the blanket.

"What was that?"

The moment recalls the September luncheon before our wedding in the courtyard of the Castle Otočec, when the waiter came to our table and apologized for the fighting in Karlovac. But there is one essential difference. At Otočec the explosion had been muffled and distant, traveling to the soles of our feet along subterranean pathways, whereas the explosion tonight detonated right outside our window. Not underground but right there in the air. In our air.

The large seamless pane of glass separating us from the outside world shudders faintly from the impact. The cords on the blinds sway back and forth like pendulums. The air outside in the abandoned street is invisibly aquiver.

Aleš looks up from the screen and out into the darkness toward the red-and-white *toplarna*, the shrouded cubes and stocky towers of the Moste industrial sector. The night is foggy, but it is still possible to see a good distance. For several weeks now the Ljubljana fog and high cloud cover hasn't lifted, and we have been locked in the dim gray bowl of the city, relatively inactive, pleasantly hypnotized by the lack of sunlight, reading, sleeping, waiting for something to happen.

"I don't know," he says. His eyes return to the screen, index fingers to the keyboard.

I lie back down on the narrow bed and pick up my book, eyes seeking out the place on the page where they left off, the end of the French diplomat's short and arduous journey.

A second massive blast scours the night.

This time Aleš gets up on his feet. I stand up from the bed. He takes the single stride to the balcony door, opens it, and steps out onto the narrow platform. I follow him. It is cold outside, a degree or two above freezing, and I am wearing only pajamas and guest slippers. A light powdering of snow still lies here and there in shallow drifts on the empty streets and in the empty market square between the apartment buildings. The streetlamps radiate a dull yellow light that is quickly consumed by the surrounding fog. A single figure, a slender male, runs down Zaloška Street in the direction of Fužine. Fužine, in contrast to Moste, is Ljubljana's true southern ghetto, a massive multiblock-long complex of apartment towers lying just inside the ring road. Serb, Albanian, Bosnian, and Croat laborers and their families occupy the miniscule and identical apartments like worker bees in the compartments of a vast honeycomb. Only the occasional Slovenian, unable to find any other reasonably priced option, moves to Fužine.

As we stand on the ninth-floor balcony of our own little hive and watch the lone figure recede down the street and disappear from view, another series of percussive blasts dances through the night around us. These are different from the previous two explosions, which had been heavy resonant booms. These are lighter, higher, almost like firecrackers skittering across the pavement, or gunfire. They go on for some time, the sharp echoes rebounding against the cinderblock buildings and finding their way up to our perch. But there is nothing to be seen out there. No indication of where the sounds are coming from. If the explosions have left any smoke, it has taken camouflage in the fog. Only a faint sulfurous odor fills our nostrils.

"I don't believe this," says Aleš.

We silently scan the streets. The silhouettes of two more figures rush in the direction of Fužine, hands in pockets, shoulders hunched against the cold.

"Could it be?" I ask, not completing the thought, letting the unfinished question hang between us.

The waiter at Otočec had apologized for the disruption from Karlovac. He had said that it was all very unpredictable. But the one thing I have learned since that day, since living in proximity to a war zone, not close proximity, certainly, but closer than I ever have before, is precisely the opposite. It is, in fact, all very predictable. You can expect to hear artillery fire along certain parts of the Croatian border. On the other hand, you can expect to travel far south along the Croatian coast without hearing anything more destructive than the sea lapping against a wooden pier or the famed *burja* wind blowing through the tops of the cypress trees. Even people who live in more dangerous locations can predict what fields and pastures should be avoided because land mines have been planted there, what settlements are populated by slivovitz-addled paramilitary units, what streets have roadblocks, at what times of day certain routes should be avoided. Sarajevans have constructed a whole new map of their besieged city in their minds, a map made up of predictions and calculations gleaned from experience and hearsay. Where it is safe to get water. When it is safe to wait in line at a certain bakery. When is the most prudent time to dash across Sniper Alley, when you have a better than fifty-fifty chance of making it unharmed to the other side. What changes in a war zone is not the ability to make predictions, or even the general accuracy of those predictions, but the gravity of what will happen if the predictions don't hold.

"It couldn't be," Aleš murmurs. But the way he says the three words sounds more like an open question than a statement. He peers out onto the familiar streets of his neighborhood, into his darkened and seemingly abandoned city.

"There's no reason for it. It makes no sense."

It defies the predictions.

Because there is no expectation in Slovenia—none at all, not even a sliver of one—that the war will migrate north again, from

Croatia and Bosnia to Ljubljana, not even to Fužine where many of the residents hold passionate opinions about the war in the south, about its various participants, about the brutal nature of the crimes going on down there, the atrocities on all sides as the diplomats diplomatically refer to the mostly one-sided conflict. Many of them came here, and most of them stay, precisely to avoid war, not to foment a new one.

"If it were . . . ," I ask Aleš, again not completing the crucial clause: "Would you stay?" I already know that I wouldn't. I knew it the moment I heard that first explosion. I suppose I even knew it back in Otočec. But tonight, the instant the sound and vibration of the blast penetrated my mind, my reading, the procession in Travnik, a wave of adrenaline pounded through my system, my heart leapt into high gear, and I made a quick mental check of the location of my American passport—in the drawer where Aleš keeps all of our *dokumenti*. I even had a sudden and absurd vision of helicopter evacuations from the roof of the American embassy (absurd, because in those days the American embassy was housed not in a stand-alone villa with a heliport but in a small suite of rooms on the fourth floor of a downtown office building). I imagined desperate people waiting in line outside the embassy, trying to pull some strings, trying to contact anyone they knew who might be able to get them out.

I love Aleš. That's not the problem. I love him even more since we've been married than I did before. And I like his country well enough. I like our life here. But I don't like it well enough to live a life of curfews and closed airports, a life of cautious predictions and catastrophic possibilities.

"Would I stay?" Aleš echoes my question. He pulls his gaze from the streets below and makes a reconnaissance of my face. He already knows what my answer would be. "Would I stay?" He says it again, with a slightly different inflection, meaning "if *you* didn't."

I can easily imagine the calculations going on behind his eyes. Whether he loves me too much to stay. Whether he loves his homeland too much to go. Whether he could bear the specter of shame that would fall on him were he to run to the American embassy with his American wife. Even after the nearly bloodless Ten Day War, a reckoning was made of who stayed—fighting with the territorial guard, manning the information center at the *Nova Revija* editorial offices, as Aleš did, writing press releases in English, even accompanying a CNN crew out to the sites of firefights, or simply continuing one's ordinary life, defiantly sipping a coffee in one of the cafés along the Ljubljanica River even as the pamphlets rained down, even as the tanks approached—and, on the other side of the ledger, who packed their bags and fled to Italy or Austria only to return two weeks later with their tails between their legs, unable to erase their miscalculation, the evidence of their cowardice, their lack of commitment.

"Oh, Aleš." I throw my arms around his neck and bury my face in the hollow of his shoulder. Suddenly, in this moment, making the reckoning of our love, of who we really are, to whom we really belong in the moment of truth, I remember the gamble I made coming here, the twin fears I faced: the war and his women. I always sensed that all the worries about war and postcommunist deprivation and only three bars in Ljubljana were exaggerated. What I secretly feared more than anything else was that he would cheat on me within months of my arrival, that I would soon be on my way back home, on a plane to New York, a divorcée at the age of thirty-two, having tossed the dice and lost. But miraculously, it hadn't worked out that way.

"I've loved it here," I whisper into his neck. "Loved this shitty little apartment. Loved my stupid language classes. Loved that ridiculous *toplarna*."

He pushes me away and frowns at me.

"Why are you talking in the past tense?"

I'm blubbering now, shivering from the cold, weeping and sniffling like an idiot.

"And you've been so good to me. Why have you been so good to me?"

"What are you talking about?"

"So loyal?"

Now he is regarding me as if I've gone completely round the bend. And yet even if he pretends not to know what I'm talking about, I know, even in my current state, why he's been so good to me, unpredictably good, a perfect husband, really. He loves me, though perhaps not enough to leave his homeland, not yet anyway. But what is equally important is that he likes to be the best at what he does: the best judo champion, the best poet, the best womanizer, and now the best husband.

I lucked out. And now this damn war is threatening to wipe out my small bit of luck just as it has wiped out thousands of lives in far more spectacular fashion. It's a selfish thought, I know, but romantic love is, if nothing else, incredibly selfish, incredibly self-regarding.

He puts his hands on the side of my arms as if to shake me, the way strong men shake hysterical women in the movies, sometime even slap them across the face to shock them just enough so they can pull themselves together. But it's hopeless. Because at that moment, another huge blast, louder and close than the previous ones, explodes right next to our ears. Several other inhabitants of Proletarska 2 come out onto their balconies. I cringe, let out a little shriek, and squat down on my haunches. Aleš looks down at me and then around toward Fužine.

"What the fuck?" He sounds mystified and amazed and outraged all at once.

"Should we do something?" I ask him. "Should we go somewhere?" I'm thinking of a bomb shelter, a basement. I don't even know if this apartment building has a basement. I already know we shouldn't bother calling the odd-numbered elevator. We should just take the stairs, two at a time if necessary.

"I'm going to make a phone call," he says.

He escorts me inside and sets me down on the bed. The Andrić book is still laying there where I left it, pages down. I hear him dial. I hear his voice speaking in low tones in the kitchen. I hear him hang up. He comes from the kitchen back into the main room.

"What is it?" I ask.

"I called the police."

"What did they say?"

He's smiling. He's almost laughing.

"What is it?" I snap at him, irritated by his sudden and, as I see it, irrational gaiety. What could possibly be funny?

He shrugs his shoulders, shakes his head, looking at me as if I may be in need of a cure at the sanitarium which happens to be located in the woods beyond Fužine.

"What's happening? Why are you looking at me like that?"

"Nothing's happening," he answers. "It's the Orthodox New Year."

"What do you mean, the Orthodox New Year?"

"It's the Serbian Orthodox New Year. They're on a different calendar, the Gregorian calendar. They celebrate two weeks after us."

I look down at the Andrić book next to me on the bed. I look back at Aleš.

"Oh, god." I put my hands up to my cheeks. I feel so stupid.

He looks down at me, his face expressing a mixture of fondness and exasperation, the kind of look with which a parent might regard a high-strung, fearful, yet still very sweet child.

"You got me going too." He also looks slightly shamed.

"Well," I say, trying to justify myself, "it was awfully loud, wasn't it? Everybody else came out onto their balconies too."

As if to back me up, a battery of blasts ricochets down the street outside. They sound quite obviously like firecrackers now. Aleš takes the single step toward the bed and sits down next to me. He turns and puts both hands on my thighs.

"Yeah, really awfully terribly loud." His voice is mocking, but his lips pressed up close against mine feel forgiving enough. He pushes me back onto the bed, reaches out a hand, and flicks the Andrić book to the floor.

"Hey, you lost my place," I protest. "It's a good book. A really good book. Brilliant, in fact."

"Yeah, I know," he says, and kisses me harder now, and pushes me over so there is more room for him on the narrow bed, his work at the computer apparently forgotten. "It is brilliant, a masterpiece. Those Yugos, they get you every time. One way or the other."

Pust

Pust parade in Ribnica

Pust—known in other European traditions as Carnavale, Fast-nacht, Mardi Gras—is another holiday that has been enthusias-tically celebrated throughout Slovenia's many federal and imperial arrangements and under all its various political systems.

Perhaps this is because, like the Day of the Dead, Pust can wear many faces, many masks. Falling in February or early March, it is above all a Catholic holiday, celebrated by both the Roman and Eastern Orthodox churches, the masked festival that marks the last feast day before the Lenten fast. But it also has pre-Christian and pagan roots, extending as far back as the Roman festival of Saturnalia. In communist Slovenia, it was celebrated in rural towns and villages as a pagan rite of spring and fertility, and in the cities as a secular sort of Halloween, with children dressing up in costumes and going door to door for sweets.

Aleš, ever mindful of my ongoing Slovenian education, sug-gests an outing to the Sunday Pust parade in Ribnica, a trading town specializing in wicker goods, the regional capital of our old stomping grounds of Dolenjska. Ptuj, in the center of the country and home of the renowned *kurent* masks, Slovenia's unique contribution to European carnival celebrations, might be a more obvious choice for a Pust destination, but it would be crowded, Aleš tells me, and this way we can stop for a walk and lunch in Travna Gora, the hills above Loški Potok.

"There will be *kurenti* aplenty in Ribnica," he reassures me.

"What are these *kurenti*, anyway?" I ask.

"They're Slovenian carnival figures," Aleš explains. "They wear huge costumes made of straw and sheepskin, with heavy chains wrapped round their waists, and cowbells hanging from the chains. The costumes alone weigh hundreds of pounds. *Kurenti* are supposed to be magical creatures from the other world that come to chase winter away and announce the arrival of spring, fertility, new life, but what they like most of all are girls. They like to grab them between their hard strong hands," Aleš warns me, "and when they do it is the custom for the girl to put a handkerchief in the *kurent's* big belt, or else who knows what he will do. Do you have a handkerchief?"

"None," I say, "just paper tissues. Will that do?"

In Travna Gora all the snow has already melted. The hills are a drab brown color, the trees leafless, but the sun, a slightly different quality in the past few days, sheds a mild and hopeful light over the barren countryside, coaxing clouds of tiny little wildflowers, pale pink hellebore, yellow cowslip, white snowdrops, up through the cover of dead leaves.

The mountain hut at Travna Gora is chock-a-block when we arrive. A group from Loški Potok has hiked up from the valley, though we see no family members among them. Aleš recognizes a few old playmates among the boisterous crowd, and the mayor is holding court. A bottle of schnapps circulates. Aleš orders two bowls of goulash and bread to absorb the alcohol.

After we're done eating, I walk into the dark tavern to find the restroom. On my way out, I am waylaid in the foyer by two figures, one very tall and one very short and both very drunk. Neither speaks to me, which is probably just as well—what with the liquor and the local dialect I wouldn't understand them anyway. The two peer silently at me through the dim interior light, as if making some sort of diagnosis, gauging what it is that ails me, what it is I need. The wood-paneled foyer is nearly black in comparison to the bright spring sunlight outside, but I can make out that the tall one holds two tiny silvery tins in his long spindly fingers. One is filled with black grease paint, the other with red.

Wordlessly, he bends down to me and begins to artfully apply the paint to my forehead, to my cheeks and chin, to the exposed area beneath my collar bones. I had stripped off my sweater at the table as I ate the steaming goulash, and now this tall silent man is making primitive markings on the bare skin revealed by the scoop of my long-sleeved T-shirt. He is very gentle and seems certain of the marks he wants to make. I stand before him, utterly still and unblinking, hypnotized by his swaying frame, by the sour smell of plum brandy on his breath, by the intent expression on his pointy red-veined face. It is his little round friend who finally breaks the spell, holding up a hand to halt the application of paint. He takes the grease tins from his colleague and hastens me back outside to rejoin my husband. Not a word has been spoken.

When I emerge, Aleš glances at my transformed visage, raises his eyebrows briefly, but like the two men inside the tavern says nothing, and soon I forget about the episode and its effects on my appearance.

Not long after lunch we are in Ribnica, a half hour away by car. Aleš parks on the outskirts of the town and we walk in past the hawkers of wicker baskets and pale wooden rakes and homemade brooms made of young birch branches. We make our way along the narrow lanes, past the baroque church, its frescoed steeple, through the crowds of people, and on to the main drag where the parade had already begun. I do not know what I expected to see: the sophisticated long-nosed devilry of painted Venetian carnival masks, the puffy inflated innocence of the Macy's Day Parade, but I am stunned by what I do see, by what I sense, by the madness unfurling in the center of this quiet little provincial town. What is going on here is far more pagan than Catholic, far more demonic and downright sensual than decent Christian society normally allows, more Dionysian Saturnalia than some genteel nod to the onset of spring.

Kurent

The ground rumbles beneath our feet.

Roaring down the pavement towards us come the wild fur-covered faces of the Ptuj *kurenti*, spinning in great circles, whipping colorful ribbons down at our feet—*snap! snap!*—jumping unbelievably high in their massive straw costumes, folding their legs beneath them, and then crashing down like a ton of male flesh and straw and clamoring cow bells onto the black pavement. Then come the *orači*: "the plowers," Aleš whispers to me. They carry curved wooden plows with which they make symbolic furrows and grooves on the asphalt as they pound past. Then the painted wooden fright masks of the Idrija *laufarji*, jeering at us with their grotesque protruding teeth, their flat painted eyes, their yarn hair swinging wildly. More and more wild pagan creatures come flailing down the street in front of us: *kopjaši*—lancers—wearing bright-colored kerchiefs, stabbing the air with sharpened spears to frighten evil sprits from the fields, *pokači*—clappers—cracking their whips, and then a huge feathery red cock proudly leading the procession from Dobropolje.

I turn to Aleš to ask him about the cock from Dobropolje. But he is gone, nowhere to be seen.

I scan the crowd behind me: strange faces, folksy pink-flushed faces, foreign Slav faces with high broad cheekbones and narrow mouths and laughing slits for eyes. I scan the street in front of me, the swaying stamping spinning figures, the dancing blades of scythes catching the glint of a suddenly sinister afternoon sun. I hear the whirring of the incomprehensible Dolenjska dialect around me, the pounding of drums under my feet, the shrill clanging of the cowbells. Suddenly, terribly, the strangeness of my situation bears down on me—my total vulnerability in this place, my almost complete isolation, the fact that I am tied to only one person, and that by the slenderest of threads. He is but a single person after all, a single life. Here one minute, gone the next. Otherwise I have nobody.

I am completely alone in this world.

The nasty taste of panic rises in my throat. I feel a sudden urge to flee to some more familiar circumstances. But I don't. I stand my ground. I'll wait right here. It's the only thing I can do. He'll find me here. And if he doesn't, I'll try and make my way back to the car, though regrettably—and this is so completely typical of me—I have no idea where it is. My poor sense of direction again. I didn't pay any attention walking into town, didn't bother to get my bearings. It didn't occur to me that I would need to.

I turn back toward the street and, feigning calm, look at the oncoming pageant. I am an ordinary bystander. I am supposed to be here. I try to smile as I contemplate the unusual spectacle. In the distance, I spot a very tall figure standing out from the rest. He is not in a group of like-figures as are most of the other participants in the parade. He is alone, a good distance from me, about fifty feet, and from where I stand, it looks as if he is clad from head to toe only in foliage and twigs. He looks like some great big man-shaped bush. And the weirdest thing of all is that this green figure has stopped dead in his tracks and is staring straight at me.

I turn and glance behind me. It's unmistakable. There's nobody else. He's looking at me. It's as if he recognizes me from somewhere, although that seems far-fetched given his likely history, given mine. But the longer he stares at me, the more I have the feeling that our encounter is somehow fated, that on some primordial level I recognize him too. Then he is on the move again, approaching, and as he comes down the street, this strange figure, this creature clothed in nothing more than forest and field, stubbornly holds my gaze. He has caught my eye through his mask of green, and he refuses to let it go. He comes closer and closer and closer, down Ribnica's main street, until at last he stops right in front of me.

The parade seems to come to a stand-still around us, to go all eerie and silent.

Nearly a head and a half taller than me, the figure leans down and pushes his leafy face into mine. I can smell him, smell the earth on him. He's deadly serious, so serious that I don't dare shimmy away from him with a girlish laugh as I might normally be inclined to do. Plus my body is still rigid from Aleš's disappearance, my mind in adrenaline-stoked survival mode.

The leafy figure dramatically lifts one of his hands high above my head and, as if following the time-tested steps of some ancient ritual, reaches down and lays a long finger on the red and black markings on my forehead and my chest. It was not me that he recognized, I suddenly realize, but the symbols, the markings from Travna Gora. Finally, he raises himself up to his full treelike height, takes one of my hands into one of his, spreads my palm, and then with his other hand digs under his costume for something, and thrusts whatever he has found there into my open hand. He curls my fingers into a closed fist and is gone, dancing back into the spinning maelstrom of the parade.

I slowly open my fingers and look down into the cradle of my palm.

"What have you got there?" Aleš is at my side.

I close my fingers into a fist and spin around to him.

"Where were you? Where did you go?" My voice shakes with accusation and sheer relief.

"I'm sorry," he says. And he does look contrite. He must have known how terrified I would be to find myself alone here. "I got pushed back by the crowd, and then I saw someone I knew, someone from high school, and I had to stop and talk to him for a second."

I exhale deeply. Someone from high school, there's always someone from high school, always someone he knows.

A lull falls over the parade. The procession seems to be coming to an end, and the closing marchers are more subdued and tame than the ones that came before. I spot a baton twirler out of the corner of my eye as she bends her knee and successfully connects with the falling silver projectile. I still recall the terrible feeling that overcame me when Aleš disappeared: the sense that I was connected to my surroundings by absolutely nothing.

"Open your hand," I say to him.

"What?"

I tilt my head and smile coyly at him, shaking off any lingering feeling of dread and isolation. I rise up on my toes and plant a damp open-lipped kiss on his mouth.

"Open your hand," I say again.

He opens his hand, palm facing upward. I empty the contents of my hand into his. It is the soft and silty flow of seed. The smell of earth.

"I want to have a baby," I say.

PART THREE

Plural

Grožnjan

APRIL 1994

With friends in Grožnjan

It is Friday afternoon. We are working on verbs again.

The class seems restless, anxious even, waiting for the bell to
release us into the arms of the coming weekend. Outside, the sky
is a pure oxygenated blue, or so it seems after the long claustrophobic winter. Small shoots have appeared on the bare branches
of all the trees along the Ljubljanica River and city's streets and
avenues, coloring the city in a rinse of pale green. The world beyond the classroom windows beckons to us, spring having arrived
in earnest, and I, for one, have special plans. We are going to the
seaside this weekend, Aleš and Tanja and I along with some new
friends, to the Croatian coast, Grožnjan, one of the old forgotten
villages on the highlands of the Istrian peninsula. It will be my
first time venturing across Slovenia's new southern border.

Today we are not expanding our vocabulary of verbs, not working on something as mundane as tense. By now we have learned

most of the tenses other than the present. We have mastered the past, the conditional, and the future and can range easily along the temporal continuum. Well, not easily, exactly.

This afternoon Gita is not introducing new information but attempting to fortify what we have learned earlier in the week. She has brought in a teaching aid, a children's counting song, with which she hopes to nail down yesterday's lesson on verb conjugations and, specifically, what is called the *dvojina* in Slovenian: the dual. It turns out that it is not enough for Slovenian to have six grammatical cases, to have three genders (masculine, feminine, and neuter), and a singular and plural form, the grammatical complexities increasing exponentially as one considers the different endings for singular masculine nouns in the first and second cases, plural neuter nouns in the third and fourth cases, singular and plural feminine nouns in the fifth and sixth cases, and so on and so forth.

No, that is not enough. Because Slovenian is also one of the few languages in the history of human languages to have a special form for two: for the two of us, the two of you, the two of them, and, maddeningly, even for those two inanimate objects over there, these two chairs (masculine), those two tables (feminine), these two eggs (neuter) being fried sunny-side up in that bloody frying pan over there (masculine singular). Aleš told me that the *dvojina* does in fact have a sunny side, namely that it comes in very handy when writing love poems, but that provides little comfort. From the point of view of most of the students in the class, not having reached anywhere near the lyrical heights needed to write a love poem, the dual just adds another layer of complexity to learn before the proficiency test we have to take at the end of the semester. Although I admit I rather do like the orderly escalating numerology of the Slovenian system: first the singular, me alone in the world, followed by the dual, me with Aleš, followed by the plural, me with Aleš plus one more. After the Pust parade, Aleš resisted the idea of starting a family right away, wanting perhaps to stay in the dual a little while longer, wanting to stay in the love poem. But I am slowly, slowly bringing him around to the idea, and he is slowly, slowly succumbing to it, realizing perhaps that in the end it is futile to try and oppose the female urge, once it strikes, to procreate.

And yet, as attracted as I am to the dual transforming into the plural, I rebel, along with the rest of the class, when confronted with one final grammatical/numerical twist in the Slovenian language—namely, that the plural form is used for only three and four, and when you get to five and above you revert to the singular. With the introduction of this rule, the whole project seemed to take on perverse, almost sadistic, dimensions. The day before, I had been reduced to raising my hand and objecting.

"But why? Why do you do that? Why do you say 'five is' instead of 'five are'? 'Six is' instead of 'six are'?"

The deep linguistic answer might have something to do with the cultural understanding of the group versus the individual, that once a group is comprised of more than four members, it becomes a thing of its own, transcends the plurality of its individual members and becomes a singular item once again. But Gita doesn't care about deep linguistic answers. She is a pragmatist above all. She wants us to learn the nuts and bolts of the language, memorize them, and be able to regurgitate them on the day of the test.

"Remember," Gita repeated her mantra, "never ask why." That's what she was always telling the evangelicals when they would cry out "why, why, why"—paradoxically, I always thought, since in other areas of life they accepted the existence of miracles and all manner of improbable events, the earth being created in seven days, for instance, or Eve being made from Adam's rib.

"Why is it 'on the university,'" they would ask, "and not 'at the university'?"

"Why is it 'small am I' instead of 'I am small'?"

So it is no wonder that we are feeling anxious on this Friday afternoon, and no wonder that Gita has felt compelled to bring in something light and entertaining to try and ease our anxiety. I glance down at the xeroxed sheet of paper Gita has distributed. The song is printed in Slovenian only, no English translation as is Gita's practice. Hers is the "don't ask why" total immersion method. I am pleased, though I understand little else, that at least I understand what the song is counting. It is one of the words that I did not write down on the first day of school when we were divided into groups, because I didn't know whether it was slang or not, didn't know whether it was vulgar or not. We will be counting *zamorčki* today: the little ones from beyond the sea. The song Gita handed out is Slovenia's variation on the *Ten Little Indians*.

In pet zamorčkov šlo je	Five little Negroes
na ta ljubljanski grad,	to Ljubljana Castle did go,
se eden je spotaknil	one tripped and stumbled
je padel v prepad.	and fell into a hole.
In štiri zamorčki šli so	Four little Negroes
po Svet'ga Petra cest',	went to Saint Peters Lane,
pa eden je bil lačen,	one got very hungry,
je padel v nezavest.	and fell into a faint.
In trije zamorčki šli so	Three little Negroes
na ta ljubljanski tramvaj,	rode the Ljubljana rail,
pa eden je razgrajal,	one caused a ruckus,
ga vzel je policaj.	and had to go to jail.
In dva zamorčka šla sta	Two little Negroes
zvečer po promenad',	on an evening stroll did tarry,
se eden je spreobrnil,	one felt the touch of God,
odšel je v lemenat.	and joined the monastery.

En sam zamorček šel je	The last little Negro
po širnem božjem svet,	to the great wide world did go,
tam se je oženil	there he found and took a wife
dobil zamorčkov pet.	and had little negroes five.

In pet zamorčkov šlo je ...   Five little negroes ...

The hand of one of the female evangelicals in the front row shoots up in the air.

"What does *zamorček* mean?" she asks.

Gita deconstructs it for her: *za* = beyond, *morje* = sea, and *ček* is the diminutive.

"*Zamorček*," Gita concludes, "the little one from beyond the sea. It's the Slovenian word for a black man or an African."

The girl who asked the question sits slack-jawed for a moment, speechless at this response. One of her coreligionists speaks in her place.

"But that's racist," he objects. "We're not going to sing a racist song."

"Well, no," says Gita, and for once she seems truly taken aback, "it's not racist. *Zamorček* is not an ugly word. It's not the same as the English word *nigger*."

It actually sounds kind of sweet the way Gita pronounces it, with a long *e* and a rolled *r*, *neeger*. All the same, the Americans in the class, myself included, draw in our collective breath at this breach of the code.

"If anything," Gita reassures them, "it's cute and endearing."

"Cute!" the woman who originally asked for the definition finds her voice.

"Endearing!" the other American joins her.

"That's even worse," they both cry out in outraged unison.

Andre sighs loudly and slides down in his chair. Xavier lays his head on the table and closes his eyes, pretending to sleep.

Even I, no fan of Slovenian bias against southerners and the words they use to express it, am disappointed. Singing would have been a nice undemanding way to fill the last half hour before the end of class. And besides, I can't help thinking that Gita has been badly treated. It's not her fault the language is so absurdly difficult. Not her fault that the evangelical churches of America saw fit to send an army of proselytizers marching into this little Catholic country.

Gita stares grimly out at the classroom.

"It's just a word," she says, "just a song. And this is Slovenia," she reminds them, "not America."

By which I suppose she means that Slovenia is not guilty for the sins of America, did not enslave the dark-skinned people that arrived on its shores from the other side of the sea, did not perpetuate genocidal war on the dark-skinned people that were indigenous to the continent until there were, quite literally, no little Indians left.

I glance down at my watch. I was thinking of leaving early today anyway. Aleš and Tanja had wanted to get on the road so we could get to Grožnjan before dark. I don't have my bike, it's in the shop, and I know from experience that this little confrontation is going nowhere. As I quietly slide Gita's incendiary handout into the pocket of my binder, close my notebook, and drop my pen into my purse, Gita stiffly points out to the now sullen and silent class the descending verb forms in the song—šli so, šla sta, šel je.

I slip out of the door just as the voices in the class, minus several abstainers, begin a somewhat dispirited rendition of the counting song. I send a cheery wave over the heads of the others to Andre and Xavier, sitting up very tall in their chairs now, their low, booming, mock-jolly voices drowning out the others.

Outside I bolt into a cab I spot waiting on Ajdovščina Square.

I sit in the front seat, which is the custom in this sometimes strikingly egalitarian, sometimes strikingly unegalitarian country. It seems that a passenger seated in the back seat of a paid cab carries an unpleasant guilt-inducing whiff of the old European bourgeoisie and their hired chauffeurs, just as rickshaws strike some contemporary Western tourists in Asian countries as carrying an unpleasant guilt-inducing whiff of colonialism.

Bowing to local custom, I slide into the front seat.

"Proletarska 2," I say. My pronunciation is so flawless, I think, my delivery so authoritative that I might even be taken for a local. Then the driver goes and ruins it all.

"Do you want me to go by Saint Peter's on Zaloška, or cross the river past Poljane?" he asks.

"Pardon?" I try to snatch some meaning out of the blurred string of words.

He repeats the question more slowly.

"Whichever way you like," I stammer. Predictably, I botch this short but slightly more complex phrase.

"You're not from here?" He turns and studies my profile.

I look down and read his name from the laminated license on the dashboard: Enver Selimović. He's not from here either. If little else, I have learned how to dissect names to figure out people's origins. The ending -ić, the Serbo-Croat patronymic, is a telltale sign of a southerner. The soft ć doesn't exist in the Slovenian alphabet (neither does w or x or y for that matter); instead it has a hard č. Eventually most southern immigrants who remain in Slovenia adopt the local-ič ending, as did, for example, Tanja

and the Gvozdenovič family. Indeed, practically the entire Slovenian national soccer team is comprised of such transformed
southerners, the Yugo effect not only encompassing bedroom
skills, but apparently finesse on the soccer pitch as well. But
whether my driver spells his name with a ć or a č hardly matters,
because Enver and Selim are both unmistakably of Turkish origin.
My driver is Enver, son of Selim: a Bosnian Muslim (or a Bosniac,
as they will later be dubbed in order to keep them straight from
the other Bosnians, Bosnian Serbs and Bosnian Croats, without
resorting to a religious label.)

"Angležinja?" he asks, delighted to have a foreigner in his cab.

"No," I shake my head, "Američanka. By way of New York City."

Enver is even more delighted by this response. Americans are,
by definition, more exotic than the British, they come from farther away, from the land of Hollywood and Marlboros, and, crucially these days, America, however lumbering and ineffective and
full of platitudes about freedom and democracy, seems more
likely to help Bosnia out of its current predicament than the even
more lumbering and ineffective European Union.

To amuse him, and to practice my Slovenian, I tell him that
unlicensed taxi drivers in New York are known as gypsy cabs. He
throws back his head and lets out a big guffaw, Gypsies having a
far more immediate connotation in Central Europe than they do
in the Bronx.

"Forget about Gypsies," I say. "What about Bosnians?"

I am not sure why I decide to pursue this line of conversation.
Perhaps because we are both outsiders in a small and extremely
homogeneous country, perhaps because I feel guilty for not having taken a stand with my fellow Americans in Gita's classroom,
for not having condemned all forms of racism, all potentially
derogatory words which are used to designate the minorities
among us. Or perhaps because I feel guilty for laughing at all the
Bosnian jokes Aleš constantly tells me, perhaps I worry that I

have bought into the stereotype that lies at the core of each joke, that Bosnians are good-natured and stupid, and by implication, deserve their fate, not being clever enough to avert it, not being savvy or modern enough to carve out a safe place for themselves in this rapidly changing world.

"What about the way Slovenians treat their neighbors?" I insist. "Their former Yugoslav fellows in brotherhood and unity? What about the way they treat Bosnians? The fact that there is no minaret in this country, no mosque?"

Which is true. In a country with nearly sixty thousand Muslims, there is not a single place of worship, not a single community center for the indigenous Islamic community. And, for what it's worth, the Bosnians are indigenous European Muslims, culturally nearly identical to the Christian population, not economic immigrants from the Middle East or Africa, not *zamorčki*. I cross my arms over my chest and turn toward the driver. I've made my case. Now my look says: go ahead, break loose, have a go at your chauvinist Slovenian hosts.

He turns his head and regards me with surprise. Certainly it must be unusual for a well-heeled American passenger, or any passenger for that matter, to show solidarity with the plight of his people or indeed his own plight: his low wages, his poor prospects in this country, the daily humiliation he gets because of his accent, his name, his nominal religion; for like most Bosnian Muslims, he may well be of the secular sort. I wait for his outrage, wait for him to offer some particularly heinous example of local prejudice. But it doesn't come.

His hands float slowly up from the steering wheel, as if the cab has been momentarily flooded by some clear viscous fluid. They hover there awhile, swimming helplessly in the air. We are standing at a red light below the gold and red mosaics of Christ and the four evangelists on the facade of Saint Peter's Church, another one of Slovenia's countless Roman Catholic churches, although this one has unmistakably benefited from the strong influence of Byzantine design elements from the East.

"What can they do?" he answers at last. "We *are* different. And Slovenia is a small nation, very small and very new. They must take care of their own first."

The unexpected grace of his remark comes as a reproach to my careless provocation, the nobility of his resignation a far cry from the posturing in Gita's classroom. I turn away from the driver for a moment, feeling unaccountably shamed, as if I've been schooled somehow. The cab slows, turns left, and comes to a stop.

"Proletarska 2," he announces pulling up at the corner of Zaloška in front of my apartment building, which today looks almost welcoming with the bright yellow forsythia blooming in the concrete flower bed at the entrance. I fumble with my wallet and pay the fare.

He takes the money, and then turns and holds out his big workman hand to me.

"It was an honor to meet you," he says in formal and strongly accented English.

I look into his dark eyes, and then take his large hand in mine and shake it vigorously.

"The honor is mine, Enver Selimović."

We take the scenic route to Istria.

We drive past Nanos, the mountain that stands guards in front of the steep stony drop to the sea, marking the divide between hinterland and coast, Alps and sea, Central and Mediterranean Europe. The locals say that Nanos is a reliable predictor of coastal weather: if it wears a white cap on its butte-like head it will be overcast and cloudy at the shore; if its head juts up into the clear blue then it promises good weather. But today we have no need of an indicator. There is not a wisp of a cloud in sight. We can practically see the distant shores of the sea from here.

Then we drive along the edge of the mysterious limestone Karst region, arid and rocky and windblown by the famed *burja*, its fauna limited to sloping vineyards, groves of misshapen olive trees, isolated stands of pine trees, fluffy pink sumac blossoms punctuating the gray-green scrubby landscape. And yet the Karst doesn't want for more abundant plant life; its wealth lies underground, in vast subterranean caverns filled with glistening limestone stalagmites and stalactites, more strange and glorious than any formal garden or cathedral made by man.

At last we make our descent to the sea itself, and are soon driving along the cypress-lined road that runs beside the little bracelet of settlements on Slovenia's abbreviated coastline—Koper, Izola, Piran, Portorož. Unlike the Dolenjska region which boasts of its authentic Slovenian-ness and fears foreign invaders, the Karst and Primorska, the Slovenian littoral, opens its face to the sea and fears nothing at all. Oddly, it does not bristle, as most of the rest of Slovenia does, at encroaching external influences, at the stranger in its midst; does not feel an inferiority complex before the vaunted advantages of the West. Primorska sits comfortably at the intersection of many cultures and tongues. It is brazenly multilingual, its hotel staff switching easily between Italian and German, Croatian and Slovenian. It flaunts its unusual taste in food (ink-black calamari, sea fish, and risotto replacing the potatoes, pork, and dumplings that are staples of the hinterland), its eccentric card games (Triestine *briscola* and *scopa* rather than the more universal Black Peter dealt out on inland tables), and most of all its lilting, singing, laughing dialect.

This comfort with the foreign seems odd only because the Karst and Primorska have suffered far more at the hands of outsiders, of Italians in particular, than any other Slovenian region.

At the end of World War I, this part of Slovenia, nearly one third of the country's present territory along with the Istrian peninsula and a part of the Croatian coast, was bargained away by the first Yugoslavia at Europe's postwar negotiating tables. It was handed over to the Italian state, which got a nice chunk of the German-speaking Southern Tyrol at the same time, as a prize for having allied itself to the western powers in the eleventh hour of the war, and despite the fact that Italian forces, after entering the alliance, went on to suffer a series of inglorious defeats.

If this region is familiar at all to Americans, it is only thanks to Ernest Hemingway and the actual and fictional adventures he described that took place on the battlefields of the famed Isonzo front where Italians and Austrians fought against each other high in the Alps and down in the Karst plains. Most American readers of Hemingway's A *Farewell to Arms* recall the tragic love story between the American ambulance driver, Tenente, and his British nurse. Slovenian readers, on the other hand, are less likely to be moved by the romance or wowed by Hemingway's minimalist literary style, and far more likely to be outraged by the long account of the Italians' chaotic retreat from the Soča Valley through the Karst villages, past Trieste, and down toward the low flat plains of the Veneto, territory that was predominantly Slovenian in terms of its ethnic makeup and language, and that, despite Italy's dismal military failures, became part of Italy after the war. It was the price that the southern Slavs paid to the western powers for independent statehood after World War I.

A steeper and more personal price, of course, was paid by the Primorska Slovenians and Croats who suffered for more than two decades under the nationalistic and Italianizing rule of the fascist Benito Mussolini, suffered until 1945 when Primorska was liberated at last by Yugoslavia's communist partisans. As a result of this particular history, you will find no faded spots on the walls in this part of the country. Tito's jocular face is still there, still looking down benignly at his grateful subjects from the damp plaster walls of wine cellars, still peeking out from the maid's chambers in seaside hotels, still occupying pride of place in the living rooms of Karst patriarchs. However you slice it—communist or capitalist, east or west—the people here feel no need to rewrite history. The people of the Slovenian Primorska relish their story, relish the charms and contradictions of their mixed culture, their multilingual tradition, and remain grateful to the liberators of the past, however flawed they turned out to be in the long run.

We make a stop in the seaside village of Piran to watch the sunset—there are five of us in the gray Clio—Aleš, myself, Tanja, Basta (a tall Croat), and a Bosnian friend of Aleš. Another carload continues on to Grožnjan without stopping. The five of us walk single file up the winding cobblestone lanes of Piran to the church. The passageways are so narrow and serpentine that you can spread your arms and touch the houses on both sides. Looking up toward the sky, you see painted wooden shutters making a playful pattern among the drab houses, celadon green, pale blue, chipped orange, and between them clotheslines stretched from window to window. Thin cotton tablecloths, brightly colored dish towels, big white ladies' underwear all flutter in the evening breeze. Looking over your shoulder, the sea is always there behind you, winking at you. Whether it is a tiny slice spied through the crack between two narrow turrets or a sudden breathtaking expanse, the rippling turquoise surface catches the peachy silvery hue of the late afternoon sun and throws it back at you.

When we reach the ramparts at the top of the hill, Aleš stands behind me, captain of the ship once again. He points a finger to the right of the horseshoe-shaped Bay of Piran.

"At the bottom of those darks hills there, where the lights are just beginning to flicker," Aleš tells me, "that's the Italian port city of Trieste, the capital of nowhere, now that it lost its Slovenian hinterland." And it is true: the industrious Slovenian port of Koper is already starting to give sleepy Trieste a run for its money.

Aleš wheels me around a quarter of a turn and directs my gaze to the left side of the darkening blue bay. I cannot help but recall the winter day just about a year ago when he gave me a similar lesson from the top of Ljubljana's castle hill, showing me the axes of a slightly different compass: Vienna, Klagenfurt, Karlovac, Trieste. And now here we are, practically spitting distance from Trieste. I let my weight fall back against Aleš, let myself sink into the embrace of my steady guide, my captain on these foreign seas.

"Pay attention," he laughs, tilting me upright again. "That landmass over there," he points to the left of the horseshoe-shaped bay, "is Croatia already. The Istrian peninsula: rich red fertile soil—*terra rossa*—olive groves, lush vineyards, once part of the Roman Empire, and then later of seafaring Venice. It is often said that the Karst has no trees because its old forests were plundered to build the great pylons of Venice's canals, to lay the floors of its splendid palaces. But Istria itself belonged to the maritime empire, manned her ships, plied her seas. That is where we will be in an hour's time."

The proximity of borders still excites me, the proximity of him.

"Let's go, then," I say. "It's getting dark."

The shack at the Croatian-Slovenian border looks provisional, as if it had been erected in a rush. For this truly is a new frontier, not a refashioned old Yugoslav one, and its exact position is still being squabbled over, not for the first time and probably not for the last in the history of these much-desired lands.

At the moment, the grasping Croatians, as the Slovenians would have it, are angling for a few more kilometers of precious coast to add to their already vast and valuable holdings. They begrudge the Slovenians their place in the Adriatic sun and their piece of the Bay of Piran, which provides direct access to international waters. The Italians, for their part, have always lusted over this prime coastal real estate, their hankering for it being known as *irredenta*, the movement for the unredeemed eastern lands of the old Roman Empire. But with the exception of Venice's reign, they have not managed to hang on to it for long and are unlikely to get it back now. Although around here, you never know; stranger geographical anomalies have been forced into existence. During the era of the Austro-Hungarian monarchy, the landlocked Hungarians had the audacity to lay claim to the distant and noncontiguous port of Rijeka, now in Croatia. Currently, Bosnia claims its own tiny bit of beachfront property: a town called Neum. As drivers make their way down the long serpentine Croatian coastal road called the *magistrala* they are suddenly interrupted by a border crossing from Croatia into Bosnia, and then five minutes later, another one from Bosnia back into Croatia. As for the rest of the former Yugoslavia, the Montenegrins have their own bit of magnificent wild coast to the south of Dubrovnik, but Serbia is frozen out; separated, under the current disposition of old republics and newly emerging nation states, from the warm waters of the Mediterranean.

This time it is the Slovenian customs officials who wave us through and the Croatians who make a big show of examining passports. Again mine receives the most attention: the lowered head curiously scanning the faces in the car, matching the faces to the pictures, and then the light of recognition: "Aha, so this is what a nonmilitary American looks like." All of this is followed by a brief consultation with Aleš, the payment of a fee, and another tourist visa inserted into my passport—this one not stamped on but stuck in. The Croatians have opted for a thick decal that puffs out the pages of the passport, making it impossible to ever close it flat again. It features a huge red-and-white checkerboard coat of arms, although no name of the newly independent state. An oversight, perhaps, in the design process, rushed as it was.

As Aleš puts the car in gear and leaves the frontier behind, all the occupants of the Clio wail in unison:

"But this was ours!"

"All ours."

"We summered here. At Poreč. At Pula. On the island of Hvar."

"I had my first kiss here."

"I learned the breaststroke."

Their cries are innocent. They do not reflect lost imperial ownership, Venice or Vienna weeping over bygone protectorates; rather they mourn the lost empire of childhood. And thus the mood continues down the peninsula: a mixture of loss and nostalgia and ironic disdain as the group reads out the new names of formerly Yugoslav, now Croatian banks, laughs at the jingoistic slogans of the struggling new state, sighs at the calls for conscripts to fight and die in the ongoing war, Croatia having already lost nearly a half a generation of young men. The string of villages begun on the Slovenian side of the border, Koper, Isola, Piran, Portorož, continues on the Croatian side, bead by bead, pearl by pale shimmering pearl: Umag, Novi Grad, Poreč, Rovinj, Pula. Only now the little settlements, the vacations houses, the winged lions carved above low stone arches, the long wooden piers and rocky beaches, the shallow coves and narrow inlets—only now all of this lies in a foreign country.

It is already dark when we arrive in the hillside town of Grožnjan: very dark, middle-of-nowhere dark. A vast constellation of stars is beginning to appear in the firmament overhead. Tanja leads us through the town, guided by the occasional streetlamp, the occasional chink of light shining through a gap in a wooden shutter.

We maneuver as if through a darkened and hushed theater on which the curtain has yet to rise.

The others who arrived before us have already lit a fire in the open hearth in the great stone house where we will be staying. Ajda, Tanja's friend, is there; it is her parents' house, and a neighbor woman has come to help open things up and air the house out. She looks the part of an Istrian matron, round and smiling, faded white hair held up with a few stray pins, faded floral apron tied round her waist. When Aleš and I enter, she catches Ajda's eye for confirmation, and when she gets it, rushes up to us.

"*Mladoženje!*" Newlyweds!

She gives Aleš a knowing wink and pats me on the cheek with a warm doughy hand, then looks long into my face, as if she is trying to find a route on an unfamiliar map.

"*Amerikanka!*" she says. "Welcome to Grožnjan. Just so you know," she adds in a whispered aside, "we Istrians have nothing to do with this war."

Aleš had told me that Istria was almost like a country within a country, hardly thinking of themselves as Croatian, let alone Yugoslav. The occupants of the peninsula tend to cast a jaundiced eye toward Venice or Vienna, Belgrade or Zagreb, whatever distant capital houses the pack of scurrilous rats that is the current ruling government.

The neighbor and Ajda guide us up to our sleeping quarters. Aleš and I are the only ones to have a bedroom of our own, a master bedroom at that, and a heated one, the tall ceramic stove in the corner already sending out waves of heat which, though invisible, seem a luxury akin to mink or ermine between these heavy damp walls. The others will sleep in whatever nooks and crannies they manage to find, wrapped in blankets and sleeping bags and woolen coats. But our bed is vast and well-covered with a lovely hand-embroidered deep-hued coverlet. It feels like the honeymoon we never had.

Aleš looks at me across the expanse of the impossibly wide bed; it's nearly four times the size of our narrow bed-couch at Proletarska. He has that playful melancholy twinkle in his eye again, as if to say, "Oh, the things we could do in a bed like this." And I look back at him with a matching twinkle, though perhaps more industrious than melancholy, as if to respond, "Oh, the things we could make in a bed like this."

Downstairs a bottle of schnapps is already circulating. This schnapps is called *travarica* from the word *trava* for grass, and that is exactly what it is made from along with a sprinkling of pine needles. It has a clean medicinal taste, no sugary echo of fruit, and proves that a society that is sufficiently resourceful and sufficiently desirous of intoxication can ferment spirits out of any green thing, however slight, that pushes its head up from the soil. Before night truly falls once and for all, the company, *travarica* or no, is in a state of admirable resourcefulness itself, roasting meat over the open fire, preparing *žganci*, a strange starchy combination of flour and potato and water, a leftover from an era when there were always too few potatoes to go around. Tanja, banging the cupboards and clamoring through the drawers of the small kitchen, has thrown herself into the mixing of dough with whatever ingredients she can find for a cake that she intends to bake, not in the oven but right in the flames of the fire. Heat is heat.

Culinary production in this part of the world is a very straightforward and uncomplicated process, which, paradoxically, can present problems to those more accustomed to recipe books and gourmet grocery stores. As much as I like the cuisine I've encountered in Slovenia—its rustic and healthy quality, its freshness, being made from ingredients that have just been plucked from the ground rather than shipped halfway around the world—I have had little luck emulating it. Because nobody writes anything down, nobody uses recipes, nobody even bothers with measuring cups and spoons. The cooks just toss in a bit of this, a bit of that, mixing it together between their bare hands until it feels right.

"How long do I need to bake it for?" I was once foolish enough to ask.

The question was met with a blank stare and a deadpan answer: "Until it's done."

When we finish eating these casually-prepared wonders, we settle into various old chairs and sofas around the renewed fire and dedicate ourselves fully to the consumption of *travarica* and to the singing of songs. Like the preparation of dinner, the process is rudimentary. There are no instruments, no lyric sheets, not even a single shared mother tongue. As for me, I can only watch the faces of the others, listen and hum, and occasionally pick up a repetitive phrase or refrain and sing along.

The evening starts slow and sad. First the gathered company sings some old Slovenian ballads, the mournful *"Kaj ti je deklica,"* about a girl who lost her young lover on the battlefield. Then we move on to Yugoslav partisan hymns, getting war from the other perspective, the heroic one, with the rousing *"Hej brigade, hitite!"* urging the soldiers to "hurry, hurry, march on!" From there, we move on to peacetime themes, love in the fifties and sixties, fulfilled and unfulfilled, favorite Italian standards in the San Remo style, and the jazzy swingy Slovenian songs that were inspired by them, *"Ne čakaj pomladi,"* for instance, from a film of the same name urging the girls not to wait for spring to fall in love but to do it now, right now. The singers sing well-known standards in Serbo-Croatian, *"Ima dana,"* and Macedonian, *"Aber dojde donke."* At certain moments some voices falter, not sure of the tune or the verse, not certain of the pronunciation of a word in a language not their own. At such times, a solitary voice rises up and pierces the smoky atmosphere and guides the others through to

Tanja and Basta singing

the next refrain. Sometimes it is Ajda's pure girlish soprano, sometimes Tanja's steamy contralto, sometimes Basta's cigarette-scarred bass, and sometimes, to comic affect, Aleš's well-meaning but tone-deaf warble. Occasionally the melody is lost altogether and the song devolves into conversation and laughter, a heated debate over the words, different versions put forth, memories of when the song was first sung and with whom.

Late in the evening and well into a second bottle of schnapps, the group launches into a spirited rendition of the inspirational "*Jugoslavija!*," a government-sponsored anthem written in the 1970s to bolster the fraying union. The verses range from Slovenia to Macedonia, from the Dalmatian coast to the rugged hills of Bosnia, from the Danube basin to the plains of Kosovo. The refrain, with its rousing cry of "*Jugoslavija! Jugoslavija!*" pulls all the disparate lands and their argumentative peoples together into one grand union.

"I love that song," I blurt when it's over. "It's a great song. Let's sing it again." The instant the words tumble from my mouth, I realize that I'm pretty far gone. The concoction of grass and pine needle has hit me hard. I'm unused to hard liquor, being more of a wine drinker, and this stuff is primitive and potent. For a moment, the only sound to be heard in the stone house is the crackling of the fire and the hissing of the chimney flue. I feel like I must have said something wrong, put my big American foot in my mouth again. But then everyone in the company bursts out laughing at the drunken foreign girl who professes love for the discarded anthem of a shamed and shattered union, a shamed and shattered people.

"It's a fake song, a fake anthem," Basta snorts. "They just made it up. They were just trying to keep everyone together."

Another pause ensues. The embers shift and fall, the flames whisper; the singers, perhaps thinking of what has happened now that the anthem has failed, now that everyone has come apart, sigh deeply.

"So what?" I break the silence. "It's a good song anyway. And all anthems are fake. All anthems are made up by someone to keep people together. That's what the definition of an anthem is. Come on," I insist, "let's sing it again."

Eventually I win. Though it has been a strict policy throughout the evening not to repeat any song, the group consents to my demand. It is a special request made by the outsider among them, and rules are made to be broken. But first they put their heads together and write down some of the lyrics so the outsider can sing along with them, one verse of which Aleš translates for me so I can see how corny and fake it really is.

I love your rivers and mountains
I love your proud peoples
From the Vardar River to Mount Triglav
To the necklace of Dalmatia's archipelago.
I love the flower and the shepherd
And the flute on which he blows.

But it doesn't matter. We're all a bit drunk now. We sing the anthem again, and though the first time through the singers had sung the rousing hymn with a sort of ironic distance, as if to make fun of the song that marked their days in the pioneer camps, their summers in the communist youth brigades, Tito's bombastic parades, the second time they sing it, it begins with a subdued and somber tone, the recognition of all that has been lost, and ends with a roar of defiant and defeated unity.

I wake up some time later. The room is black, the shutters closed. I have no idea what time of day or night it is. I am not immediately certain where I am. I do not, to my immense surprise, have a hangover. I shake my head to confirm. No headache. My mouth is parched, though it has a vaguely spearminty taste; a benefit, I suppose, of drinking schnapps made of green foliage rather than rotten sugar-laden fruit.

But I'm terribly thirsty. I need water. I push the heavy coverlet off of me and swing my feet over the edge of the bed. I can hear Aleš breathing on the other side of the vast expanse of mattress. I have only blurred recollections of the night before and how it ended, our drunken withdrawal from the living room, our greedy giddy love-making on the continent of the Grožnjan honeymoon bed, the snoring oblivion that followed.

I lower my feet to the floor. The tiles are shockingly cold. The ceramic stove has long since ceased giving off any heat, the embers within having turned to ash hours ago. Somewhere on the other side of the blackness, I spot a narrow chink of light. I stand up and move toward it, holding my hands out in front of me in the darkness, moving one foot after another in small cautious steps across the icy floor. When I arrive at the chink of light, I push the curtains aside and move my hands over the cool panes of glass, exploring, until I find the clasp on the wooden sash, unhook it, and pull the windows inward. Cold air and a little more light seeps in between the slats of the shutters. I run my hands over their chipped splintery surface and again locate the clasp on the frame. This time I push outward.

First there is the audible explosion of dust motes in the air. Then light, so much of it that my pupils violently contract.

Off in the distance, the sea, the blue sea, endless and diamond-sharp. And here, down below, the town itself, Grožnjan, sprawling out from the foot of this cold stone house, at the top of this red-earth hill above the sea. Grožnjan, which, like its fellow Istrians, doesn't seem to care much for the war going on in this country, for the endless machinations of state and empire, armies and ethnic cleansers. Here it stands, stone upon stone upon stone, as it has stood for hundreds of years.

A smooth old fountain in the middle of a square.

The disintegrating walls of an abandoned house, green ivy pushing from the inside out, climbing up through the ruins of a chimneystack.

A freshly painted turquoise door.

A pair of iron chairs beside an iron table.

Two empty espresso cups on the table.

And the stupefying Mediterranean sun pouring down over it all.

After the excesses of the previous night, the song and the drink, I don't imagine that anybody else is up at this hour. I have forgotten my thirst for the moment and lean out the window drinking in the morning. Suddenly from below, from somewhere outside of my field of vision, a raspy female voice begins a mournful dirge. It must be one of our group, for amazingly, I recognize the song, not from the night before, but from another time, another place. The song is from Prekmurje, the eastern Pannonian region of Slovenia that borders Hungary and is, like Istria, almost another country within a country. I recognize the song because it was on a CD of Slovenian ethno-folk music that Aleš gave me back when our affair was new, back in my apartment on Twenty-Fourth Street. I remember listening to the song in my empty apartment after Aleš had returned to Slovenia. High above Third Avenue, I listened to its slow drone, its infinite melancholy, and I remember wondering at the time, as a siren screamed down the avenue and the yellow cabs hooted and the restless city hummed, who wrote this song? Who sings it? Is such slow-motion pathos even possible anymore?

Back then, the song's plaintive repetition seemed other-worldly to me.

Vsi so venci velji,	All the wreathes are white,
vsi so venci velji,	all the wreathes are white,
vsi so venci velji,	all the wreathes are white,
samo moj zeleni.	only mine is green.
Ar ga jes zalejvlen,	Because I water it,
ar ga jes zalejvlen,	because I water it,
ar ga jes zalejvlen,	because I water it,
svojimi skuzami.	with my tears.
Če bi moja skuza,	If my tears should fall,
če bi moja skuza,	if my tears should fall,
če bi moja skuza,	if my tears should fall,
na kamen spadnola.	upon a stone.
Kamen bi se razklau,	The stone would break,
kamen bi se razklau,	the stone would break,
kamen bi se razklau.	the stone would break,
na dvouje, na trouje.	into two, into three.

"Aleš," I turn my head and whisper back into the dark room. I want him to hear it too. And I want to show him the view from our window. *There*, I would say, turning him one way, *there's the sea. And there, the coastal town of* Novi grad. *And here all round, the hillside settlement of Grožnjan.* I want to show it to him. It's so beautiful. But he sleeps on.

Standing barefoot in our Grožnjan wedding suite, I realize that I have begun to understand the bottomless melancholy of the song. I remember the cry of "*Jugoslavija!*" the night before, how it gathered up all these lands in its triumphant refrain, and now I hear this other, much sadder refrain, and I imagine tears falling softly onto what was once so very solid, breaking it apart, into two pieces, then into three, and then it crumbling altogether.

Slovenia, Croatia, Bosnia, Macedonia, Montenegro, Serbia, Kosovo.

I want to tell Aleš that I think I am beginning to love more than just him, that I am beginning to love these unfortunate lands as well, this homeland of his, his country, not only the present one, but the many ones that came before. All the fragments, all the broken pieces.

The Bureau for Babies

Ljubljana pharmacy

By summer I am pregnant.

What I failed to anticipate when that pagan fertility figure in Ribnica first planted the seed in my hand, or even during all the subsequent rolls in the marital bed that would serve as the launching pad for the project, was that each of life's great milestones—migration, marriage, birth, death—is accompanied by a certificate, by a *dokument*. In other words, each necessitates a trip into the bureaucratic maze.

So I am waiting in line again. This time at Šlajmerjeva 7, the woman's clinic at the Ljubljana medical center that lies, fortunately for me, between Zaloška and the river, easy walking distance from my proletarian neighborhood of Moste. Slovenia is small enough that many of its babies are born in the same place, right here on this very street, in the new maternity hospital next door. The unfortunate thing is that the bureau for babies is not much more cheerful than the bureau for foreigners. At the front of the large entry hall, which resembles a dilapidated turn-of-the-century Austro-Hungarian railway station more than a medical facility, there is a glass window behind which tight-lipped uniformed officials, nurses this time, stand and process applicants, all female, that line up on the other side of the window with little booklets clutched in their hands.

The booklets are not passports but little orange health-insurance pamphlets (which one day soon, even as the national health care system is eroded by private enterprise, will be replaced by magnetized cards; progress of a sort). The booklets, which must be regularly stamped either by one's employer or by the unemployment office, prove that one has up-to-date national health insurance. Naturally I don't possess such a booklet. All I have is my own American passport, which I have a feeling will buy me no favors here, and Aleš's proof-of-insurance booklet that I have borrowed for the occasion.

When I arrive at the head of the line, the white uniformed nurse frowns at these offerings and pushes them back over the counter toward me. I inform her in my now quite serviceable Slovenian that I have a Slovenian husband (employed), a legal residence permit (still valid), an appointment with a gynecologist (who speaks English, I hope), and, most important of all, that I am pregnant. The last item I report with a slight blush. I am only just getting used to it myself. The Slovenian word for pregnant is *noseča*, which means carrying.

The nurse takes no notice of the blush.

"Do you have a national identification card?"

"No, I'm not a citizen," I explain. "But I do have insurance through my husband."

I push my passport and Aleš's health insurance booklet back over the counter again. She pushes them back.

"You'll need your own," she says.

I shrug, as if to say, "What can be done?" The state can't control everything. It happens even to noncitizens. I pat my flat stomach and give her a beseeching look.

"You can see the doctor today," she relents, "but you'll need to get one of these. Your own, not your husband's."

She taps a sharp fingernail on Aleš's orange booklet. Meanwhile from beneath the counter she pulls out a clean white folder and another booklet, navy blue, slightly larger than the orange one, featuring a minimalist sketch on its cover: the curved outline of a kneeling mother holding the curved echo of a baby in her arms. It is, the nurse informs me, my maternity booklet, and I must bring it with me each time I come to see a doctor in this office. It will contain all the data of the pregnancy and eventual birth.

"It is an extremely important *dokument*," she says gravely.

I nod obediently. Despite her stern bureaucratic demeanor, I am thrilled. This somehow makes it official.

Then she proceeds to fill out the basic information on the first page of the maternity booklet and on my virgin white medical file. Name, address, age, blood type, special medical conditions, etc. She writes in a neat hand, even-sized letters, almost as regular as a type-writer. I'm beginning to warm to her. She's competent, and competence is as important as human kindness in such situations.

She copies out the necessary insurance information from Aleš's booklet, and then when she comes to the space on the file where she would ordinarily write in my national identity number, she opens a drawer and rummages through it for a while. Whatever she is looking for, she cannot find right away. The line of waiting women extends behind me but that doesn't seem to trouble her. She turns and walks toward her neighbor's drawer a few steps away and, frowning, rummages through that one as well. Finally, after some time, she finds what she's looking for: a red felt-tip pen.

She returns to the counter where I wait with my file. Armed with the pen, she writes—this time in bold red capital letters—a single word in the empty space. Then she flips the folder open and writes the same word two more times—also in bold red capital letters—on the backside of the clean white folder.

She is taking no chances. She is making absolutely certain that any medical professional who happens to pop up between my stirruped feet in this medical facility, anyone who happens to prod one of my organs or to measure the heartbeat of my unborn baby, will know that the body being prodded and measured is not the body of a Slovenian citizen. The word she has written in big red letters is: TUJKA. Foreigner. Feminine singular.

I stare down at the word. Then I stare into the face of the unsmiling white-clad woman who stares coldly back at me. She pushes the material across the counter to me and instructs me to take it down the hall to examination room number one. I turn and glance down the hall in the direction she has indicated. The corridor is lined with narrow wooden benches that are occupied by rows of motionless women staring into space, some with huge bulging bellies teetering over the narrow confines of the bench toward the floor, threatening to topple the whole precarious structure. Here, as at the hair salon, the concept of a fixed appointment has not yet developed. There are only two time slots offered to women who call on the phone: morning and afternoon.

My gaze returns to the nurse who is now clearing the deck for her next supplicant. I decide to turn the other cheek. I beam at her, sending her my biggest, broadest, most foolish American smile.

"*Hvala lepa, sestra!*" I articulate the words energetically, using all the muscles in my mouth, just as Gita has taught me over the course of the last year. Thank you, sister. All nurses in Slovenia are addressed as sister, male nurses presenting a confusing anomaly in this society, not unlike pregnant foreigners. I turn and walk down the hall, past all the waiting women perched on the edges of the wooden benches like so many round-chested birds on a telephone wire, and when I come to the door marked 1, I give it three sharp cheerful knocks. There is a brief rustling behind the door and then it is opened by another white-uniformed nurse. She only opens the door a crack, but nevertheless I confer on her another smile as wide as the crack in the door is narrow.

"Good day, sister," I almost salute her, clicking my heels together, and handing over my new maternity booklet along with my red-stained medical folder.

She gives me a cold stare—it must be part of their training—and takes the offered items.

"Wait outside," she says, and shuts the door in my face.

Kill them with kindness. That's my new strategy. That's how I will survive nine months of regular contact with the medical bureaucracy. Teach by example. Show them how to grease the wheels of everyday life with a smile and a friendly word.

On the one hand, such a strategy is not difficult in my current state. For I am content; supremely content. Though my midriff has not yet started to expand, I feel as benign and pacifistic as a round-bellied Buddha. It feels natural for me to take an indulgent and generous attitude toward the peculiarities of my adopted country. This little country, after all, has given me a wonderful husband, will soon give me a baby, and has tossed free medical care into the bargain. Who am I to complain or criticize how things are done around here? And anyhow, now I have become a sort of country myself. I too am hosting a strange new life, a little colony of growing cells.

On the other hand, it also becomes clear that my benevolence will have to extend beyond my monthly visits to Šlajmerjeva. It turns out that the homogenous Slovenians have more than one way to skin a cat. The medical bureaucracy has agents fanning out far beyond the clinic center. These agents are purveyors of folk wisdom and wives' tales, and they are everywhere. Mothers-in-law, fellow passengers on the bus, fruit and vegetable vendors at the market place, little old ladies riding their bicycles to Žale ready to shake a crooked finger at you if you are dressed improperly. It is a nationwide conspiracy.

Of course, I already had some exposure to folk wisdom during my first year in Slovenia. It started with a trickle of tea and honey and lemon for the sniffles, extract of bee pollen and sugar for a sore throat, sage leaves soaked in warm milk for laryngitis. It started with those lunches at the Gotska apartment when Mija offered me a pair of guest slippers and my one rash effort to decline them.

"But your feet are bare." She followed me around the small apartment from room to room, plaintive and insistent, holding a pair of the frumpy slippers in her hands. I refused to take them. It already seemed imposition enough that I had had to part with my Kenneth Coles.

"I'm perfectly fine," I assured her. "And I'm not barefoot. I'm wearing socks."

But Slovenians have no word for *stocking feet*. They only know a binary relationship when it comes to feet. Either you are shod—*obuta*—or unshod—*bosa*. There's nothing in between, as good an example as any of how language determines categories, determines how we view the world, and how we define ourselves in relationship to that world. And in the world of Slovenia, if you are unshod, the consequences can be dire.

"But you'll get a bladder infection," Mija fretted.

"A bladder infection?" I turned toward Aleš for a translation.

"The cold will travel up through the floor," she pleaded with me, "into your feet, up your legs, into your internal organs."

I looked down at the offered slippers. It crossed my mind to bring up Louis Pasteur, the germ theory of disease, the progress that had been made in the field of medicine during the last two centuries, but in the end I decided against it. I didn't have the vocabulary, not to mention the sheer energy and willpower, to battle such convictions. I took the slippers, dropped them onto the lethal floor, and slid my stocking feet into them.

Then there was the whole related question of drafts, of air moving from one place to another. A peculiar phenomenon can be observed at Ljubljana intersections on sweltering summer days. I remember the first time I noticed it. It was only a few months ago, before I knew I was pregnant, during an early summer heat wave, when Aleš slowed the Clio at a red traffic light in front of the train station.

"Why are they doing that?" I pointed to the several lanes of cars in front of us, which, like us, had stopped at the traffic light.

"What?"

"Why have they all opened their front doors?"

And indeed all the cars stopped at the light had their doors swung open on the drivers' side as they waited for light to change from red to green. Aleš turned to me and gave me a look that suggested that I perhaps was suffering from a bit of sunstroke myself.

"Because it's hot."

That was indisputable. It was over a hundred degrees Fahrenheit and most cars in Ljubljana in 1994, all those Yugos and Fičos and Zastavas, didn't have air-conditioning. Apartments and offices and grocery stores had a similar lack (and still do) despite the occasionally intense summer heat.

"Why don't they roll down their windows, then?" I asked, sending Aleš's sunstroke look right back at him.

"Because then there'd be a draft in the car."

"But the air is hot," I pointed out. "Very hot."

It doesn't matter. No distinction is made between hot and cold air. Drafts of whatever temperature cause a wide variety of ailments: cold, flu, fever, earache, migraine, arthritis, rheumatism, kidney stones, infertility.

The light turned green. All the doors on the cars in front of us snapped shut in unison and the vehicles lurched forward in a wave of secure airtight motion.

"Well, if you believe that," I challenged Aleš, "why are our windows open?"

"Because," Aleš flashed me an impetuous grin, "I'm taking my life in my hands with you." And then he peeled out with a loud screech, the sudden wind in the car making our hair fly wildly around our faces.

But now that I'm carrying, everything has changed. First of all, Aleš is not so devil-may-care anymore. He may have been willing to take his own life in his hands, and mine, but not, it turns out, the life of our future child. He has suddenly become conservative. He has joined the purveyors of wisdom with phrases like "doctor knows best" and "better safe than sorry." He can no longer be counted on as my ally in such matters, and such matters are multiplying fast. Now that I am more than one lone lunatic American driving through a summer day with my windows rolled down, the volume, variety, and intensity of the folksy advice increases, and much of the advice touches on activities that, however trivial in the face of new life, are important to me. And, anyhow, I'm starting to realize that in the sensitive sphere of baby-making—maybe it's the hormones—it often feels as if one's very identity is at stake.

I must not read during pregnancy, or my eyesight will be ruined.

I must not cry, or my baby will have a sour temperament.

I must not eat in-season fruit, or my child will be allergic to those fruits when he or she is born (and this in the summer season of July and August when, after a barren winter of cabbage and turnips, the market tables are piled high with strawberries and peaches and slick-skinned nectarines).

FORBIDDEN BREAD

Indeed, I must not eat any raw fruits or vegetables, or I will get heartburn.

If I have heartburn, it means the baby will have lots of hair.

I must not wash my own hair for three weeks after the baby is born.

I must not bathe or something will swim up there.

I must wrap my breasts in warm wet towels so my milk will come in.

I must eat doughnuts with stewed apples and rhubarb so my milk won't dry up.

I must, I must, I must not.

And though I first assumed that folk wisdom was a quaint Old World way of explaining things, of laying responsibility for misfortune on some higher power—nature or fate or the weather—it turns out that it's exactly the opposite. The final consequence of all those dictates and prohibitions is to lay responsibility for everything bad that can happen, from allergies to blindness to bladder infections, on one person's head: the mother's. My head.

Every culture has its version of folk wisdom, I know that, although you don't usually realize it until you're swimming against the current of another culture. In America it is science and rationality, individual freedom, and the pursuit of happiness. Yet even though I understand all of this, as the Slovenian advice piles up higher and higher I am beginning to feel homesick: homesick precisely for rationality and science, freedom of choice, privacy, to each his own. I want all those old ladies to shut up and leave me alone. Now for the first time since I've been here I badly want to go home. I want my own feminist-lawyer mother at my side during this crucial time of my life: my mother who loudly scoffs over the telephone when I tell her that Slovenian women must press with a scalding iron the inside of each and every miniscule item of baby clothing that will eventually make contact with their child's skin, and not my mother-in-law, who offers to do all that

232

ironing for me. Accepting such an offer would be tantamount to surrender, tantamount to accepting their view of the world, and losing my own.

As each day passes, I am finding it harder and harder to maintain my patience and tolerance, my sunny equilibrium. As each day passes, it is becoming ever clearer that I *am* an outsider here, that perhaps I always will be, and that Aleš is increasingly siding with *them*. That nurse was right, after all, when she wrote that single word on my file: TUJKA.

Sometimes it's better to face such things head on. In red ink.

In the fall we pay a visit to Pavel's twin brother, Peter, who lives in Ljubljana. His son, Vito, Aleš's first cousin, and his wife, Mojca, live in the family house and have recently become parents for the first time. They have a six-week-old baby son.

By this time, things are moving along for us as well. We have, unbelievably, moved from Proletarska into a bigger apartment in a brand-spanking-new complex closer to downtown, just behind the train station. Not a barn in sight. We have four separate rooms: a bedroom with a real queen-sized bed, a living room, a kitchen-dining area, a bathroom with a full-length bath and a normal flush toilet (without the inspection shelf), and a balcony that is more than just a slice of storage space hovering above the abyss. We could actually put a table and chairs out there and still have room for a potted oleander and a baby swing. I have at long last retrieved the boxes that accompanied me across the ocean a year ago and have been stored all these months in the Debeljak cellar. I have put down the Oriental carpet and hung the framed prints and the mirror.

For the first time, it feels as I am building a real home here.

Though it did feel strange and a little sad to leave the Proletarska studio. Aleš and I were like a pair of twins that had suddenly burst free from the claustrophobic confines of a shared womb. In the first days in the new apartment, we found ourselves trailing each other from room to room, always staying close, very close. It felt weird and, yes, drafty to be in separate rooms after such a long stay in one. Too much air, too much space. We had to relearn the art of being apart.

And not only has our living space grown, but my belly is growing too. It has not yet reached Buddha-like proportions but is round enough to sweep my hands around its circumference in a pleasing arc. My breasts have nearly doubled in size, an unlooked-for bonus as far as Aleš is concerned. And I actually felt the baby moving the other day when I was sitting in the middle of the living room unpacking books and CDs. It felt as if a butterfly had unfolded its wings high in my abdominal cavity, just beneath the breast bone. I froze for a moment there in the middle of the floor, book in hand, waiting to feel it again, wanting to feel it again. When I didn't, I stood up gingerly and resumed the placement of books on the shelf, and, only then, as if waiting for my movement, did the butterfly open its parchment wings again.

On the visit, I hold Mojca's baby boy flat on my lap, placing his small round head in the palm of my hand, practicing for my own. Aleš talks loudly to his Cousin Vito and his Uncle Peter, telling of his most recent publications, his most recent television appearances, ignoring the baby. Sometimes it seems he wants to hold the whole thing back, to pretend it's not happening. I worry that only now, with fatherhood, will Milena's prophecy—he won't lift a finger—be realized.

Mojca is tall and lovely and self-confident, a picture-perfect mother. She used to be a fashion model. She invites me into the bedroom where she will change the baby's diaper.

"Why do you do it like that?" I ask.

We are standing above the bed looking down at the wriggling baby. I stumble over the words, aware that I must express myself carefully, that something might be wrong. The baby is wearing, if I am not mistaken, three diapers: a disposable paper next to his skin, then a thick cloth diaper, then another wrapping sort of thing with strings attached. It all looks terribly complicated.

"Like what?" Mojca turns her lovely broad-planed face toward me. She hasn't taken offense. She is all warm maternal efficiency, turning the baby this way and that in the many layers of white billowing material and strings and tape. Presumably, somewhere in the middle of the confusion of child and fabric, lies a little pile of mustard-yellow baby shit.

"Why is he wearing so many diapers?"

"Well, for his hips, of course."

"Oh, I'm sorry."

There is something wrong, and she's so calm and glowing and untroubled. I really admire her. I'm not sure I would be so composed if my baby arrived with some sort of problem, some physical infirmity.

"What's the matter with his hips?" I ask in a sympathetic whisper.

She turns sharply to me. Now she is offended. "Nothing," she says. "All babies wear them. It's called wide diapering—*na široko*. So their hips and legs will form properly. So they won't have to wear leg braces later on. It's to prevent," she searches for the English word, "is it rickets?"

I'm stunned. I've never heard of rickets. Or if I have, it was in some nineteenth-century novel that took place in the sooty sun-deprived urban slums of the industrial revolution. Mojca has finished diapering her baby, has lifted his bottom and put all the padding back underneath it, turned him face down, then face up, tying strings back and front. In the process, she has reversed the proportions of an ordinary infant. Now his bottom is nearly twice as big as his head, the mass of diapers reaching nearly to his ankles. Dangling his legs or kicking his little feet up into the air would be a physical impossibility. I lay a hand on the orb of my own stomach.

"All babies?" I ask.

Maternity school is the place where the medical bureaucracy and folk wisdom intersect. Men are required to attend maternity school (and pay a small fee) if they want to be present at the birth of their babies. Women are strongly encouraged to attend, and no doubt female attendance would also be made mandatory if it weren't for the inconvenient fact that, whether they attend or not, those babies are on their way out.

Aleš and I sign up for our session of maternity school in January and February, some two months before I am due to give birth on March 7. Over the course of six weeks, a squadron of sisters gives us the full official version on double diapering (we practice on plastic dolls), the strict necessity of ironing (even if the babies' clothes have been boiled at ninety degrees Celsius and have bounced around for an hour in one those new-fangled Italian tumble dryers), and most importantly on how to give birth diligently. We are told that the more *pridna* we are, the better and safer it is for our babies. Screaming, weeping, moaning, and any other such nonsense are all a wasteful dissipation of energy that could be better dedicated to the birthing process. We look at slide shows of a woman with her legs tucked neatly under her chin, a slimy little head crowning between them, and on the woman's face, an expression of extreme meditative calm.

"I don't think I can do that," I whisper to Aleš.

The afternoon after the last class and the issuance of Aleš's certificate, we have lunch at the Gotska apartment. I have decided to make an announcement that I have been thinking about for some time. It might seem insignificant or trivial, but for me it has enormous symbolic value. It is nothing less than a declaration of independence. I am not sure why I do it among the wider family; perhaps because deep down I realize that my real target is my mother-in-law and not Aleš, who despite his certificate takes a backseat in such matters. Plus my instinct tells me that in Slovenia these sorts of issues involve the whole extended family, if not the wider sphere of society and culture.

But since I cannot address the wider sphere of Slovenian society, I deliver my announcement to Mija and Pavel and Aleš. After finishing a copious vitamin-filled lunch, I stand up, maneuvering my now truly massive belly around the table in the narrow dining nook. The baby gives me a sudden kick, thrusting straight outward, as if to warn me that this might not be the best idea, but I don't care. I clear my throat and begin.

"I am not going to be diapering my baby *na široko*."

Three pairs of eyes turn toward me. That certainly got their attention. Mija and Pavel look aghast. From the expression on their faces, I might have told them that I wasn't planning to breast feed the baby, or feed it at all.

"One diaper does the job just fine," I say and smile reassuringly, making an effort to radiate waves of self-confidence and certainty that I don't actually feel. I am alone in this. I am going against a whole country, a whole medical establishment. Whatever meager knowledge of these matters I brought with me from America seems pretty unreal right now, intangible in the face of the monolithic and concrete opinion that surrounds me.

"Erica . . ." Aleš tries to stop me. I know he is about to come up with one of his better-safe-than-sorry lines, but what he is really doing is defending his parents from me, choosing their world over mine.

I hold up a hand to shush him.

"Try to understand," I say to them directly, "these aren't scientific facts. They're just cultural differences, minor details, really, but details that are important to me in the long run, important for me as a new mother. I need to do things my way."

It is a plea from the heart, and yet even as I say the words I know how they are being interpreted. That how I *feel* is more important than anything else, more important than the baby's health and safety, more important than the remote possibility of some crazy hip condition. But in fact it is more then mere selfishness. I am thinking of the baby too. I don't want my child to be raised with the constant fear of death and disease, the grim conviction that the world is a treacherous place filled with dangers that must be constantly guarded against: cold tiles, cold breezes. The reason we waited six weeks to visit Mojca's baby is because that's the old peasant way. There's a saying that a little coffin waits beneath a mother's bed for the first six weeks of her child's life. And that's real for these people; three of Pavel's siblings died in infancy. But it's not real for me, and I don't want any little coffins, imaginary or not, anywhere near my baby. I want my baby to love fresh air, to seize the world with its hungry little hands. Or put another way, with age-old stereotypes, I want my baby to be an optimistic can-do American, not a defeatist death-obsessed European.

Mija finally finds her voice.

"It is important in the long-run, precisely in the long-run," she says. "You don't want your baby to wear leg braces, do you?" Her voice is soft and coaxing as she summons up the inevitable scare tactics. I knew they'd be used. I've had six weeks of them at maternity school. I pause and take another breath.

"Come on," I turn to Pavel, the more rational of the two, the one who admires mechanical wonders and scientific accomplishments, the one less inclined to burst into tears at the slightest provocation. "You don't really believe this stuff. You have to put it in proper perspective. I mean, you spent your whole childhood without owning a pair of shoes, and now you think if I walk around your carpeted apartment in stocking feet, I'm going to drop dead from pneumonia."

I turn to Mija. True to form, she is blinking away tears. But I forge on. "And you: you yourself told me what it was like when Aleš was born. How he arrived on Christmas Day in the middle of a freezing winter, how you used to fill the stove as much as you could before you climbed into bed with the tiny baby, how you woke up in the middle of the night, and the fire was out, and when you opened the baby's diapers to change him the steaming warmth of them hissed into the freezing cold room. You could see your own breath. You could see the baby's breath. You were barely twenty years old. You had no idea what you were doing. You didn't go to maternity school. Aleš didn't eat a banana until he was fifteen years old. He didn't see a pineapple until he went to New York City, and he's fine. He survived. Just look at him." I gesture toward Aleš, who is glaring at me furiously.

"You must diaper the baby *na široko*," says Pavel.

It is, I realize, as close as it comes to a direct command. The discussion suddenly seems to have taken on a gravity far greater than its subject. My legs are trembling beneath me. The baby sends a sharp kick down into my pelvic floor. I have no idea what that's supposed to mean, but the sudden pain only makes me all the more insistent, all the more resentful.

"Why?" I demand. "Why must I?"

And somehow I know what his answer will be before he even says it. It is the mistake of all cultures, big and small, the tendency to extrapolate, to believe that everyone is like you, that everyone has the same values, everyone wants what you want.

"Because," he responds, "it's universal."

Wednesday. March 7, 1995. I wake up with a dull pain low in my belly. Right on time.

I have an appointment on Šlajmerjeva that day, morning slot, and my doctor confirms that I am in labor. I should go home and have a bite of lunch, relax a while, and then head back to the maternity hospital.

"Take your time. Pack a bag. You'll be fine," she says and gives me an encouraging smile.

She won't be there. That's the practice in Slovenia. Midwives attend to the laboring women. Doctors only come in an emergency.

At a little before five, Aleš drives me to the maternity hospital, and I check in. I'm feeling pretty good, just these periodic spasms, a little more frequent now, not too intense. There's a young woman in the waiting room who looks to be a lot farther along than me. She's walking up and down restlessly. She has the haunted intensity of an animal. At one point she squats down low to the floor and lets out a long low howl. Her face is a snarl of pain. She doesn't look anything like the woman in the slide they showed at maternity school.

At a little before seven, I'm in my room. Not a private room but a cubicle separated from other similar cubicles by movable barriers. Aleš is at my side, looking terrific in his surgical green scrubs. We hold hands and wait, talk in whispers, monitor the time between contractions on the wall clock. We occasionally hear the exertions of women on the other side of the barriers. One in particular is letting out ragged screams now and then. At one point, she lets out a shrill *"pička ti materna!"* It is one of the vulgar expressions I didn't write on the form the first day of language school, the classic Mediterranean insult, the one that means your mother's you-know-what. Aleš catches my eye and

grins. It hadn't occurred to me before, but it's not so inappropri-
ate under the present circumstances. I assume it's the voice of
the girl I was watching in the waiting room. She must be almost
done by now. But I'm still OK. I'm still handling it. I'm doing my
breathing exercises, holding Aleš's hand, white-knuckling it a bit
now, trying to emulate the nirvana-like facial expression from the
slide.

At a little before eight, I'm not so OK anymore. This is too
much, I think. I want to go home, but I can't. I've got to go
through with it. There's no other way. Finally I give in and let out
a suppressed scream of agony.

At the sound of the scream, my midwife enters the cubicle.
She shoos Aleš away from the bedside. She wants a private word
with me. She doesn't need Aleš to translate, presumably because
what she needs to say is straightforward, can be conveyed without complication. She sits on the bed next to me. She takes my
two hands in hers and looks intently into my face, woman to
woman. Then she lets go of my hands and lifts a finger to her lips
in silent warning.

"Ssh, *gospa*," she admonishes me. She's actually calling me
ma'am. I can't believe it.

"But that other girl," I whimper. I gesture in the general direction of the howling and swearing. "That other girl is—"

"That other girl," and now the midwife moves in closer to my
face and fixes me with an even more meaningful stare, by which
I infer she is about to impart some crucially important information, "that other girl is Macedonian."

I nod desperately, holding on to her eyes. I know what she's
talking about. I know exactly what she's talking about. She's referring to the primitive Balkan south. She's talking about letting
go, about losing control, and she's urging me not to do it. She's
urging me to hold on. I feel the next contraction rearing up like

a wave on a distant horizon, heading my way, preparing to crash over me.

"OK," I nod at the midwife like a child. I want to be good. I really want to be good.

At a little before nine, the game is up. There is no escaping it, I am Macedonian now. I have completely surrendered to my southern impulses. I have reverted to some primordial and prelinguistic state. I understand not a word of Slovenian, and I'm not sure I would understand English if it were spoken to me. For his part, Aleš is also stunned by the intensity of the moment, its wild emotion, my obvious and total loss of control, and as with his father's toast at our wedding in Otočec, he completely forgets to translate the midwife's increasingly exasperated instructions. I am writhing on the table, screaming with abandon, crying out for someone, anyone, to help me.

By nine, I have a baby girl.

The next morning I wake up in a room in the maternity ward. I nursed the baby in the darkness before dawn, but now she is asleep in her transparent Plexiglas bassinette. The rounds of doctors and nurses have come and gone, breakfast has been eaten and the tray taken away, visiting hours have not yet begun.

I peer through the Plexiglas at my first child, her perfectly formed rosebud lips, her tiny button nose, the blue veins gliding across her forehead, her parchment-thin eyelids. She's so lovely I'm tempted to wake her up, to lift her up out of her nest, but I resist. I may not know much about child-rearing, but I do know that you're not supposed to wake a sleeping baby. Instead I slide gingerly down to the end of my hospital bed and scoop my maternity booklet out of the pocket where it has been deposited next to my medical chart. I look at the cover of the blue booklet for what must be the hundredth time—the curvy outline of the kneeling mother and child—and my hearts swells with satisfaction.

I did it. I'm a mother now.

Suddenly all the fuss about double diapering, ironing, dough-nuts and stewed apples seems utterly trivial, my feelings of alien-ation completely exaggerated, my worries about Aleš's loyalty and commitment misplaced. I am content again, benevolent, serene. I flip through the pages of the book, past the columns of ever in-creasing numbers indicating my weight in kilograms, ultrasound results, monthly blood pressure and urine tests. I turn to the last page, to the climax of the whole story.

Klara Debeljak (we named her after my grandmother, Clara, but with a K to honor her Slavic blood, her Slavic home.)

Baby girl

Date of birth: March 7, 1995

Weight: 3.190 kilograms

Length: 52 centimeters

Diameter of head: 35 centimeters

It's all there. The physical measures of one healthy baby girl, my baby girl, our baby girl. Then my eye wanders to the bottom of the preceding page and a series of boxes I hadn't noticed be-fore. There is a box checked to indicate that I attended maternity school, and then there is a section that the midwife fills in after the birth, evaluating the success of the maternity school's peda-gogical efforts.

There are three boxes. With a jolt, I see where the midwife's pen came down. I see where she wrote an X so emphatic that it escaped the confines of the box. A wave of shame rushes through my body so forcefully that I think my milk is coming in or that my hormones have finally run completely amok. I drop the little booklet on the bed and lift my hands to both cheeks and discover that they're hot and wet.

At precisely that moment, a soft knock comes at the door. Mija and Polona, followed by Aleš and Pavel, pad quietly into the room. No one brings flowers; flowers are not allowed in the maternity ward as the fragrance is said to be harmful to mother or baby, I can't remember which, but they bring expressions of anticipation, joy, rapture even. This is the moment they've all been waiting for. The first baby in the family. The first grandchild.

When they see me sitting on the bed, in my pale green hospital gown, sobbing, the two Debeljak women rush forward.

"But what's the matter?"

Aleš had called them the night before. He had told them that everything was all right. The baby was healthy and beautiful, fifty-two centimeters long, head measuring thirty-five centimeters. The last he saw of us we were being rolled away in a gurney though the dim corridors of the hospital, Klara wrapped in a blanket tucked in my arms, me so entranced that I almost forgot to say good-bye. Everything was absolutely fine.

"What is it?" Aleš asks, concerned. He takes a quick peek at the peacefully sleeping newborn in the bassinette. "What's wrong?"

I am crying so hard now I can barely manage to catch my breath. I can hardly speak. I just open my mouth and the words tumble out of it.

"I flunked."

It's absurd, but I'm used to doing well on tests. It was bad enough last summer when I got a lousy fifty-eight percent on the Slovenian language test. But at least that was a passing grade, and it was the second highest in the class. That was some comfort. But this isn't even passing, and it is not an exam I can go back and retake. I hold out the maternity booklet open to the page where the midwife had marked the box beside the word bad, not even unsatisfactory, but just plain bad. I sob the word in Slovenian.

"*Slaba.*"

Mija sits down on the bed beside me. "Let me see that," she says. She is, after all, the person in the room with the most experience in these matters. We all watch her as she studies the page in question. I am still sniffling loudly, gasping for air. She pauses to look briefly at the data listed under the child's name. She lays a finger softly on the word Klara. Then, to my amazement, she flicks the booklet away from her with a gesture of disgust.

"Nonsense," she makes her judgment. "Absolute nonsense."

And this, after nine months of standing shoulder to shoulder with the Slovenian child-rearing establishment, and against me, on every single aspect of giving birth and raising children. The magnitude of the gesture astounds me.

"Look at her." She points at the baby sleeping in the bassinette, while at the same time pulling out a tissue from her pocket and wiping my wet cheeks. "How can you think you've flunked when you see her? You've passed with flying colors. She's perfect."

And now we all gather around and stare into the Plexiglas bassinette. The baby lies on her side, with a rolled-up cloth diaper at her back, propping her up so she doesn't roll, that being the current wisdom about the safest sleeping position.

"Look at all that hair," Mija whispers.

Babies on my side of the family usually sprout their first tufts of pale fuzz sometime around their second birthday. Nora, the niece who came to our wedding the year before, didn't have a single hair on her head. But this newborn child has a crown of wispy dark hair framing her pink face. I realize, with a start, that she is quite obviously a Debeljak, quite obviously a member of this wild-eyed black-haired clan of southern Catholic Slavs. All of a sudden, her hands stretch outward spasmodically. Two perfect little hands, ten perfect little fingernails. Her lips purse and make a sucking movement. All five adults gathered around the little bed gape in astonishment at these feats.

"Isn't she amazing?" I sigh.

"Is she eating enough?" Mija brings us all back to earth with the single obsession that is shared by the whole Šlajmerjeva medical institution, the single obsession that is shared by this whole country of Slovenian women brought up in food-scarce postwar Yugoslavia. The maternity-ward nurses even roll over a little scale before and after feedings, just to make sure the milk is going where it's supposed to go. But at this point, I don't really know how to answer the question. I mean, how much can a person eat in the first nine hours of life?

"She's wonderful," I say. "She's a good little ..." And now I cast about in my fledgling Slovenian vocabulary. Aleš had warned me in the months before I gave birth that I was at a dangerous point in both my Slovenian language skills and my driving skills. I had in recent months finally gained the courage to zip around Ljubljana in the little gray Clio, sometimes even making an illegal left turn, or parking with two tires on the sidewalk, two tires off. This dangerous point, Aleš defined it for me, is that window of time when self-confidence outstrips actual ability. Now casting about in my Slovenian vocabulary and coming up short, I make up a word. Compensating for its massive complications as a language, it is quite easy to make words in Slovenian. Cash register—*blagajna*—becomes cashier, *blagajničarka*. The verb "to sell"—*prodajati*—becomes salesperson, *prodajalka*. I know the verb for "suck"; it is *sesati*, so I just make the word for sucker.

"She's a good little *sesalka*," I say.

And as happens all too frequently when I try to express myself in my adopted language, everyone in the room bursts out laughing.

"What did I say?" I ask.

Aleš is wiping tears of mirth from his cheeks. The others are trying to master their glee. But it's one of those infectious things. It's like crying. Once you start, it can be awfully hard to stop.

Klara opens her eyes now, makes her little hands into fists, and stretches her mouth open into a yawn. These new tricks serve to shift the tone in the room momentarily away from ridicule and back to awe. I stand up and lean over the bassinette, very carefully picking the baby up, cradling her small black-haired head in the palm of my hand. Mija is sitting silently on the edge of the bed watching, slate-blue eyes brimming. She can hardly believe it when I carefully, very carefully, lay the child in her arms.

"Seriously," I turn to Aleš again, "what did I say?"

Sometimes, of course, when self-confidence outstrips ability and knowledge, amazing things happens, miracles even. A particular uncanny instance of parallel parking, for example, in a teensy spot on the left-hand side of a narrow and crowded cobblestone lane in the baroque center of Ljubljana. Or a gutsy little territorial guard that overcomes the third largest standing army in Europe in just over a week's time. Or a New York woman, a financial analyst, who against her own judgment and the judgment of pretty much everybody else she knows, marries the most flagrant womanizer she's ever met, a poet of all crazy things, and moves to his tiny new country halfway across the world.

Mija is still holding the baby, cooing at her.

"What did I say?"

"You said," and now Aleš moves around to the other side of the bed and sits down beside me. He peers into my face. It looks as if he loves me, as if he's proud of me, and grateful for what I've given him, a little earlier than he wanted it, but all the same. And he looks relieved too, relaxed now that all these months of transition are over, this process—so strange and disorienting at times—of expanding first from the singular to the dual, and now, miraculously, to the plural. He gives me that devil-may-care grin that had been somewhat absent in recent months and kisses me long and hard on the lips. "You said that she's a good little mammal."

Now it's my turn to give him a long quizzical look. I suddenly remember how handsome he'd been in those green surgical scrubs the night before, and it crosses my mind that maybe he should have been a doctor instead of a poet, that breaking the news to my American family about the whole marriage and move to Slovenia might have been easier that way.

"I don't think that's funny," I say.

For without meaning to, I stumbled onto a quality far more universal than double diapering, a quality that encompasses us all, a bigger tent than culture or language or religion, than nationality or ethnicity, than humanity, even; a tent that accommodates the whole species and then some.

And, besides all of that, Klara really is remarkable.

"She is a good little mammal," I say proudly. "A great little mammal."

The City and the Child

Aleš and Klara, six days old

No cry, really, is meaningless. Only when an archangel
appears, like a blue gentian on a mountain slope, do we know,
if only for an instant, our native land. Your Babylonian
moan won't die away. That's why poets never sleep. The task

seems clear now: this will be a chronicle of pain.
The size of a melting glacier. Which floods poppy fields
and villages, targets painted on the portal's slender frieze,
the lush filigree of Turkish silver: each tear deepens you.

You stand on the immovable rock. The world around you crumbles
into the abyss. You drink the water of life, drawn from the mouths
of those who breathe with you. Each morning, they come to witness

your rebirth. Like this poem. It won't be long before an avalanche
silences it. But a thousand cries will spring up in its place. For the love
Flowing through your veins is the seed, the blossom, and the fruit.

—Aleš Debeljak, *The City and the Child*

When Klara is a month old, my mother and my sister, Rachel, and my niece, Nora, now two years old, arrive from California, landing at the little airport that lies in the shadow of the Kamnik Alps not far from Tanja's house in Medvode. The same airport from which they departed some eighteen months before, after our wedding at Otočec.

Leaning over the new baby, fussing with the yards of billowing white material, one grandmother on one side, one grandmother on the other, the culture clash we experience seems to explode harmlessly above our heads like a sweet-smelling cloud of baby powder. In the hospital and afterwards, I had succumbed to the overwhelming pressure of the society around me, all those nurses and midwives and in-laws, and began to double-diaper Klara. My mother looks on at this spectacle but discreetly withholds comment. My sister, in contrast, stridently insists that I am the mother. I should do things the way I see fit, not the way others see fit.

As for Mija and Pavel, they are relieved that I have come around to their way of diapering at least. For the time being, they remain stuck in a state of hovering and breathless adoration, accompanied, predictably enough, by acute fits of worry about every little thing that might go wrong. This naturally drives me crazy most of the time, though sometimes it strikes me as sweet. It took me a while, but I now recognize that there is at least one positive element to folk wisdom. In America, when you catch a cold, the most common response is simply: "So what? Get over it." In Slovenia, when you catch a cold, the first reaction is: "It's your fault. You must have left the window open in the car, or neglected to wear a hat to cover your ears." But then, as if to counter the unkindness of the accusation, they drown you in the most marvelous concoctions of hot steeped hand-picked forest tea, special honey harvested near a fragrant grove of acacia trees, spoonfuls of sugar soaked in bee pollen and fresh lemon juice that must trickle slowly, slowly down in order to soothe your sore and aching throat. There is, in the end, a measure of love in that.

As for Aleš, he has settled ecstatically into his new role of father, determined, as with so many other segments of his life, to be the very best at it. In the hospital he had covertly studied a young father carrying his new baby (his second) casually in one hand while gesturing effusively with the other. Now that he's home, Aleš saunters happily around our apartment emulating this young father: Klara slung over the crook of one arm, the telephone against his ear, crowing to all his friends about the joys of fatherhood. There is much more Slovenian spoken in our home now. Aleš has reverted to his own childhood language with Klara, transforming her name into a series of Slavic pet names—Klaruška, Klarica, Klarka—which would have puzzled her namesake, my grandmother, but seems to delight the baby.

A thick snow blanketed Ljubljana in the weeks after Klara's birth, but by the time my family arrives from America, the weather is balmy and unseasonably warm. Ignoring the six-week peasant rule about the little coffin under the bed, we go on short outings with the baby, around Ljubljana and its outskirts. We take a boat ride on Lake Bled where the heavily clad and heavily perspiring oarsman glances disapprovingly at the baby and warns us of the dangers of spring air. We take a short hike up to the source of the Sava River. On the day before my family's departure, we go for a stroll in the main market, alongside the Ljubljanica River and Plečnik's classical arches, walking in the direction of the Three Bridges, the same walk I had taken on my first day of school.

Suddenly there is a terrible commotion behind us. A small platoon of women, fruit and vegetable vendors with their scarves tied beneath their chins and their aprons round their waists, have abandoned their stands and are storming after us, calling out to us. Something has gone wrong. They are in a frenzy, and their attention falls entirely upon our little group.

With my mother and sister on Castle Hill

My mother, alarmed, stops and turns back toward the women. "What is it?" she asks, addressing nobody in particular.

"They're saying something to us," says my sister, looking to Aleš for assistance. "What are they saying to us?"

One of the running and exclaiming women holds something small and pink in her hands.

"*Copatek! Copatek!*" she calls out in a tone close to anguish. We stop as a group and turn to face the women. Nora cowers behind Rachel, eyes wide, little hands gripping her mother's coat. "*Nogica! Nogica!*" the women cry out, as they bear down on us with a terrible urgency. And then we stand there at last, the two groups facing each other like rival gangs, American and Slovenian women, Aleš between the two.

"Klara's lost a slipper," explains Aleš.

The first word, *copatek*, is the diminutive for slipper; the second one, *nogica*, the diminutive for foot. Slovenian is a language that lends itself to babies. There is a whole new vocabulary I must learn, new versions of words I thought I already knew: *pupati* for eat, *papati* for drink, *lulati* for pee, *čičati* for sit. The vendors are in the grip of a collective panic, desperate that the baby's little foot will get cold, and god only knows what the consequences of that will be. In the view of the Americans present, of course, there is no real emergency, no immediate cause for alarm. Klara's little foot is not bare at all: she is wearing a pajama outfit with feet in them, little woolen socks, and on top of that is wrapped in a blanket. Anyway, what's the harm of a little fresh air? Aleš and I squat down beside the stroller.

"H*vala*," I say, accepting the knit slipper from one of the women.

The market women lean over us, watching our every move, making sure we get it right. They didn't leave their stands unattended and run all that way for nothing. I nervously tug the little slipper onto the baby's foot and securely tie the yarn laces. The women nod and cluck in response. My mother and sister and Nora look on wordlessly.

"H*vala lepa*," I say again.

Aleš and I catch each other's eyes over the stroller, acknowledging to each other that this will be the shape of our shared life for some to come. But it's not so bad. It's probably not all that different, in the general scheme of things, than the lives of other new parents, the main difference being that we have substantially more items on the agenda that call for negotiation and compromise. Offsetting that, of course, our field of potential discovery and wonder is that much wider.

When we get home that evening, I get a call from New York. It's Tina. She's received Klara's birth announcement in the mail.

"She's gorgeous," Tina gushes over the phone. "Absolutely gorgeous."

I glow with pride. I can't help it. But then Tina bursts my bubble.

"But what's she wearing? What's with all those diapers?"

And that is how I end up renegotiating my decision to double-diaper. This time vanity is the motivating factor: I want nothing to mar Klara's beauty. It turns out, as global marketers have long known, vanity is far more effective in its transformative power than any notion of cultural independence.

Klara diapered na široko

Later the same night, euphoric about the baby's new and lithe appearance, I offer to drive my mother home in her uninsured rental car back to the Proletarska apartment, where she is staying. Her first reaction to the style of driving on Ljubljana's streets was, like mine had been when I first arrived, fear and intimidation. So Aleš and Polona and I have taken turns ferrying her around. Once free of the tiny parking place where Aleš had somehow managed to squeeze the car earlier that day, I jauntily swing the car into reverse and plow it directly into a cement barrier that I somehow managed to overlook. We're both fine, although the rear fender is badly banged up. My self-confidence is too, which on this occasion had far outstripped my ability, as Aleš had predicted.

The next day at the airport I cry at the departure gate as my mother and sister and little Nora prepare to go into the boarding area and then to the airplane that will take them home. I pretend that the tears are due to my guilt over the smashed car but I know otherwise. I know that this is a real departure, a real ending, in the way that their postwedding departure hadn't been. I had already sensed this finality, this sadness before. In the instant Klara was born, when she emerged from my body and I looked at her for the first time, I felt, along with the joy and the accomplishment and the sheer relief from physical pain, a flash of a new and more metaphorical pain. In that moment, I caught a glimpse of real exile. I realized that I had been playing at it up until then—playing house, playing foreigner—and now, with the arrival of this child, the game was over. This was real.

I suppose that wherever a child is born—whether in the same hospital as its mother was or half a world away—its arrival always thrusts its parents into a symbolic realm of exile: exile from one's own childhood. With the child's first ferocious breath, one's youth becomes a thing of the past. Most parents have the luxury to pretend, for a while at least, that they can relive their own childhood through their child. The child will walk the same streets as they did, go to the same schools, speak the same language. But I couldn't enjoy that illusory luxury even for a second. Thousands of miles, a culture and a language, separated me from the scenes of my childhood, and in the moment of Klara's birth they fell away from me as heavily as a stone. Looking down at the little girl's unfamiliar face framed in dark hair, I felt the invisible safety line that had connected me to home weaken and fray. I felt, in that moment of joy, displaced at last.

And that is why I cry at the airport. Because they're leaving, really leaving me now.

"Good-bye! Good-bye," I call out through my tears.

"Good-bye," My mother calls back to me through hers.

"Good-bye."

And the sliding doors glide shut, cutting off my view of them. I stare for a second or two, bereft and seemingly all alone in the world, at the blank whiteness of those doors.

Then Aleš turns to me and places both of his thumbs on my cheeks and firmly wipes away the tears. I let out a long shuddering sigh. We both reach down at the same time and place a hand on the curved handle of Klara's car seat. She is sleeping in the shell of it, oblivious for now to the historic events taking place all around her. We lift up the seat, letting it swing gently between us, and walk from the airport and out to the car.

Together.

Plural.

The three of us.

Nineteen ninety-five was indeed an eventful year.

Not only was our first child born on March 7, 1995, but the war in Bosnia lurched to a horrific, unsatisfactory, but nevertheless relief-inducing halt.

In July 1995, eight thousand Bosnian Muslim men and boys were murdered by Bosnian Serb forces in the fields in and around the safe haven of Srebrenica under the timid and watchful eyes of UNPROFOR, the inappropriately named United Nations Protection Forces. On August 28 the second massacre in the Markale marketplace occurred in the center of besieged Sarajevo. In the first incident, a single shell fired from Serb positions had killed sixty-eight people, most of whom were waiting in line for water; 144 were wounded. In its late summer repetition, a shelling of the same target brought a harvest of thirty-seven dead and ninety wounded.

These events and others triggered the American-sponsored and Croatian-implemented Operation Storm, which drove Serbian forces and civilians, Tanja's aunt and uncle among them, out of the Krajina regions of Bosnia and Croatia, as well as the NATO-led Operation Deliberate Force that bombed Serbian positions in Bosnia and finally brought the war to a sputtering and inglorious end. Inglorious for all involved—the perpetrators, the victims, the late-to-act saviors. There were no heroes, no celebration, no parades, just a weary and shamefaced relief. It was finally over, and thus the Babylonian moan that was Yugoslavia, at last, did die away. On December 10, 1995, the Dayton Peace Agreement, essentially formalizing the ethnic segregation that had been accomplished during the years of fighting and civilian atrocities, was signed by all concerned parties.

In response to this event-filled year, during which the immense happiness of becoming a father mingled strangely with the grief caused by the final demise of the country of his own childhood, Aleš wrote a collection of poetry titled *The City and the Child*. The city of the title was Sarajevo, the child Klara.

In 1996, I returned to the maternity hospital on Šlajmerjeva and retook that test, giving birth to a son, Simon, on November 28. And I went back again in the spring of 1999, one child for each of the three little boxes in the maternity booklet, and gave birth to a second son, Lukas, on March 31, 1999, a date that coincided, oddly enough, with the final paroxysm of the dismemberment of Yugoslavia: the war in Kosovo and the subsequent bombing of Serbia by NATO forces. As I sat cross-legged in the bed at Šlajmerjeva, nursing my third child through the middle of the night, I listened to the sounds of the maternity ward around me: the soft footfalls of nurses in the corridor, the occasional choked cry of a newborn, the low murmur of a mother's voice, and also to the distant roar of the NATO fighter planes that had taken off from the Aviano Air Force base in Italy and were flying over Slovenian airspace on their way to their midnight bombing raids in Serbia. It seemed incongruous: the sounds of new life and new death occupying the same dark night.

But amazingly, once again, these unfortunate lands survived even this latest pounding, standing up after the dust had cleared, resentfully brushing off their knees, and continuing the sometimes glorious but mostly muddled business of living.

The baby, Lukas, turned out to be colicky, crying inconsolably during the first six months of his life. No wonder, what with all that racket right at the beginning.

And we survived that too.

Ljubljana
MARCH 2008

Lukas, Klara, and Simon

"Shut up, or you'll walk home."

I turn and holler toward the back of the car, which is no longer a little gray Renault Clio, but a silver Ford Focus station wagon. Lukas and Simon are waging war over the limited and by any objective measure undesirable territory of the backseat. Klara, who turned thirteen ten days ago, has graduated, to her immense relief, to the front seat. Her curls, still abundant, have turned from black to light brown, a change that started already in the first months of life when she miraculously transformed, practically overnight, from black-haired southern Slav to towheaded angel. Now she is on the slow voyage back to black, or perhaps to some way station in between. She still has her perfect rosebud mouth, though now it is regularly coated in various shades of shiny-wet lip gloss. In fact, she is applying a fresh layer right now, using the rearview mirror, blithely disregarding both the mirror's primary function and the ruckus taking place in the backseat of the car.

If the boys did walk, they'd probably make it home faster. The traffic, as usual at this time of day, is utterly horrendous. Ljubljana's streets remain as narrow and charming as the day I arrived fifteen years ago, and its drivers as crazed and semi-suicidal. The difference now is that these same crazed and semi-suicidal drivers are no longer confined to sputtering little Yugos and Zastavas and Fičos, but instead are maneuvering great big wide-bodied Mercedes and BMWs and SUVs down the narrow arteries of the city. Fortunately I do not have to suffer through the morning rush hour. I work at home, having changed career paths, leaving financial analysis behind me once and for all and becoming, after the years of study with Gita and others, a translator from Slovenian into English, a decently paid, much in demand, and well-respected job here. But later in the day, I am transformed into the equivalent of the American soccer mom, taxiing the children to and from various extracurricular activities—soccer, of course, and expressive dance, and scouts—and often finding myself trapped in the agonizing midafternoon jams. Today, I have made a much regretted detour in order to stop at the outdoor market in front of our old apartment building at Proletarska 2. It is, as luck would have it, a stone's throw from our new house, which lies on the other side of the railroad tracks in the direction of the Žale cemetery.

I wrest the rearview mirror away from Klara and reposition it properly, glancing, as I do, toward the now silent backseat. Long-haired Simon, sullen and impassive, gazes out the window at the street. Nine-year-old Lukas, the sensitive youngest child, is livid and red-eyed. He has inherited his grandmother Mija's propensity for tears.

"Hey, I'm sorry," I say, "I shouldn't have said shut up."

Lukas glowers at me, lips quivering. I will not be so easily forgiven.

"You can pick out whatever fruit you want at the vegetable stand."

He considers the offer. I'm sure he'd rather have his pick of something less healthy, but still the calculating look in his eyes suggests that he thinks he might gain something from the deal.

"Cherries," he replies, exacting the highest possible price for my sin.

"No way," I say. "They won't have them."

I scan Zaloška for a parking place. The outdoor produce markets have changed in the fifteen years I've lived here. There are imports now, strawberries from Spain throughout the winter, sometimes even hothouse blueberries. But cherries in March: not a chance. There is also not a chance of a legal parking place—that much hasn't changed—so I pull all four tires of the car up onto the sidewalk and put the hazard lights on.

"Wait here," I order Klara and Simon. "If they try to give me a ticket, run and find me."

Lukas and I head over to the Albanians with our basket. There's a new guy manning the fruit stand, someone I've never seen before. I look over the goods, grab a head of lettuce, a yellow squash, a red pepper, and cast an eye over the tiny tangerines. Maybe they would satisfy Lukas. But the little boy has other ideas.

"Look," he says triumphantly, and points to a small box right at his eye level.

Containing valuable cargo, it sits next to the man's cash register. It is filled to the brim with dark red swollen cherries. Lukas reaches out a greedy little hand.

"They have them," he says, transfixed. "I knew they would."

He speaks English to me, as is our custom. All three children are comfortably bilingual, though in different ways and to different degrees. Klara, perhaps because she is the eldest, speaks an eerily authentic variant of California Valley girl English, as if she is channeling the schoolmates of my youth. Simon has a cool and blasé Slavic accent. Lukas tends to mix the two languages without noticing it, sowing confusion when chattering to his monolingual relatives.

I grab the little boy's hand just as it is about to seize a fistful of cherries.

"Lukas," I say, "look at the price of them. It's highway robbery."

"But you promised . . ."

Years ago I used to despair of the winter produce in Slovenia. I thought if I saw another beet salad or learned another way of preparing cabbage or potatoes, I would get on the next plane and go home. But now I have become as parsimonious as an old Slovenian housewife. I disapprove of all the imported out-of-season food. It usually doesn't taste as good, and besides, with everyone in the world talking about eating local, it seems a shame for Slovenia to toss aside the habits and knowledge acquired over generations of how to carefully husband one's resources, how to use everything, waste nothing.

I eye the vendor suspiciously.

"Where are they from?" I ask the man. Now I speak Slovenian.

He grins broadly at me.

"Where are you from?" He heard us speaking English between ourselves.

"I asked you first." I point at the cherries.

"*Angležinja*?" he guesses.

"The cherries?" I insist.

"They're from Chile," he relents, putting his five fingers to his lips and kissing them enthusiastically. "Delicious," he says with the melodramatic exaggeration of the born salesman. "As sweet as your first kiss. All the way from South America."

"Well, I'm all the way from North America, and my first kiss wasn't that sweet. It sure wasn't that expensive."

"*Amerikanka!*" he crows happily.

I nod wryly. After the last few years of unilateral American foreign policy, ill-advised wars, squandered sympathy in the wake of 9/11, and general arrogance and incompetence, Albanians, both those from Kosovo and those from Albania proper, are virtually the only people on the face of the earth who still view America with that same old combination of rapture and awe. Even the gratitude of the Bosnians has lost some of its ardency after a decade living in a moribund state born of compromise rather than principle. But this fellow is clearly in the throes of full-blown America adoration. Last month, on February 17, the Kosovo Albanians declared independence from Serbia after nearly a decade of being ruled by a UN governing body, and before that, nearly a century of being ruled, apartheid-style in the last years, from Belgrade. America was among the first governments to extend recognition to the new state. All of which may explain why this fellow is smiling ear to ear, holding up his hands, looking at me as if I were some long lost lover who happened to turn up at his fruit stand. But then just as quickly, he turns serious.

"There was a war here once...."

The Albanian fruit seller begins in a once-upon-a-time sort of way, as if he is going to tell me a fairy tale or some ancient legend about the famed fourteenth-century battle on the Kosovo fields, or the turning back of the Turks at the gates of Vienna, or a terrible skirmish between the armies of the Ottoman and Austro-Hungarian empires.

"I know," I say, trying to stop him. "I remember it. I was here."

"My little brother," he continues unperturbed, "about the same age then as your little boy is now, at home in Kosovo, in the fields. He went out to play and he stepped on a mine." At this point in the narrative, the man stops speaking and throws his arms up into the air and looks down at his legs behind the counter as if they've been blown clear off, a shocked and mournful expression on his big face.

Lukas's hand, which has been hovering eagerly over the cherries all this time, waiting for the go-ahead, drops to his side. He stares at the man, cherries momentarily forgotten. The story has caught his attention: a boy about his age, an explosion, legs ripped off, blood, mayhem, all gripping stuff.

The man, eyes shining, continues.

"The Americans were still there then," he says, "and they evacuated him. They flew him to some military hospital in Germany, and then all the way to America. He had many operations, three in as many years. But he walks now, my little brother, and he talks too, in English, just like your boy. He lives in Cleveland. He's going to go to college next year. He's a good boy, a good American boy. Land of opportunity," he concludes with barely controlled emotion, lips trembling, tears still standing in his eyes.

I sigh. I have, over the years, become leery of acting as a representative of my homeland, even its positive side: the occasional generosity of America, its continued though tarnished ability to inspire hopes and transform individual lives.

"How much do I owe you?" I jiggle the coins in my hand.

"Cherries," Lukas hisses under his breath.

"No," I say irritably, "they're too expensive. We'll get tangerines instead."

Witnessing this exchange, our Albanian salesman rushes out from behind his stand, small brown paper bag in hand. He stuffs the bag with cherries and hands it to Lukas with a pat on his head.

"For my American friend," he says.

Lukas grins happily. He doesn't give a hoot about American foreign policy, just as he doesn't give a hoot who gives him the cherries or who pays for them, just so long as he has that sweet dark juice on the back of his tongue. He is, in fact, exactly what I wanted my children to be: not fearful or demure, but an optimistic, can-do, seize-the-world-with-both-hands little boy. I nudge him sharply, sending him a significant glance.

"Hvala lepa," he mumbles. Then he pops a Chilean cherry straight into his waiting mouth.

We all live in history, though most of the time we aren't that keenly aware of it.

Changes occur incrementally in our everyday lives, in our markets, written about in the columns of small print in our disposable daily newspapers, and the great sweeps of history, the profound transformations of society and worldview, often go virtually unnoticed, hammered out behind closed doors, veiled in propaganda.

That was not the case, however, in the time and place where I experienced the first decade of my marriage. During that brief period, a number of historical processes were played out in a way that was starkly visible to the naked eye. Nearly every day, decisions were made or events occurred that we knew would coalesce to form tomorrow's reality, its most basic foundational blocks. On the most obvious level, countries were being constructed and deconstructed all around us. Constitutions were being written, flags and passports and visas designed, national anthems resurrected or discarded, borders redrawn, political parties formed. All of the elements that tomorrow would be taken for granted as if they had always been there, as if they had always constituted reality, like the Bill of Rights and flag and borders of my own homeland, were being established, set in stone right then in the everyday flow of our lives.

At the same time, the opposite process was occurring. What had been the life-forming structures of yesterday—its wallpaper, its furnishings—faded and disappeared with an almost inconceivable rapidity, being relegated first to the category of vaguely remembered history, then history-book history, then ancient "what does it matter anymore" history. When the Albanian Kosovar fruit vendor said to me in that never-land fairy-tale voice of his, "There was a war here once," he wasn't so off base. Although he was referring to the Yugoslav wars of secession that ended within recent memory, to some he might as well have been speaking of an ancient Balkan battlefield. To many of the young people growing up in this region today, many of whom, like my own children, were born not in Yugoslavia but in one of its now seven successor states, Yugoslavia seems not much more real or concrete or immediate than its predecessors: the Austro-Hungarian and Ottoman empires. For them, the late twentieth-century siege of Sarajevo might just as well be the seventeenth-century siege of Vienna. At its most concrete, Yugoslavia provides a font of nostalgic Balkan pop songs that the Slovenian kids like to dance to at their nightclubs and parties. The kids to the south have no doubt inherited a more dangerous legacy, but both sorts are just kids, immersed in the everyday immediacy of their lives.

Today a Slovenian father might ask his young son, "Do you know who the partisans were? The home guard? Do you know who Tito was?"

And the son might answer him, "Tito? Wasn't he some politician or something?"

"*Some* politician. He was *the* politician. *The* icon. He was the way we started school every morning of our lives, fists thrust up above our heads, throats full of his name. S *Titom najprej!* With Tito onward!"

Some politician indeed.

And so slowly, during my first decade in Slovenia, I came to understand that back in 1991 when I lay beside my exotic black-haired Slovenian poet lover in my apartment on Twenty-Fourth and Third Avenue, and he told me, through those long lovely wakeful nights, all his childhood tales, all the stories from his homeland, I had made a fateful error of context. I thought then that I was practicing for the future, learning what I needed to know should I ever travel to his country, should I ever happen to live there. But, in fact what I was learning had little to do with the future and almost everything to do with the past. Even at the moment when our two heads were resting side by side on that pillow in that darkened bedroom, when his words were floating lazily up toward the ceiling, the fascinating stories he told me about Trieste and Klagenfurt, east and west, were already receding into history, already belonged to a dying world, would soon be fit only for the ashen pages of some rarely opened book.

On a less exalted level than the great empires and figures of history, but in some ways even more important, are the unsung fixtures of our everyday lives: the water-saving toilet bowls with their odd little inspection shelves and the peculiar half baths that populate our worlds. And all those are gone now too. I remember vividly when I first came to Slovenia in 1993 and found myself immersed in the very particular postcommunist atmosphere of drab ale-houses and kitschy sixties-style hotel lobbies, all tossed up in a bizarre mixture with the almost feudal peasant ways of the villages. I remember how fascinated and bemused I was, but at the same time a little bit embarrassed by it too. It was all so foreign and old-fashioned compared to what I had left behind, so primitive and unaesthetic. It seemed in some ways to reflect poorly on the choices I had made: of husband, home, new life. I wanted Slovenia to hurry up and get modern. I wanted Ray-Bans and Benetton and two-ply toilet paper, and I didn't want to have to drive all the way to Trieste or Klagenfurt to get them.

Then to my amazement my wish was granted, almost in the blink of an eye, it seems, looking back at it all now. Nobody in Slovenia today would dream of driving down to Italy or over the Alps to go shopping, unless it was for a bargain or some chic cosmopolitan outing. The unquestioned atmosphere of the country, the primary underpinning of national character, shifted practically overnight from scarcity to abundance, from having too little to having too much. And as we all entered the era where even diehard capitalist countries began to realize that it actually is possible to have too much of a good thing, that the earth itself might begin to stagger under the weight of it all, I regretted my fervent wish for Slovenia to hurry up and get modern. I belatedly realized that there was much to admire in the lifestyle of Mija and Pavel, Tanja and her mother, all the residents of Loški Potok and other Slovenian villages. That it was a very good thing to know how to light a fire without lighter fluid, how to bake a cake in the open flames, how to collect tea from the plants on the forest floor, how to make sweet syrup for juice from the blossoms of lilac bushes or the pale fresh tips of pine trees that burst forth in the spring.

But by the time I came to that realization it was too late. The transition was over. The rural life style of Loški Potok was as dead as the cosmopolitan multiethnic marvel that had been Sarajevo. And anyway, I also realized that such knowledge, such habits of living, have to be burned into a person by experience. It's no good trying them on a like a new coat. They don't stick.

All of which is to say that this story, my story, is also ancient history now. Nearly everything described on these pages no longer applies. The following, therefore, is a list, no doubt incomplete, of amendments and corrections:

Slovenia, a full-fledged member of the European Union as of 2004, is no longer located in the Balkans, at least not as measured by the company it keeps or by the kind of coffee it drinks (espresso coffee now being the rule in most homes and restaurants) or by the widespread use of guest slippers (Kenneth Coles are now allowed indoors).

The Slovenian tolar no longer exists. In 2007, three years after joining the European Union, Slovenia adopted the euro as its currency. All extant tolars were destroyed, making it one of the shorter lived currencies in history and dispatching, as is only appropriate, I suppose, the melancholy face of the poet Prešeren from paper money to the rather more useless paper of poetry collections. And, of course, Slovenians no longer keep a collection of Austrian shillings and Italian lire in their drawers just in case they need to cross a nearby border in a hurry, these currencies having also been phased out of existence. Strangest of all, there are no more German marks with which to price truly valuable objects—apartments and cars, houses and salaries. The only people who still enjoy the reputable Old World value of that once so-solid European currency are the Bosnians, whose monetary unit remains the convertible mark and is calculated on some phantom notion of what the German mark might be worth if it still existed today.

There are no more official borders to cross, at least not between Austria and Slovenia, Italy and Slovenia, Hungary and Slovenia. The new cordon sanitaire between civilized Europe and Balkan chaos, the legendary south, now lies on Slovenia's border with Croatia, although that too will surely change with time.

Unlike the tolar and all those border crossings, the gaudy *toplarna* still stands, though it burns a cleaner fuel now. However, it is no longer surrounded by the Moste industrial zone, but instead by a vast sprawling shopping mall known as BTC. It's a destination neighborhood that easily rivals the city center. It is the fastest-growing and most vibrant area of Ljubljana, exploding with multiplex cinemas, international clothing stores, Italian furniture stores, discount food stores, health spas, gyms, tennis courts, indoor swimming pools, electronic bowling alleys, and computer arcades. Ljubljana's baroque center and what was once Tito Street have become, by comparison, sleepy backwaters.

The shantytown made up of scruffy vegetable patches that once surrounded Žale cemetery is gone. The municipal authorities swept it away. Many of the larger vacant lots and plots around Ljubljana have been snatched up by moneyed commercial interests as real estate values rise. There are no barns in the city anymore, no cows, no rows of lettuce and cabbage and beanstalks. You are no more likely to spot a horse-drawn cart piled high with straw on the streets of Ljubljana than you are on Park Avenue.

Mirko and Ivanka, in Loški Potok, no longer run the village *mlekarna*. They do not collect milk from the other mixed farmers in the village, nor does anybody else. For there are hardly any mixed farmers in Slovenia's villages anymore. Mixed farming is no longer profitable or necessary for the supply of food. It is easier and much less labor-intensive to pay a visit to the nearest supermarket. A growing proportion of Slovenia's milk is imported from Hungary and other neighboring countries.

Ivanka and Mirko's son, Janko, did get married despite his family's hardworking reputation. He married a pretty widow from the village and they now have a young son.

Tanja graduated from college.

So did Polona.

Languid afternoon visits were supplanted by jobs and families and maneuvering through afternoon traffic jams.

Tanja's mother in Medvode got central heating.

There are more than three bars in Ljubljana.

Babies still wear two diapers, though the practice is in decline.

"We're home."

We tumble into the warm house: school bags, soccer jerseys, shin guards, basket of produce, winter coats, scarves, lip gloss, and all.

"Hey," says Aleš, "what have you got there?"

He is standing in the front hall, the welcoming papa, looking at Lukas, whose face is covered from cheek to cheek with sticky red juice.

"Cherries," answers Lukas with enormous satisfaction, the brown paper bag, now wrinkled and stained, still gripped in his fist.

"Cherries?" Aleš stares at me. "In March?"

I shrug as if to say, "What can you do? The times, they are a'changing."

"Where are they from?"

"They're Albanian cherries," I say, and give him an ironic look, "from Kosovo."

"Wow," Aleš responds, with mock appreciation. "Cherries from Kosovo. That really is forbidden fruit."

And in that instant, we catch each other's eyes over our children's heads, both of us remembering that first dinner at Marion's restaurant so many years ago, remembering that I'm not supposed to be here. I was his forbidden fruit, his forbidden bread, the thing he was supposed to resist, the American girl he meant to leave firmly behind where she belonged, in America, while he started a new life in his new country. In that instant it almost feels as if we would both go back to Marion's if we could, that we would do it all over again; or at least we would pause for a little while and tell the children about it before it's completely forgotten. We would go all nostalgic and misty-eyed about the olden days as parents are pathetically inclined to do.

But we never seem to have time for that. The demands of the present are always so pressing.

Lukas is just now using the relatively unsoiled white cuffs of his long-sleeved shirt to wipe the splotches of red from his face. Klara is giving her father an adolescent-girl "hi Daddy" hug while at the same time frisking him for his cell phone, which has better games on it than her old model. She is, unbelievably, almost as tall as he is. Simon has kneeled down on the floor, flung open his school bag, and turned it fully upside-down, pouring out its chaotic contents in order to find the history test on which he got an excellent grade that day. Simon does, as a point of fact, know who Tito and the partisans were. He even dressed up as a partisan soldier for Pust this year, red star and all, which pleased his teachers but mystified his fellow students, who were more likely to be clad in Superman or Osama bin Laden costumes.

"I'll say they're forbidden fruit," I remark, the passing nostalgia of the moment overtaken by the practical, "at twenty euros a kilo."

"Give me one of those," says Aleš, never much good at resisting the forbidden. He leans over to Lukas, pauses to wipe his face with a tissue, and reaches into the brown paper bag for a cherry. After rummaging around for a second, he pulls one out and pops it into his mouth. "Mmm," he sighs, closing his eyes. "Cherries from Kosovo. Tastes like independence."

"I want one too," I demand, and reach into Lukas's wrinkled and smudged bag, but there's none left. It's empty. Aleš got the last one. My shoulders sag.

"Here," Aleš offers. He brings his face toward mine, gesturing as if to give me what is left in his mouth of the little piece of fruit.

"Ugh," grimaces Klara.

But I lean over and kiss him anyway. I get a faint echo of cherry, but mostly it's just an ordinary kiss.

"Mmm," I sigh, closing my eyes. "Tastes like love."

Reading
Guide

READING GUIDE

1. What is the significance of the book's title? How does the notion of forbidden bread differ from forbidden fruit? How does this proverb play itself out over the course of Erica and Aleš's love affair?
2. Slovenia is a new and almost completely unknown nation at the beginning of the book. What sometimes ironic terms does Aleš use to define and distinguish his country? What anecdotes does he tell? How does this differ from the way the citizens of larger nations define themselves?
3. In New York, before her departure, Erica struggles to explain why and where she is moving. Discuss the different responses she gets from Americans, Western Europeans, and Eastern Europeans. Is the negativity of the responses only because of the war unfolding in that part of the world? Or are there other factors involved?
4. Erica visits Slovenia once before deciding to move there, and does research about the new country and its neighbors. How prepared do you think she really is for the move, and how likely did it seem that it would succeed? Did her romance with Aleš work out against all the odds, or do you think these types of relationships—between people of different cultures—often do succeed?
5. Erica is shocked but amused by the Slovenian vulgarities and jokes she learns, many of which disseminate clichés about the various Yugoslav peoples. The horror of the Yugoslav wars of secession does nothing to slow the flow of such humor; if anything it produces its own brand of jokes. Discuss the use of ethnic humor and slurs in such situations. Is it only insulting? Or can it deflate some of the tension among peoples? How does it differ from the use of humor in America?

6. In the chapter "Klub Drama," Erica meets Tanja. Why does she befriend her? How is Tanja's lifestyle distinctive? Why is she so amused by Erica and Vitaly's efforts to communicate with each other?

7. In the chapter "Loški Potok," Erica meets her rural Slovenian relatives. What kind of lifestyle does she discover there? What does the term *po domači* mean? How do her impressions of life in small Slovenian towns and villages reflect on American city life or even suburban life?

8. In the chapter "The Bureau for Foreigners," Erica once again enters Slovenia's bureaucratic maw. Though ultimately successful, it is an upsetting experience. Why is she given special treatment? How does that treatment make her feel? At the end of the chapter she concludes that every nation has its southerner. What does she mean by that? How does this truism apply to Slovenia? Bosnia? Kosovo? America?

9. In the chapter "Fužine" (and in earlier chapters such as "Medvode" and "Septentrion"), Erica reports and reflects on what it is like to live in relatively close proximity to a war zone: the fear and everydayness of it, the predictability and unpredictability of it. Discuss how this differs from more common depictions of war.

10. There are a number of episodes throughout the book that describe the Slovenian language school. Who is attending the school, and what fault lines emerge within the class? How do the Americans respond to the song *Five Little Negroes*? Do you think this is an appropriate response? What does the scene with the Bosnian taxi driver suggest about the possibility of different approaches to the age-old problem of ethnic divisions in society?

11. In the chapter "Grožnjan," Basta says that the song *Jugoslavija!* is a fake anthem. Erica retorts that all anthems are fake. What does this exchange, and other elements in this chapter,

reveal about the arbitrariness of national arrangements and patriotism? Is this particular song dismissed only because of the ultimate failure of the Yugoslav union? What are the implications of this for the generations of people that thought of themselves as Yugoslav above all?

12. Throughout the course of the narrative, there are a number of universal events that seem to unite people and erase cultural differences. Other things—folk wisdom and local traditions, for example—tend to emphasize differences. Discuss these events and dynamics and how the narrator and her family, old and new, negotiate the intercultural terrain. Do you think immigrants to America encounter similar situations?

13. The surprised exclamation *"Amerikanka!"* is the response of many Slovenians and former Yugoslavs, from customs officials to the peasant saleswomen in the market place, when faced with the unusual presence of the narrator in a country that has relatively few foreigners. Describe the range of responses she receives from various locals. Does the perception of America and Americans change over the course of the book? Why?

14. The narrative takes place during a key phase of Slovenia's development: its birth as a nation-state and its transition from socialism to capitalism. What changes are observed during the course of the story? What is gained during these years? What is lost? Is the end of socialism an unmitigated good?

15. As an American marrying into a traditional Slovenian family, Erica has to adapt to many different social and cultural norms, deciding what customs to adopt, and what role to play within her new family. How do you think she deals with this challenge? How does Aleš help guide her through this process, if at all? Do you think Erica, as we see her at the end of the book, is more Slovenian or more American?

ABOUT THE AUTHOR

Erica Johnson Debeljak has published three books in her adopted country of Slovenia. Her essays and stories have appeared in many American publications and have been translated into several other languages. She received her MFA in creative writing from the University of New Orleans. She lives in Ljubljana with her husband and three children.

NORTH ATLANTIC BOOKS
INTERNATIONAL LITERATURE

Since 2006, the mission of North Atlantic Books International Literature has been to publish fiction and literary nonfiction to help foster connections between writers from diverse international cultures and their English-speaking readers around the world. Inspiring literature from different cultures has the potential to awaken us to the situation of others, widen our conception of what it is to be human, and develop our own values as a country involved with other countries. North Atlantic Books as a nonprofit independent publisher has embraced from its beginnings in 1974 a belief that the personal is political, that one's own country and mores are not separate from or independent of other nations' challenges.

Some of the international books we have published to date:

Alamut
A novel by Vladimir Bartol, translated by Michael Biggins (Slovenia)
$16.95, ISBN 978-1-55643-681-9, 400 pages (November 2007)

Angels Beneath the Surface: A Selection of Contemporary Slovene Fiction
Edited by Mitja Čander with Tom Priestly (Slovenia)
$15.95, ISBN 978-1-55643-703-8, 192 pages (March 2008)

Guarding Hanna
A novel by Miha Mazzini, translated by Maja Visenjak-Limon (Slovenia)
$15.95, ISBN 978-1-55643-726-7, 288 pages (June 2008)

Belonging: New Poetry by Iranians Around the World
Edited and translated by Niloufar Talebi (Iran)
$18.95, ISBN 978-1-55643-712-0, 256 pages (July 2008)

Bringing Tony Home
A novella and stories by Tissa Abeysekara (Sri Lanka)
$19.95, ISBN 978-1-55643-757-1, 224 pages (November 2008)

The Feline Plague
A novel by Maja Novak (Slovenia)
$15.95, ISBN 978-1-55643-764-9, 304 pages (March 10, 2009)

For information contact Lindy Hough, Publisher and Executive Editor, North Atlantic Books, ldh@northatlanticbooks.com.